THE TINWORKING LANDSCAPE

OF

DARTMOOR

IN A EUROPEAN CONTEXT - PREHISTORY TO 20TH CENTURY

Papers presented at a conference in Tavistock, Devon,
6-11 May 2016 to celebrate the 25th anniversary of the DTRG

Edited by

Dr Phil Newman MCIfA, FSA

DARTMOOR TINWORKING RESEARCH GROUP

2017

For
Helen Harris
pioneer recorder of Devon's industrial archaeology

Published by

Dartmoor Tinworking Research Group (DTRG)

Publication No. 5 July 2017

Copyright © Dartmoor Tinworking Research Group and individual authors

All rights reserved.

No part of this publication, including images, may be reproduced, stored in a retrieval system or transmitted in any form or by any means, electronic, mechanical, photocopying, recording or otherwise without the prior permission of the authors.

ISBN 978-0-9529442-4-9

www.dtrg.org.uk

Front Cover: Aerial view of the central part of Hexworthy Tin Mine (Hooten Wheals), showing evidence of medieval and post-medieval tin streamworks, post-medieval openworks, and surface remains of 19th-20th century mining (Damian Grady © Historic England Archive).

Rear Cover: A tinner's view of Dartmoor hills and tinworks in 1671 (Philosophical Transactions **5**)

Typesetting and layout by the editor

Printed by Short Run Press, Sowton, Exeter

Contents

Tom Greeves	The World of the Dartmoor Tinner: An Historical Context 12th to 20th Century	1
Richard Scrivener	Tin Deposits of the Dartmoor Granite	15
Henrietta Quinnell	Dartmoor and Prehistoric to Early Medieval Tinworking	19
Phil Newman	Mining for Tin on Dartmoor in the Eighteenth to Twentieth Centuries: The Landscape Legacy	27
Tom Greeves	Lodges and Mills: The Field Archaeology of Tin Accommodation, Stamping and Smelting on Dartmoor	55
Simon Hughes	The Hemerdon Project	77
Peter Herring	Tinworking in the Cornish landscape	83
Gerhard Brügmann, Daniel Berger, Carolin Frank, Janeta Marahrens, Bianka Nessel, Ernst Pernicka	Tin Isotope Fingerprints of Ore Deposits and Ancient Bronze	103
Petr Rojík	Leats and tin streamworks of the 16th century in the Krušné Hory / Erzgebirge, Czech Republic	115
Michael Rund	National Cultural Monument Jeronym (Hieronymus) Mine, near Rovna, Czech Republic	125
Beatriz Comendador Rey, Emmanuelle Meunier, Elin Figueiredo, Aaron Lackinger, João Fonte, Cristina Fernánz, Alexandre Lima, José Mirão, Rui J.C. Silva	Northwestern Iberian Tin Mining from Bronze Age to Modern Times: an overview	133

Acknowledgements

Sponsors: Devon Archaeological Society; Northern Mine Research Society.

The editor is grateful to Dr Tom Greeves for assistance and support.

મ The Tinworking Landscape of Dartmoor in a European Context: Prehistory to 20th Century

The World of the Dartmoor Tinner: An Historical Context 12th to 20th Century

Tom Greeves*

The legacy of the Dartmoor tinner is all around us – apart from the Dartmoor tinworking landscape itself, many fine Devon churches and dwellings of the medieval and later period could not have been built without wealth generated at least partly from tin. Even four hundred years ago, in about 1600, when the Devon industry was in relative decline, tin was still considered to be the most important of all metals produced in the county, and the mining industry as a whole of greater significance than seafaring, being surpassed only by farming and the woollen industry (Blake 1915, 347-8). John Hooker, whose opinion this was, stated of tin that there is 'not a better merchandyse' in terms of trade with 'other countries and nations'. His contemporary, Richard Carew of Cornwall, expressed the same sentiment, and saying 'Tin... is always requisite, always ready for our service' (Carew 1602, 25). It is John Hooker who has given us the first and most vivid description of the Dartmoor tin labourer: 'there is no labourer to be compared unto him: for his apparel is coarse, his diet slender, his lodging hard, his feeding commonly coarse bread and hard cheese, and his drink is water, and for lack of a cup he drinketh it out of his spade or shovel: and he goeth so near the weather as no man can live more frugally and nerer than he dothe. His life most commonly is in pits and caves under the ground of a great depth and in great danger because the earth above his head is in sundry places crossed and posted over with timber to keep the same from falling' (Blake 1915, 342).

I want to introduce you to some of the tinners whose lives and stories were intimately connected with Dartmoor, spanning eight centuries of documented history. But first let me summarise the stannary system. 'Stannary' is a word derived from the Latin word for tin – *stannum*. A stannary is a tinworking district administered by a stannary or tin court (which was judicial, and also a court of record) based in a town (Fig.1). In Devon there were originally three stannaries, probably dating from at least about AD 1200 (but possibly with much earlier origins) administered from three towns – Chagford, Ashburton and Tavistock. They were joined by Plympton St Maurice in 1328 (Pennington 1973). Dartmoor, for much of the high medieval period and later, was thus divided into four regions, with specific boundaries meeting at the central point of a prehistoric

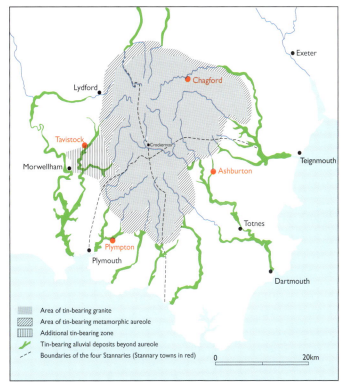

Figure 1 Map showing stannary boundaries and towns.

---

*Cultural Environmentalist. Email: *tomgreeves@btconnect.com*

The Tinworking Landscape of Dartmoor in a European Context: Prehistory to 20th Century

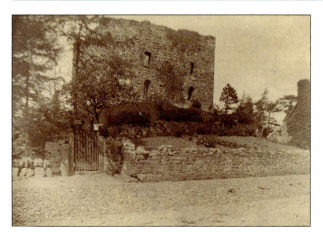

Figure 2 Lydford Castle about 1880 (Greeves collection).

Figure 3 Crockerntor (Elisabeth Stanbrook).

cairn known as Broken Borough, now in Tor Royal newtake near Princetown (Greeves 1981, 391-394). Each stannary had distinct characteristics in terms of its tin-related geology and the extent of streamworks or lodeworks, and also in terms of access to the sea (and hence trade). By King Edward I's charter of 1305 a stannary prison was confirmed at Lydford, in the castle there (Fig. 2), which had been built as a royal prison in 1195 (Greeves 2005). It was also the seat of power for administering the royal estate of the Forest of Dartmoor. It has been suggested that the Lord Warden of the Stannaries may have held courts there (Summerson 1987, 72), but there is no documentation to support such a supposition.

The stannary courts were viewed with suspicion by many – in about 1540 Tavistock's court was said to be 'of quyke spede' (Greeves 1981, 47), and in 1614 a Buckfastleigh resident described the local stannary bailiffs (presumably of the Ashburton court) as 'poore men, of smale creditt or estimacion' and as having spent their 'whole estate in boowsing and drincking and other lewde vices' (Stoyle 1994, 17).

The stannary towns were also 'coinage' towns to which the tinners were required to bring their ingots of tin metal for assay, weighing and taxation (at a rate of 1s 6¾d per hundredweight, which varied between 100 and 120 lbs) (Lewis, 1908). The word coinage seems likely to be derived from the French 'cogner' = 'to strike', or 'coin' meaning 'stamp' or 'die', rather than referring to a corner of the ingot being struck off as some have argued. An expert assayer would have been able to judge the quality of a block of tin by striking it and assessing its relative hardness or softness (soft tin was the finest quality). This system seems to have developed in the thirteenth century, and was confirmed by King Edward I in 1305. The earliest detailed records of coinage for Devon date to 1302/3 (Greeves 2003).

Because of the strategic importance of tin, medieval and later monarchs had an interest in it. By charter (King John's of AD 1201 is the earliest we know of) the tinners of Devon and Cornwall were exempt from normal taxation and had privileges in terms of where they could work for tin. Ultimate administration was overseen by the Lord Warden of the Stannaries, appointed by the Crown. Beneath him was a Vice-Warden for each county. Each stannary court had its own officials of steward, bailiffs and sergeants, and a jury of twelve tinners was selected from twenty-four nominated (Pennington 1973).

Of the greatest interest for Dartmoor is that the tinners of Devon held their own occasional Great Courts or Parliaments, which enacted statutes for managing the industry. We know of nine Great Courts held at the central location of Crockerntor between 1474 and 1600 (this is probably a complete record), and of another four held in Tavistock, after adjournment from Crockerntor, between 1663 and 1710 (Greeves 1987; Greeves & Newman, 2011). The last known assembly was in Moretonhampstead in 1786. The outdoor gatherings at Crockerntor (Fig.3), in the heart of Dartmoor, 1300ft (nearly 400m) above sea level, attended by ninety-six tinners elected by their fellows, and by royal officials and probably hundreds of others, must have been extraordinary occasions (Greeves & Newman, 2011). That held on 27 October 1600 was attended by no less a person than Sir Walter Ralegh, then Lord Warden of the Stannaries. The Cornish tinners also had their Parliaments or Convocations, but they were significantly less democratic, with only six jurates from each of four stannaries, and they do not have as long a surviving documented history as the Devon ones (Pennington 1973).

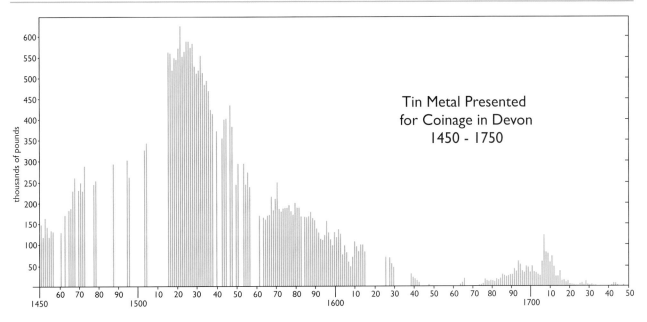

Figure 4 Table showing official production of Devon tin, 1450-1750.

The stannary system in Devon was maintained until the Civil War of the 1640s, which had a devastating effect on the industry, bringing activity almost to a standstill (Greeves 1981). However, the significant revival of the industry in the late seventeenth century seems to have operated within a functioning stannary system of courts, which do not appear to have become defunct until the mid-eighteenth century. A letter from John Elford of Sheepstor (1670-1748) in 1732 mentions that 'the Courts are not [now] kept' and queries how 'Rapparees' can be dealt with without Courts, prison, Steward or Warden'[1]. The only part of the stannary system that continued to operate in a more or less traditional manner was that of the occasional coinage of tin. The last coinage of tin in the county took place at Morwellham in 1838 (Booker 1967, 28).

Production of tin fluctuated considerably over time (Fig. 4), with different stannaries experiencing different fortunes (Greeves 1992c). Our present state of knowledge can point to relatively prosperous periods for Devon in the late twelfth century, the early fourteenth century, from 1450-1600, and for several years around 1700. A revival of activity in the late eighteenth century led to a lively few years in the mid-nineteenth century when about fifty tin mines were operating within the county (Newman 2010). Mining continued into the twentieth century with several mines still operating before the First World War. Between 1854 and 1920 some sixty-six mines are recorded as having produced some 6,000 tons of dressed tin ore within Devon (Burt et al. 2014, 36 + Table 20, 74-5). In the 1920s on moorland Dartmoor only Golden Dagger Mine was a significant enterprise, and it closed in November 1930. Some efforts were made to revive it over the next decade but the Second World War intervened (Greeves 2016, 130-135). In the second half of the twentieth century, there was a little activity at Owlacombe Mine near Ashburton, and in the Tamar valley, but probably the most significant work was on the Kester Brook near Ashburton in the 1970s, where alluvial tin was exploited successfully by John Walbeoffe-Wilson (Greeves 2008, 38-9). In the twenty-first century, a major potential tin producer (of up to 1000 tonnes per annum as a by-product of tungsten production) is now in operation at Drakelands Mine, Hemerdon, operated by Wolf Minerals.

From the mid-twelfth century we have the first names of people interested in tin – Hugh of Chagford and his wife Alice who reserved the right to work tin near Chagford Bridge in about 1150 (Greeves 1981, 28), and Guy de Bretteville's 'men of Sheepstor' ('Sitelestorra') who were digging illegally within the king's forest (the whole of Devon was subject to forest law at this time). Joel of Ashburton was a key figure from 1169-1188 in which year he fell foul of the authorities and was fined 100 marks (£66 13s 4d), a huge sum (Finberg 1949, 158). In 1184-5 several Chagford persons were fined for illegal smelting of tin (Finberg 1949, 182 n.8) including Eilwald a smith ('faber'), so probably our first named tin smelter, and Ailric of Corndon ('Querendon') (Anon 1913, 160-161). In 1198 an important tinner within the historic parish of Tavistock is named – Roger Rabi was almost certainly from Rubbytown (SX 435741),

The Tinworking Landscape of Dartmoor in a European Context: Prehistory to 20th Century

Figure 5 Foundations of medieval longhouse at Gutter Tor, Sheepstor SX 579668 (Tom Greeves).

Figure 6 Sibilla of Murchington ('Morcheton') near Chagford listed as an exempt tinner in 1347 (TNA/E363/4).

on the western edge of the great mineral-rich ridge overlooking the River Tamar and only a few miles from Tavistock. In that year he was appointed a juror by William de Wrotham to look into practices within the stannaries (Finberg 1949, 158).

Surviving records are often about matters that have gone wrong - legal disputes or accidents. In the early 1280s William Voyla was killed by 'part of the cliff' falling on him at the head of the River Meavy near modern Princetown when digging with three colleagues, two of whom came from known nearby farms – at Peek and Horseyeat in Walkhampton parish. Robert of Ford was equally unlucky when working in a tinwork at Blachford (Blakeworth) north-east of Cornwood for he too was 'crushed by a heap of earth' and killed instantly[2]. Robert Richeman of Shaugh was another killed in a thirteenth century tinworking accident (Fox 1999, 325).

In 1281/2 Walter of Gutter Tor ('Gotetorr') within Sheepstor parish stole tin to the value of two shillings and was outlawed[3]. Remarkably we can still see the foundations of a substantial longhouse in which he lived at SX 579668 (Fig.5). Isobell of Nosworthy ('Northeworthi'), with Hugh of Newleycombe ('Nywelecomb'), Richard of Middleworth ('Middelworth') and Richard of Stanlake ('Stenylake') were from a group of farms, all in Walkhampton parish, who took tin ingots to Ashburton in 1303 – a distance of twelve miles (19 km) as the crow flies, very probably along the ancient route marked by crosses on moorland – the 'Maltern Way' (Greeves 1998; 2003). In the same year, Robert of Littleweek ('Litelwyke') presented nearly 11,000 pounds weight (4.83 tons) of tin metal at Chagford, on which he paid tax of 150s 7¼d. This represented more than 10% of the county total, and would probably have required more than fifty packhorses to carry it. In the same year Walter Wallyngs presented at Ashburton the third largest quantity of 5,262 pounds (2.35 tons), but within a couple of years was in Lydford gaol, indicted for the murder of his nephew at Holne (Greeves 2003)[4].

With tin being such a valuable product, smuggling must have been extensive. In Totnes in the early fourteenth century seven ingots of unlawfully acquired tin were found 'hidden in a stable, dungheap and elsewhere' next to the Chapel of St Peter, close to the quays in Little Totnes, and John Janet and Ivo Hyne of Totnes were accused of smuggling them (Greeves 2014). This incident occurred at a time of considerable prosperity and activity within the industry. In 1314 the men of Devon complained that the tinners were annually destroying more than 300 acres of farmland, wood, meadow, houses and gardens (Finberg 1949). In the National Archives in London are documents listing hundreds of names of Devon tinners claiming exemption from Edward III's wool taxes in the 1330s and 1340s. These included Sibilla of Murchington ('Morcheton') near Chagford in 1347 (Fig.6), and William of Combestone ('Comereston'), senior and junior, in 1336-7 and 1341-2, who lived on a farmstead overlooking the River Dart south of Dartmeet, on the western moorland edge of the parish of Holne (Greeves & Stanbrook 2013)[5]. By the early 1370s one in 20 of the male population of Devon was involved directly in tinworking (Fig.7), with many ancillary activities involved as well – such as charcoal-making from peat or wood (Fox 1999, 325).

More than a century later, John Hanworthy (a variant of Hannaford) of Combestone in Holne parish was presenting small quantities of tin at Ashburton, and was elected as a jurate by his fellow tinners to attend a Great Court at Crockerntor on 11 September 1494 (Greeves 1987). Many such tinners (occasionally women) were not landless impoverished labourers but members of prosperous farming families indulging in tin. This seems to be the pattern across Dartmoor with farming families holding shares or actively working tinworks or mills for crushing and smelting.

Bovey Heathfield was a great centre of tinworking

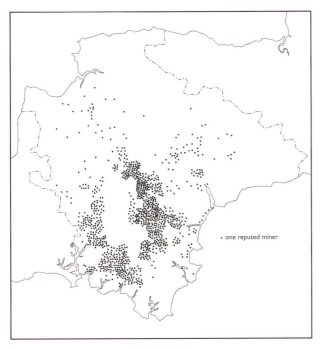

Figure 7 Distribution of tinners in Devon in 1373 (from Fox 1999, Map 40.4).

in the medieval period, and much larger in extent than it now is (Greeves 2008). A dispute involving a leat near Liverton is recorded in the early fifteenth century[6]. Joel Underhays accused Ivo Baggetor of diverting water from a leat which led from Ivo's land in Liverton to Joel's tinwork on Heathfield. The leat and its precious water must have been of some considerable significance as Ivo was 'attached' (i.e. ordered to appear in court) by means of the seizure of four oxen and six cows of his which were impounded at Dunnabridge on the Forest of Dartmoor. However, Ivo and five others broke into the pound and released the cattle. Besides giving us insight into the 'wild west' of Dartmoor, this is a nice example of how it is essential to recognise the integration of farming and tinworking on Dartmoor, which I believe to be inseparable.

On 23 June 1475 at Buckland Monachorum, tinner Henry Wynneslond sold 214 pounds weight of corrupt tin to widow Agnes Staunton[7].

Sometimes major landowners and lawyers were involved. Sir Thomas Fulford of Dunsford was accused of abusing stannary law in the late fifteenth century (Greeves 2008, 22). In September 1470 Fulk Fitzwaryn headed a group of nineteen tinners, seemingly an adventuring company in their own right, as they together presented fifty-three ingots at Ashburton weighing a total of nearly 3 tons of metal, and may well have been working very productive tinworks on Holne Moor, possibly at Ringleshutes (Greeves & Stanbrook 2013). Nicholas Radford, the best known lawyer in mid-fifteenth century Devon, was called upon to resolve a dispute between tinners on north-east Dartmoor (Greeves 2010).

A unique description of a tinner in the sixteenth century appears in a journal kept by his grandson, rather than from a legal document. John Furse (*c*.1481 – *c*.1549/50) 'had a great delight to be a tinner', owning two hundred tinworks in Devon and Cornwall, and a tin mill at Lydford, and a share of another in Okehampton parish. He was 'decent and trim in his apparel' and 'great and clean grown strong' and a great wrestler ('wraxseler'). He was an attorney and for sixteen years was Steward of the Stannary (probably Ashburton). He enjoyed life, and at Swimbridge near Barnstaple in North Devon at Christmas allowed the practice of the 'lord of misrule' with minstrels and eight tall fellows in his livery. He is buried in the chancel of Great Torrington church (Travers 2012, 43-47). His son, also called John (*c*.1506-1572), who inherited tinworks and tin mills from his father, was 'very strong lusty and well tried for wrestling, leaping, casting of the bar and also with his sword and buckler' (Travers 2012, 55).

The well-known case of Richard Strode MP, imprisoned in Lydford for three weeks in 1512 by the tinners, for attempting to introduce a bill into the Westminster Parliament which would have curtailed their activities, and which was something expressly forbidden by their Great Court of 1510, still receives attention worldwide, as it seems to have led to the principle of parliamentary privilege (Finberg 1949; Greeves & Newman 2011). But an equally remarkable incident, starting in the same year, relates to John Cole of Slade in Cornwood. He was immensely rich, a gentleman and a tinner. For some reason he, his son Thomas (also a tinner) and thirteen others in two separate raids broke into a pound on Dartmoor and seized forty cattle and ten horses, and also sixteen stray bullocks. For each offence they were fined 100 marks (£66 13s 4d). John Cole then masterminded an assault on 20 October 1512 by his son Thomas and nine others on three stannary bailiffs who were carrying sixteen ingots of tin to Exeter, valued at £36 (45 shillings each). The officers had previously confiscated the ingots from Thomas Cole as they had not been stamped and registered with his 'hote marke'. Each offender was fine 100 marks.

By early 1514 John Cole was in Lydford gaol, but on 21 March fifteen men (comprising tinners, farmers, two grooms, a butcher and a carpenter) gathered at

Figure 8a (top left) Ducks Pool Stream, Saintonge jug (scale 15cm) (Tom Greeves); b (top right) Upper Merrivale tin mill, sherd from North Devon jug c. AD 1600 (P. Miatt); c (bottom left) Upper Merrivale tin mill, clay pipe bowl AD 1650-1670 (P. Miatt); d (bottom right) Upper Merrivale tin mill - glass from Netherlands (?), c. AD 1600 (P. Miatt).

Bridestowe and, led by Thomas Cole, riotously broke into the prison and released him. Another fine of 100 marks was imposed on each of them. Remarkably, although Henry VIII issued a general pardon in 1515, he specifically excluded both John and Thomas Cole. However, it seems they evaded justice as the fines were never paid (Greeves 2005).

The accidental death of Nicholas Eveleigh of Parke, an important lawyer in his own right, happened at Chagford stannary court on 6 March 1618, where Eveleigh was Steward. A 'graceless varlet' swore to God that, if he told a lie, then the building 'may sodainely fall upon my head', which it promptly did, despite being solidly built and there being no unusual weather conditions. Eveleigh and nine others were killed and seventeen badly injured. Beside his estate at Parke, he had one house and two shops in Lombard Street in London, as well as corn mills and the rectory at Bovey Tracey, and woodland in Lustleigh[8]. Eveleigh has an elaborate tomb in Bovey Tracey church (Greeves 2008).

Perhaps the closest we get to a labouring tinner's world, to support the view of John Hooker, is through eyewitness accounts concerning Antony Giles of Walkhampton in the mid-seventeenth century. In October 1640 he was accused of stealing sheep and was required to open the door of 'a little house' he had by his tinwork. In it, a great earthen pot contained 'almost a whole sheep salted'. At his home by the parish church was found 'about half of another sheep powdered' i.e. preserved. Giles claimed that a dog had killed the sheep and had partly eaten the beast. He recovered what he could 'except one of the shoulders and part of the breast which the dog had spoiled', and pulled the wool off the dead sheep and hid it underground. More portions of sheep were found preserved at Giles's house by the church in Walkhampton (Greeves 1992a).

From occasional finds of pottery and other artefacts from both lodges and mills, and from excavations at Upper Merrivale, we can begin to add even more substance to this world – ceramic vessels from France, jugs from North Devon, clay tobacco pipes, even fine glass reaching high moorland locations (Fig. 8). John Elford, landowner and tinner of Longstone, Sheepstor - sculptor, artist and poet, both parliamentarian and royalist - whose family were much involved with tin for generations, placed

Figure 9 Wine bottle seal of John Elford of Sheepstor 1661 (drawn by Francis Stanbrook).

his family crest and motto on his wine bottles in 1661 (Fig. 9) – DIFFICILIA QUA PULCRA – 'It is not easy to achieve beauty' (Greeves 2011).

From the mid-seventeenth century we have the first image (Fig.10) of how the tinners perceived Dartmoor. Published by the Royal Society in 1671, to accompany a paper almost certainly written by a west Dartmoor tinner, it is of the greatest interest as it shows different ore bodies and means of prospecting them, besides showing Dartmoor as being a bounteous source of tin, with breast-shaped hills and its main rivers running from north to south (Anon 1671).

Much Devon tin was exported – through Exeter, Teignmouth, Totnes/Dartmouth, Morwellham and Plymouth. Merchants were vital to the success of the industry. Several are mentioned in a Pardon Roll of King Henry VIII dated to 1509-1514: Robert Wyndeyate of Widecombe, John Herte of Bovey Tracey, and John Braban of Bovey Tracey (Anon 1920a, 203-234). In 1522 Thomas Harries, tin merchant of Moretonhampstead, was given official protection in the retinue of Lord Berners, Deputy of Calais (Anon 1920b, 1019-1020). William Periam/Peryam, an alderman of Exeter, whose will is dated 20 February 1551/2[9], seems to have greatly enriched himself at least partly through tinworking in Devon. In the 1520s and 1530s he presented some of the largest quantities of tin metal at Ashburton coinages (Finberg 1949)[10]. He owned a grand house in Moretonhampstead which was leased to the Stonyng family[11]. Geoffrey Babbe, William Giles, Peter Buggins, Walter Buggins, Henry Carswell,

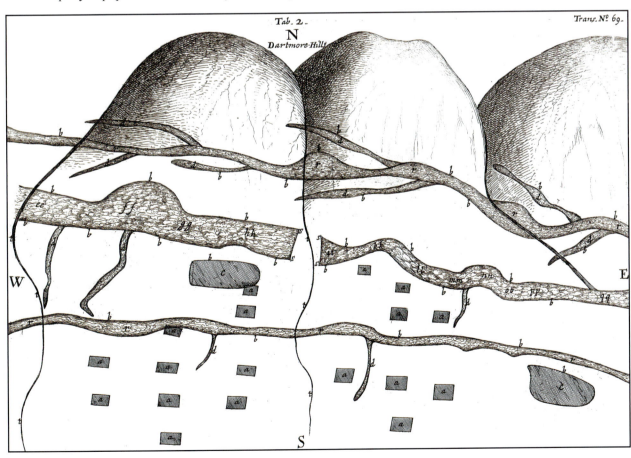

Figure 10 A tinner's view of Dartmoor hills and tinworks in 1671 (Anon 1671).

The Tinworking Landscape of Dartmoor in a European Context: Prehistory to 20th Century

Figure 11 Buildings at Vitifer Mine, North Bovey c. 1910 (Chapman & Son).

Figure 12 Miners at Vitifer Mine, North Bovey c.1910 (Chapman & Son).

Figure 13 Waterwheel at Hexworthy Mine c. 1905 (photographer n/k).

John Giles, William Giles, Alan Hakewell and Walter Smith, all of Totnes, were other merchants in the sixteenth and seventeenth centuries who must have dealt in tin (Greeves 2014)[12].

Sometimes merchants met with misfortune. In March 1597 Nicholas Glanville (Glanvil) of Tavistock placed seventeen pieces of tin in the *Unity* ('unetye') of Plymouth destined for London, but the ship and tin 'was taken by the Dunkirkers' ('dunkerkes')[13]. He is almost certainly to be identified with 'Mr Glenvile of Tavistock' who was named as one of the most important merchants dealing in tin in 1595, along with 'Mr Bab' and 'Mr Seret' of Totnes (Mizui 1999, 207).

In July 1599 James Bagg was corresponding with Filippo Corsini regarding his dealings in ten thousandweight of tin at Tavistock with the mother of Tobias Glanville[14]. He proposed taking the tin to his own house and having it cast into bars and then packed into barrels. According to Caroscio[15], the tin trade in the sixteenth century was largely controlled by Flemish merchants, but in the fourteenth century it had been an Italian monopoly, especially of the Bardi and Peruzzi families. Majorca was a major trading centre from which tin was shipped on to Genoa, Pisa, Florence, Naples and Venice (Hatcher 1973).

Cornwall and Devon seem always to have been closely connected in matters of tin and other affairs. From the late seventeenth century onwards numerous tinners working on Dartmoor are recorded in parish and other records as being from Cornwall. But the migration was not only in one direction – in the 1580s we know that Barnard Webb from Meavy, owner of Devon tinworks since the 1560s, was a tinner living at St Just in west Cornwall (Greeves 1992b, 4).

Tavistock always had a particularly interesting relationship with Cornwall, being so close to the county boundary. A special Court for the Stannaries of Cornwall was actually held in Tavistock on 27 August 1571 (Pearce 1725, 154-5), dealing mainly with the preservation of harbours from silting with tinners' waste.

A major figure in west Devon tinworking in the early 1700s was Richard Balhatchett, surely a Cornishman. He was a jurate for Tavistock stannary at the Crockerntor Great Court held on 23 September 1703 (adjourned to Tavistock). He worked Furzehill/Forest Hill Mine at Horrabridge (Brooke 2001, 11; Greeves & Newman 2011, 34) and presented very large quantities of tin in Tavistock in the early 1700s. In a period of 18 months between 4 March 1705 and 19 September 1706 he presented no fewer than 405 ingots, a much larger quantity than any of his fellow tinners. The total weight was 117,464 pounds = 52.44 tons. Each ingot weighed an average of 290 pounds[16]. Incidentally, he was one of the so-called 'rapparees' referred to by John Elford (see above).

In the spring of 1752 a Devon tinner, Capt. Edmund Moore, died in London. He was 'first a working tinner, then captain of a tin work, afterwards supposed to have acquired a good fortune, and to have been concerned in most of the mines in England'. He was buried in the churchyard at Whitchurch adjoining Tavistock and, when digging his grave, 'the workmen struck into a lode of tin ore: so that he now lies buried amidst that about which he was employed during almost the whole course of his life' (Polwhele 1806, 129-130n). He was a lessee of 'Caple Tor' mine in the Tamar valley and is recorded as buying copper ore (Patrick 1983), and was also involved in exploiting lead mines in the Mary Tavy area (Risdon 1811, xviii).

Harold Fox surmises that the medieval stannary town of Chagford was 'an especially unruly town' and notes that in 1431-2 many men were involved in major disturbances there, involving fists, knives and daggers (Fox 2012, 78). Three hundred and sixty years later, on 12 November 1793, a colourful incident occurred in the town concerning sixteen or seventeen tinners 'with Bludgeons under their coats', many of them Cornish, from Vitifer Mine, objecting to some of their number being arrested for breaking 'the windows of a publick-house where they were refused an immoderate quantity of liquor'. One of the group was Zacharias or Zachary Pascoe, who headed a list of ten names, eight of whom were from Cornwall. He was aged 45, from Wendron in Cornwall (as were three others) and had a wife and three children (Greeves 1992b; Crowden 2007). They threatened 'that the Town of Chagford would be Levelled to the Ground in About three Weeks'. The bells of the church were rung as an alarm and twenty-seven townsfolk gathered to protect their property and to pursue the tinners, who continued to Cheriton Bishop, to the house of the Justice of the Peace, Mr Foulkes, where their comrades were being held. This was some eleven miles (18 km) from Vitifer Mine from where they had set out that morning, and their zeal was significantly diminished by the time the men of Chagford caught up with them 'under a hedge' and they were all, except one escapee, arrested (Greeves 1992b, 8). In November 1793 a newspaper reported

Figure 14 Underground at Golden Dagger Mine c.1910 (Chapman & Son).

Figure 15 Henry (Harry) 'Silvertop' Warne (1877-1942) at Golden Dagger Mine, late 1920s (photographer n/k).

that the leaders 'were delivered to a press-gang, and conducted on board the tender at Dartmouth'[17]. Zacharias, however, seems to have remained on Dartmoor, and died in 1843 aged in his nineties (Crowden 2007).

In the nineteenth century newspaper reports and other accounts give us a yet more detailed picture of life among Dartmoor's tinworks. Men were employed underground, with sons joining them at the age of about sixteen, having previously worked on the surface. If poorly ventilated, conditions could be grim, with candles going out and men suffocating – one miner in the 1830s claimed that the lack of air shafts at Birch Tor Mine 'killed scores of miners'. Women and children were employed on the surface, sometimes 'crying of the cold' on the exposed dressing floors. Accommodation was notoriously bad, with beds having a succession of occupants for twenty-four hours, and the lawlessness of Dartmoor was compared to the penal colony of Botany Bay in Australia (Greeves 2016, 38). A local farmer's wife complained of miners washing in streams (Broughton 1971, 15). Women were employed on larger mines for domestic work such as washing laundry – one of these was Jenny Jenkins at Ailsborough Mine in 1815[18]. From the 1860s, but mostly of the early 1900s, we have our first photographic images (Greeves 2016) of mines (Fig.11) miners (Fig.12), mine machinery (Fig.13) and even of underground conditions (Fig.14).

Let me introduce briefly three persons connected with the last years of Dartmoor tinworking. First a working tinner – Henry 'Silvertop' Warne (Fig.15). Born in 1877, he was from a longstanding mining family. At the time of the census in April 1911 he was living at the Temperance Hotel, Postbridge run by his brother Solomon and his wife Mabel. Another brother, a sister, and another miner also lived there. Harry, as he was known, was recorded as a tin miner and 'hewer undergound'. By a remarkable coincidence, staying in the hotel at the same time was Ernest Rutherford, pioneer nuclear physicist, with

Figure 16 William Ambrose Grose (1886-1994) (B.Julyan).

Figure 17 Donald Smith (1907-1993) on left, with Jim Webb, at Golden Dagger Mine c. 1927 (photographer n/k).

his wife Mary and others, including the grandson of Charles Darwin. Although by all accounts a loving husband and father, Harry's demon was drink and he spent a disproportionate amount of his wages at the Warren House Inn, causing great hardship for his wife and daughter. He worked at Vitifer and Golden Dagger, both underground and on the surface. He died in 1942 (Greeves 2016).

The remarkably long-lived William Ambrose Grose (1886-1994) (Fig.16) was from generations of a Cornish mining family. His father managed Hexworthy Mine for several years around 1900 and William lived there as a teenager. His recollections have enabled us to participate in the mine, miners and his home life (Greeves 2016).

Finally, I would like to mention Donald Smith (1907-1993) (Fig.17), born in a public house in Hertfordshire who, thanks to an entrepreneur aunt of his, was given a job at Golden Dagger Mine in late 1925 as electrical engineer, having previously worked in theatres in London! Within about two years he was in charge and, with a combination of remarkable practical ability and force of character, kept tinworking on Dartmoor alive until November 1930. He eventually had a successful teaching career in Brighton. His photographs and memories bring alive these final important moments in Dartmoor's long tinworking story so far (Greeves 2016).

As a coda, I would like to reveal an exciting discovery during preparation of this conference, of a lead matrix of a unique Devon stannary seal (Fig.18), thought to be of the seventeenth century. This was probably used in one of the Devon stannary courts either as a badge of office, or as a back-up copy of a seal perhaps in precious metal. Let us imagine this was once in use here in Tavistock. It was located recently in Australia and has now travelled back to its home county where, hopefully, it will remain. The design of the conference medallion is an acknowledgement of its significance.

The world of all these people, stretching over eight centuries, is still with us. Through richly varied documents, combined with the physical remains, we can begin to read the landscape in human terms – with living men, women and children who knew the same tors and streams as we do, even if their lives were immeasurably more difficult than ours.

I will conclude with a poem titled 'Crockerntor'

Figure 18A & 18B – Lead seal matrix for Devon stannaries, probably 17th century (Chris Chapman).

CROCKERNTOR

Here, between the rocks, the hardened lumps
Of grey flecked granite
Windswept, as they all are,
Outlines engrained on memory,
The mist outrigging each outcrop
Each party of silent travellers wedged
Between the morning wind and the ghosts of tinners
Who came here once to debate and argue
Pay tribute, weigh up their grievances,
Pre-cursor of democracy that outlived their veins of cassiterite
The burrowed streams, washed and panned, refined,
Their common sense, the common cause,
Pounded out with adits and blowing houses,
The stannary laws that clothed each
Town like a roughspun cloak, and steered each destiny
Within the history of that metal.

Gathered in all weathers, beneath the sharp skies,
Four paths at least and a fifth from the north west
They returned each bearing tokens,
A strange reminder of what was.
Each name called out, half familiar
Though five centuries have passed
Caught on the wind and carried in a-long
Out a-long, down a-long lea.
Uncle Tom Cobley and all tethered in the sunlight,
One path for each town,
Like the spokes of a giant wheel
Time revolves within the minds
Of those that choose to listen.
Digging deeper, there is always a rich vein
A silent watchman echoing in the old shaft.
A Parliament within the giant stones,
A reminder of sturdy men, independent and resourceful
Dartmoor lives shaped and furrowed by the wind's water,
Surviving the bog, the rough saddle,
Stirruped, the weather tapping on their shoulder

by James Crowden, composed in 1994 at the time of a celebration of a 500th anniversary of a tinners' Great Court. His poem is part of a limited but fine tradition stretching from Edmund Spenser in 1596 who wrote in *The Faerie Queene* of the River Dart 'nigh chockt with sands of tinny mines' (Spenser 1596, Bk IV, canto XI, stanza 31, line 5), to Anne Born whose poem 'Tin', inspired by the story of William Grose mentioned above, was published in 1989 (Born 1989), to Alice Oswald in 2002 who conjured up some of the tinners themselves (Oswald 2002, 10), and also to Jim Causley who will be performing, on our last evening, his song 'Pride of the Moor', composed in 2015[19].

Acknowledgements

I am grateful to Elizabeth Rutledge for help with reading medieval documents, to James Crowden for telling me of the account in the *Oxford Journal* relating to the Chagford riot, to Chris Kelland for telling me of some early 16th-century merchants, to Ian Mortimer for information on William Peryam, to Francis Stanbrook for drawing the Elford seal, to Henry Summerson for some late 13th and early 14th-century data, to Chris Wordingham for transcripts of early 18th-century coinages, and to Phil Newman for considerable editorial input and assistance with illustrations.

Notes

1. Cornwall Record Office/ME 2736. 'Rapparees' was a term originally used of Irish brigands.
2. The National Archives/JUST 1/186.
3. TNA/JUST/1/186.
4. TNA/JUST/1/188.
5. TNA/E363/4.
6. TNA/SC2/166/44; C1/68/52.
7. TNA/SC2/168/35.
8. Plymouth & West Devon Record Office/81H/3/11.
9. Devon Heritage Centre/337B/MF/135 (62).
10. TNA/E101/272/4.
11. Personal communication from Dr Ian Mortimer.
12. TNA/C21/3.
13. TNA/SP 46/41 fo.28.
14. PWDRO/1082/5.
15. Personal communication from Dr Marta Caroscio.
16. DHC/5533Z/BA/1.
17. *Oxford Journal*, 23 November 1793.
18. PWDRO/874/50/2.
19. The song is recorded on Jim Causley's CD *Forgotten Kingdom* (2015)

Bibliography

Anon 1671 'An Accompt of some Mineral Observations touching the Mines of Cornwal and Devon...' *Philosophical Transactions* **5**, 2096-113

Anon 1913 *Pipe Roll Soc* 34, 31 Henry III

Anon 1920a *Calendar of Letters & Papers Foreign & Domestic, Henry VIII Volume 1, 1509-1514*

Anon 1920b *Calendar of Letters & Papers Foreign & Domestic, 14 Henry VIII*

Blake, W J 1915 'Hooker's Synopsis Chorographical of Devonshire' *Rep Trans Devonshire Ass* **47**, 334-48

Booker, F 1967 *Industrial Archaeology of the Tamar Valley*. Newton Abbot: David & Charles

Born, A 1989 'Tin' *Rep Trans Devonshire Ass* **121**, 37-41

Brooke, J 2001 *The Kalmeter Journal*. Truro: Twelveheads

Broughton, D G 1971 'The Land Half Made' *Kingston Geological Review Research Seminar Issue No.2, April 1971*, **1 no.6**, 1-25

Burt, R et al. 2014 *Mining in Cornwall & Devon – Mines & Men*. Exeter: Univ of Exeter Press

Carew, R 1602 *Carew's Survey of Cornwall*. 1811 edn. London: J. Faulder

Crowden, J 2007 'The Chagford Riot and Pascoe's Well' *Scryfa* **9**, 70-7

Finberg, H P R 1949 'The Stannary of Tavistock' *Rep Trans Devonshire Ass* **81**, 155-84

Fox, H 1999 'Medieval Rural Industry' in Kain, R & Ravenhill, W (eds) *Historical Atlas of South-West England*, 322-9. Exeter: Univ of Exeter Press

Fox, H 2012 *Dartmoor's Alluring Uplands- Transhumance & Pastoral Management in the Middle Ages*. Exeter: Univ of Exeter Press

Greeves, T 1981 *The Devon Tin Industry 1450-1750: an archaeological and historical survey*. (Unpublished PhD, Univ of Exeter)

Greeves, T 1987 'The Great Courts or Parliaments of Devon Tinners 1474-1786' *Rep Trans Devonshire Ass* **119**, 145-67

Greeves, T 1992a ' "Almost a Whole Sheep Salted..." – Tinners and Walkhampton in the Early 17th Century' *Dartmoor Magazine* **29**, Winter 1992, 6-8

Greeves, T 1992b 'Adventures with Fiery Dragons – the Cornish Tinner in Devon from the 15th to the 20th Century' *J Trevithick Soc* **19**, 2-17

Greeves, T 1992c 'Four Devon Stannaries: A Comparative Study of Tinworking in the sixteenth century' in Gray, T et al. (eds) *Tudor & Stuart Devon – The Common Estate & Government*, 39-74. Exeter: Univ of Exeter Press

Greeves, T 1993 'The Good Life? – The Westcountry Tinner AD c.1500-c.1700' *J Trevithick Soc.* **20**, 39-47

Greeves, T 1998 'Dartmoor's Oldest Moorland Route – The Maltern Way?' *Dartmoor Magazine* **51**, Summer 1998, 6-8

Greeves, T 2003 'Devon's Earliest Tin Coinage Roll 1302-3' *Rep Trans Devonshire Ass* **135**, 9-29

Greeves, T 2005 'Dartmoor and the Tinners' Charter of 1305' *Dartmoor Magazine* **78**, Spring 2005, 8-10

Greeves, T 2008 'Tinners and Tinworks of the Bovey Tracey area from Prehistory to the Twentieth Century' *Rep Trans Devonshire Ass* **140**, 15-43

Greeves, T 2010 'Early Tinworking on the East Okement River' *DTRG Newsletter* **39**, July 2010, 7-12

Greeves, T 2011 'The Elford Seal 1661 – 350 Years Old' *Dartmoor Online*, Autumn 2011

Greeves, T 2014 'Totnes 1904 – Devon Sheet 121.05' *Old Ordnance Survey Maps – Totnes 1904*. Consett: Alan Godfrey Maps

Greeves, T 2016 *Called Home – The Dartmoor Tinner 1860-1940: Photographs and Memory*. Truro: Twelveheads Press,

Greeves, T & Newman, P 2011 *The Great Courts of Devon Tinners 1510 and 1710*. Dartmoor Tinworking Research Group Publication No.2

Greeves, T & Stanbrook, E 2013 *Combestone Farm, Holne, Devon – A History*. (Unpub report)

Hatcher, J 1973 *English Tin Production and Trade before 1550.* Oxford: Clarendon Press

Lewis, G R 1908 *The Stannaries – A Study of the Medieval Tin Miners of Cornwall and Devon.* 1965 edn, Truro: Bradford Barton

Mizui, M 1999 *The Interest Groups of the Tin Industry in England c.1580-1640.* (Unpub PhD, Univ of Exeter)

Newman, P 2010 *Environment, Antecedent & Adventure – Tin and Copper Mining on Dartmoor, Devon c.1700-1914.* (Unpub PhD, Univ of Leicester)

Oswald, A 2002 *Dart.* London: Faber & Faber

Patrick, A 1983 'Copper Production in the Tamar Valley in the Eighteenth Century' *Tamar* **5**, 35-42

Pearce, T 1725 *The Laws & Customs of the Stannaries in the Counties of Cornwall & Devon.* London

Pennington, R R 1973 *Stannary Law – A History of the Mining Law of Cornwall and Devon.* Newton Abbot: David & Charles,

Polwhele, R 1806 *The History of Cornwall, Volume 7.* London: Cadell & Davies,

Risdon, T 1811 *The Chorographical Description or Survey of the County of Devon.* London

Spenser, E 1596 *The Faerie Queene.* London: W. Ponsonby

Stoyle, M 1994 *Loyalty and Locality – Popular Allegiance in Devon during the English Civil War.* Exeter: University of Exeter Press

Summerson, H 1987 'Crime and Society in Thirteenth-Century Devon' *Rep Trans Devonshire Ass* **119**, 67-84

Travers, A (ed) 2012 *Robert Furse – A Devon Family Memoir of 1593.* Devon & Cornwall Record Society, n.s. **53**. Exeter

Tin Deposits of the Dartmoor Granite

Richard Scrivener*

In terms of its geology, Dartmoor is defined by a large granite mass or 'pluton', with an area exceeding 600 km^2, and its surrounding belt of thermally altered rocks, the 'metamorphic aureole'. Within the granite and its aureole, the bedrock is cut by numerous quartz veins, some of which carry tin in the form of the tin dioxide, cassiterite and these have formed the basis of the former mining activity. In addition, the former weathering and erosion of the tin-bearing veins have led to accumulations of gravel containing granular cassiterite and these were also an important source of the metal. In this account, the tin-bearing veins will be described in the first part, followed by the gravels derived from them.

The Dartmoor Granite is the easternmost and largest of the plutons, which together constitute the exposed part of the large granite massif or 'batholith' of Southwest England. Isotope geochemical studies carried out in the last 40 years suggest that the granite was emplaced as molten magma, at a relatively high level in the earth's crust some 280 million years ago, during the early part of the Permian period. After emplacement and crystallisation, the solid granite cooled slowly to a temperature of 300 to 350° C over a period of about 3 – 4 million years. During the cooling of the solid granite, tectonic fracturing took place along faults and thermal, saline fluids, emanating from the magma, circulated in them, forming veins, some of which carry tin. Most of the veins trend east to west or ENE to WSW: a later set trend roughly north to south, but within the granite these are mostly barren.

The tin-bearing veins are relatively simple in terms of their mineralogy and structure. The mineral assemblage present in most veins is of quartz (silicon dioxide), tourmaline (a complex silicate mineral with boron and iron), cassiterite (tin dioxide) and iron oxide minerals such as haematite and goethite. A notable feature of the Dartmoor Granite veins is the almost complete absence of sulphide minerals such as pyrite (iron sulphide) and chalcopyrite (copper-iron sulphide), which are important constituents of veins elsewhere in the peninsula. In terms of their form, most of the veins are extensional (pull-apart) structures, with a zone of tourmaline on either margin, then a zone of quartz with cassiterite and tourmaline, and a central core of quartz or quartz with iron oxide minerals. This zonal scheme is quite general, but may be disrupted by later fracturing and tectonic disturbances. In the Birch Tor area of central Dartmoor, the tin veins are notable for the presence in them of specular haematite. The distribution of the main Dartmoor veins and their principal commodities is shown in Fig. 1.

Most of the veins are narrow structures, seldom exceeding 1m in width and within them, the tin ore

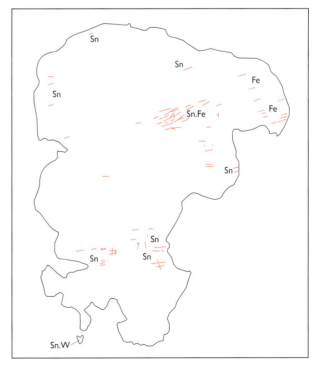

Figure 1 Sketch map showing the general distribution of metalliferous lodes in the Dartmoor Granite.

---

*Geologist. Email: rcscrivener@geologist-uk.com

tends to occur in patchily distributed aggregates or 'bunches'. An example of a rich ore specimen from a vein at Headland Mine (East Birch Tor) is shown in Fig. 2. The length of veins at surface varies considerably, but seldom exceeds 1000m, and is mostly much less. In some places it appears that groups of narrowly spaced, parallel veins occur: these are known as 'sheeted vein complexes' of which the best known example is the large deposit at Hemerdon in south Dartmoor, currently being worked for tungsten and tin.

Mining the veins underground was achieved by excavating the payable ore and then, if necessary, stripping the wall rock to obtain a working width. The ore was then crushed to an extent depending on the grain size of the contained cassiterite. Much of the Dartmoor cassiterite is relatively coarse, so crushing to a granular or coarse sandy state would facilitate liberation of the tin oxide from the waste ('gangue') minerals. After crushing, the ore was subjected to hydraulic washing treatments to separate the dense cassiterite from lighter minerals, such as quartz and tourmaline. The tin concentrate thus produced was then smelted with carbon to reduce the tin oxide to metallic tin. These processes involved considerable skill on the part of the operatives: for example, great care had to be taken in smelting to avoid the re-oxidation of the molten metallic tin.

The weathering of the tin-bearing veins described above took place over very long periods of geological time, subsequent to the uplift and exposure of the granite pluton at the end of the Permian period. In particular, weathering during the Cenozoic epoch, from 65 million years before the present to the beginning of the glacial episodes, some 1.5 million years ago, resulted in the deep alteration of the granite, with very widespread kaolinization (clay alteration) and weakening of the rock structure. The enhanced precipitation during and after the glacial period effected transport and re-deposition of this weathered material in fluvial and periglacial deposits along water courses and in places adjacent to the vein outcrops. These gravel deposits include granular cassiterite ore (or 'tinstone'), which has a substantially greater density than the general weathering products of the granite host rock. Cassiterite is also inert and extremely resistant to erosion, so that these tin-bearing gravels have the capability to survive over long periods of geological time.

Exploitation of the bedrock tin veins and the gravel deposits derived from them has formed the basis of the Dartmoor tin industry over the period

Figure 2 A specimen of rich tin ore from Headland Mine (East Birch Tor), Dartmoor. A zone rich in black tourmaline forms the margin of the vein on the right-hand side of the specimen. Aggregates of brown cassiterite crystals with white quartz form a broad central zone, while white quartz and haematite are present on the left side of the specimen, which would have been the centre of the whole vein. Scale in inches.

from the recent past, going back to the Early Bronze Age. Key features in the long-term survival of this industry have been the considerable volume of the material involved, the simple mineralogy and the extent to which granular cassiterite has been released from the bedrock deposits.

The Dartmoor tin veins have strong similarities with deposits in granitic rocks elsewhere in southwest England. The association with the mineral tourmaline is also notable in the granites of Land's End and St. Austell and is present to some extent in the other granites and their satellite bodies. Another mineralogical association of tin deposits is the presence of veins bordered by an assemblage of quartz and white mica, sometimes with topaz. This is the so-called 'greisen' association, named because of the German language term referring to the grey colour of the vein margins. In continental Europe most of the tin deposits have this greisen association rather than the tourmaline-quartz assemblages commonly met with in Cornwall and Devon. Examples of greisen tin deposits are to be found in the Krusne Hory/ Erzegebirge mining districts of the Czech Republic and Germany respectively and in the northern part of the Iberian peninsula. It is important to note that both tourmaline associated and greisen deposits have a considerable density contrast between the very dense ore mineral cassiterite and the waste or gangue minerals such as quartz, tourmaline and micas. This means that, in broad terms, the similar simple hydraulic separation and beneficiation techniques can be employed for both groups of deposits. In the case of tin deposits with a more complicated mineralogy and, perhaps a strong sulphide association, such as exist elsewhere in southwest England and in some districts of Europe, more complicated separation techniques are required. This factor has undoubtedly been a profound influence on the early and extensive development of the tin industry within the Dartmoor granite.

Dartmoor and Prehistoric to Early Medieval Tinworking

Henrietta Quinnell*

This paper presents a summary of the evidence for tinworking before the full Medieval period on Dartmoor and draws together the data scattered through a variety of sources including that from the recent Early Bronze Age Whitehorse Hill cist burial investigations. The earliest definite evidence for tinworking on the Moor comes from the Middle Bronze Age settlement site at Dean Moor. Data from presumptive wreck sites off the South Devon coast are summarised. Attention is drawn to recent geochemical work. This has great potential for providing information from sites both on the Moor, and away from it especially in the sediments of river valleys. The further development of techniques for geochemical analyses in future years may be expected to provide a much clearer picture of the importance of tin from pre-Medieval Dartmoor than at present.

It is now well established that metalworking was introduced into Britain by the 25th – 24th centuries BC as part of the range of new ideas and practices of the Beaker 'people'. During these centuries copper and gold alone were used, which allows this period to be described with some confidence as Chalcolithic (Allen et al. 2015). A small part of the copper used may have originated in Southwest Britain (Bray 2012), but much of it derives from the excavated copper mine complex at Ross Island, Western Ireland, in association with Beaker pottery (O'Brien 2004). It has also been suggested that many of the earliest Irish gold artefacts have a pattern of trace elements and lead isotopes in their metal indicating a 'Cornish', not an Irish, source (Standish et al. 2015). Analysis of this pattern in copper, gold and tin currently give similar chemical signatures across Devon and Cornwall. There is a tendency, even in modern literature, to use 'Cornwall' where Southwest Britain would in fact be more accurate.

Beaker finds are generally sparse across Southwest Britain and burials with Beakers have not yet been found in the region before around the 23rd century BC, the broad date for the introduction of bronze and so the working of tin. The scarcity of early Beaker burials in the region means that there are few early associations here for copper alloy artefacts. The knife dagger from Fernworthy, Chagford, from a burial in a pit beneath a barrow, associated with a Long Necked Beaker, jet button and flint knife, probably dates to the 22nd or 21st centuries BC: this object is the earliest associated metal artefact from any Beaker burial from either Dartmoor or from Devon or Cornwall (Gerloff 1975, 165, No 280).

By the mature Early Bronze Age, broadly 2000 – 1500 BC, the use of bronze, and so of tin, is well established across Britain, with Devon and Cornwall providing the only potential sources for the latter. From this date onward, a range of copper alloy artefacts has been found in Cornish stream works: the earliest of these is the axe of Trevonissick type from Carnon Valley (Penhallurick 1986, *fig 98*). The artefacts from stream works are supported by finds such as ingots in other contexts and demonstrate extensive tinworking in Cornwall during the period covered by this paper.

But Cornwall and Devon differ. Cornish tin grounds are more integrated into the areas suitable for lowland settlement than those in Devon, and this may be reflected in the practices associated with their working. The author considers the late Roger Penhallurick (1997, 28) probably correct in interpreting the range of finds from Cornish tinworks as symbolic offerings, or in modern archaeological parlance acts of symbolic or structured deposition (e.g. Garrow 2012). It is also likely that the location of tinworks made knowledge of significant finds more readily available to local antiquaries than any

*Email: *H.Quinnell@exeter.ac.uk*

from the more remote works of Dartmoor. It will be shown below that definite evidence for the working of Dartmoor tin does not begin to occur until at least the Middle Bronze Age, rather later than in Cornwall. It is quite possible that early knowledge of Cornish tin grounds was related to the sources of Neolithic Cornish axes (O'Brien 2010). It is now known that two of the principal axe groups, I and XVI, were at least partially sourced to stream and drift cobbles, and this early use of sub-surface deposits may have made prehistoric activity in the river valleys of Cornwall better understood and more accessible than those in Devon (Jones et al. 2013; 2015). In any case we must not assume that modern economic models were relevant to the early stages of metal extraction. The description of Bronze Age social structures and economy put forward as a background to prehistoric tinworking by Herring (1997) still, in the author's view, cannot be bettered.

Two Early Bronze Age sites in Cornwall merit comment, before this paper moves on to concentrate on data from Devon: one revives earlier work and the other looks to the future. At Caerloggas ring cairn on the St Austell granite the author's excavation in 1972 found seven fragments of tin slag, still some of the earliest known in Europe (Miles 1975). Six of these came from the laid turves covering the interior of the ring cairn, the seventh from disturbed material above them. A fragment of a Camerton-Snowshill dagger from the same turves looked like 'glass' as did the slag, which was why it was analysed and not treated as intrusive. The only date for the site is that provided by the dagger fragment, which is of a type for which a date as early as the 18th century BC is now considered possible (Jones & Quinnell 2013). This slag has been studied on several occasions subsequent to the analysis published by Leo Biek in the excavation report (e.g. Shell 1978; Salter 1997) and provides still valuable reference material for prehistoric tin slags (e.g. Malham 2009). All analyses shows a high tin content with small globules of pure tin. Its chemical signature and quality are consistent with 'crucible' smelting of prehistoric type.

Tregurra Valley outside Truro relates to recent work by the Cornwall Archaeological Unit (Taylor 2014). It contains a long sequence of pits from the Early Neolithic to the Early Bronze Age, many with structured fills (Anderson-Whymark & Thomas 2012). Several Early Bronze Age pits, with radiocarbon dates including 2025-1775 and 1866-1631 cal BC, have large quantities of cassiterite and one at least also has crushed cassiterite found by checking the residues from wet-sieving primarily intended for the retrieval of charred plant materials. Checking such residues for crushed cassiterite should in future be routinely considered for post-excavation work on prehistoric sites in Southwest Britain: Tregurra Valley itself lies some distance from a tin ground. The analysis of the Tregurra Valley material, currently ongoing, joins Caerloggas in providing data on Cornish tinworking in the Early Bronze Age. There is rather more frequent evidence from sites such as Tremough, Penryn, from the Middle Bronze Age and later (Jones et al. 2014).

In Devon the only significant find of tin in the Early Bronze Age comes with objects from the Whitehorse Hill cist excavated in 2011 on Dartmoor: the cist has a range of radiocarbon dates indicating 1800-1600 cal BC for the objects deposited within it (Jones 2016). The cist burial, a cremation of a young adult (female by association), had unusual preservation of organic materials and jewellery including artefacts of tin. The cremation and a basket of woven lime bast were wrapped in a bear pelt and laid over a textile and calfskin 'drape'. The basket contained two sets of turned spindle wood studs, a flint flake and a necklace of probably two tin beads, seven amber beads, 92 Kimmeridge shale beads and 110+ clay beads of a probable local clay. There was also a bracelet of cow hair which originally had 35 tin insets although a few of these had degraded. One tin bead from the necklace survives well and consists of a short length of tin wrapped around a central perforation; the presence of the second tin bead is a possible interpretation of some decayed fragments: the bead has no close known parallels although there was an early find, now lost, of a segmented tin bead from the burial at Sutton Veney G11c in Wiltshire (Penhallurick 1986, Fig 24). The bracelet with tin insets also has no known parallels. Analytical work (PXRF) established that the material involved in these items was indeed tin, but no isotopic examination which might have given pointers for potential source material was carried out because of the lack of current reliable comparanda. It is uncertain how far the burial of tin artefacts in a Dartmoor cist indicates local tinworking, particularly as the other non-local materials used in the jewellery may be considered to have acquired significance from their distant sourcing (Sheridan in Jones 2016). The tin used as inlay on one of the jet buttons from a burial at Rameldry in Fife is another rare example of surviving metallic tin from the Early Bronze Age (Sheridan et al. 2003) and this may be considered to have acquired some status by its distance from the metal's source.

Also relevant to the use of tin in the Early Bronze Age is the identification of tin in the glaze of faience beads such as in those from Culbin Sands, Morayshire: tin is usual in faience beads in Britain (Sheridan & Shortland 2004). How far the 'magical' properties of the shiny silver appearance of fresh tin artefacts, transformed in appearance from the dull cassiterite pebbles of which they were made, was significant to those who made, exchanged and used them must remain a matter of debate. Tin is present, more locally, in faience beads from a pit within a ring cairn at Shaugh Moor on the southwest edge of Dartmoor, which also contain traces of zinc, considered to indicate a possible use of china clay (Peek & Warren 1979). The use of a locally dug material, as with the clay of the 'local' beads from the Whitehorse cist, demonstrates exploration and understanding of materials dug out of the earth: such exploration could have led to the discovery of sources for metalworking materials.

There was extensive settlement of Dartmoor by the Middle Bronze Age (e.g. Fleming 1988) and a plot of hut circles alongside stream works of medieval and later date indicates potential tin grounds which could have been worked (Gerrard 2000, *fig 4*). Yet there is scant evidence of actual tinworking on the Moor. The only secure data are that from the Dean Moor enclosed settlement in the Avon Valley excavated 1954-6. Here Hut 7 produced a 3.2mm globule of smelted tin within a burnt spread around a hearth and Hut 5B a cassiterite pebble trodden into the floor (Fox 1957). The ceramics from this site can be now confidently dated to the period 14th-12th centuries BC in the light of current knowledge of Trevisker ceramics and their development (Quinnell 2011). The reconsideration of tin slag from a hut circle at Metherel, redeposited during the late Medieval period, indicates that this was of pre-medieval date and could relate to prehistoric activity (Malham 2009, 427-31).

There is, in mainstream literature, no record of prehistoric finds from Dartmoor tinworks as there is in Cornwall (e.g. Pearce 1983). However, Pearce's (1983, *fig 4.14*) map emphasises a concentration of copper alloy finds from the Chagford and Taunton phases of the Middle Bronze Age around northeast Dartmoor. Pearce's catalogue of artefacts can, however, be extended a little (information T Greeves).

A comment on a palstave from Drewsteignton (Pearce No 226) reads 'a portion of a bronze *cake*, whatever that may be, was said to have been found by it' (Rowe 1896, 121). This *cake* may have been an ingot: several ingots of copper alloy are listed for Devon and Cornwall by Pearce (p.384) but none from so close to Dartmoor. A low-flanged unlooped palstave was found in 1925 by Redvers Webb in the area of Golden Dagger mine, close to Soussons Down (Bellamy 1998, 123): this closely resembles Pearce's No 192 from Bovey Tracey, and is waterworn. This may come from reworking of alluvial ground and has spent some time in a river. This is in private ownership, while the current location of the ingot is unknown.

There is every reason to suppose that bronze making flourished in Devon in the Middle Bronze Age, however much or little metals were worked on the moors at this time. Pearce (1983, 107) has suggested a distinctive type of palstave, which she terms 'Crediton', to indicate a spread in Devon and their presumed local manufacture. She also considers that the three rapier moulds, all paired bivalves, known from Devon - Nos 263a and b from Chudleigh Knighton and No 244 from Holsworthy - may show some local traits (ibid). The Chudleigh Knighton moulds have benefited from further studies, on their location by Greeves (2008) in a valuable study on metalworking in the Bovey Tracey area, and by Berridge (1986) on the context of their deposition. Berridge shows that, while each pair was buried together face to face, one of each pair had been damaged before burial, a fact not demonstrated by previous illustration (e.g. Pearce 1983, *plate 134*), and their context appeared that of deliberate deposition when they could not, or had been caused not, to be usable.

The sites of three presumed wrecks on the South Devon coast are relevant to our understanding of early metalworking in Devon. Two lie off the coast just east of Salcombe in Moor Sand Bay. The presumed wreck site now known as Moor Sand was first located in 1977: the metalwork which represents it was published in 2013 (Needham et al.). A scatter of some 30 artefacts, copper alloy and a little gold, lay fairly close in shore. Its publication dates these broadly to the 13th century BC and the earlier part of the Penard period; most may probably not be of British manufacture. While this small cargo is informative about many aspects of metalworking and the exchange of artefacts at the end of the Middle

Bronze Age, it does not directly contribute to the sourcing of tin. However, diving continued in the Moor Sand area and, while work on the Moor Sand publication was in progress, located a larger group of Bronze Age metal artefacts. These are now referred to as Salcombe B, to distinguish the area from a post-medieval wreck site Salcombe A.

Some of the Salcombe B material was included in the Moor Sand publication, but more was retrieved after the volume was prepared. The Salcombe B artefacts are deposited in the British Museum, and many details and images have been made electronically available by the Museum (www.britishmuseum.org/research/search_the_collection_database.aspx). Brief details are provided in the update to Pearce's 1983 South Western Bronze Age metalwork volume (Knight et al. 2015). The Salcombe B assemblage is larger than that at Moor Sand and lies slightly further out to sea (Needham et al. 2013, *fig 1.11*) but overlapping a little with it. Some of the artefacts published belong to the Late Bronze Age 1000 – 800 BC. The assemblage includes 282 copper alloy ingots and 42 tin ingots. The tin ingots are generally round or circular and appear to have been found mostly in a close area away from other finds. A paper on their composition and microstructure has now been published (Wang et al. 2016), demonstrating that the ingots were of very pure tin, but further work, on tin and lead isotopes, is needed, both from the ingots and from other relevant material, before any comment upon source can be made. Wang et al. suggest that the ingot group may date either to the Penard period of Moor Sand or to the Late Bronze Age date of Salcombe B.

The report on Moor Sand includes details of 18 other prehistoric marine sites with metalwork around Southern Britain (Needham et al. 2013, *fig 4.1*), of which 16 lie to the east of Salcombe, between Dorset and Essex, and no others in Devon. None has any tin artefacts.

The third presumptive wreck site is that discovered in 1991 off Mothecombe in Bigbury Bay (Fox 1995). This is sometimes referred to as 'Erme Estuary' and was evidenced only by some 40 tin ingots. These were mostly oval or round, but a few were rectangular and a couple H-shaped (ibid *figs 5-7*); most weighed less than 1.5kg but eight between 4 and 7kg. It is notable that there is no other associated material, a fact which might indicate different exchange conditions to those relating to the two Salcombe wrecks. The report on the Salcombe B ingots examined two of the Bigbury Bay ingots and the results, while small scale, indicated rather different smelting and refining traditions for the two ingot groups. Aileen Fox in her publication made it clear that the ingots could not be dated, but indicated a possible early Post-Roman date. In this she may have been influenced by a misunderstanding of the data, then unpublished, on the ingot from Trethurgy in Cornwall and also by a then recently published radiocarbon date for ingots from Prah Sands near Marazion (Quinnell 2004, 73-6, *fig 47*). The Bigbury ingots may in fact date anywhere within the prehistoric to Early Medieval periods.

At Tor Royal, near Princetown, detailed study of a peat core supported by many radiocarbon dates has demonstrated enhanced tin levels likely to derive from airborne dust from fairly local tin smelting (Meharg et al. 2012). The pattern of these levels suggests sporadic working through the Iron Age to the Roman period and then a stable high level from *c.* AD 100 to *c.* AD 400 and again from AD 700 to AD 1100. The depth and nature of the peat deposits did not allow conclusions for the period before the Iron Age. This evidence is the first substantial data for tinworking for the prehistoric period, and demonstrates the importance that geochemical studies allied to radiocarbon dating now have. It is pertinent that this comes in a period, the Iron Age, when evidence for activity on the moor has been largely absent (Silvester 1979). However, it can be demonstrated that parts of Devon may have been largely aceramic in the 1st millennium BC (Quinnell 1999, 53), a situation highlighted by the small assemblage of Early Iron Age date recently retrieved in the research excavation of a hut circle at Teigncombe (Gerrard 2016). The potentially hidden nature of much of the evidence for later prehistoric activity on Dartmoor is also highlighted by the recent work on peat cores from the high moor with dates in the 1st millennium BC from levels with palaeobotanical data for tree clearance and subsequent open grazing (Fyfe & Woodbridge 2012).

With the Iron Age, data from literature of Greece and Rome begins to be relevant but much of this is at least secondhand and very muddled, and it should be noted that no reliable references to a Phoenician trade in tin with Britain are considered to exist. A good modern account of the formation of this literature and its reliability is given by Cunliffe (2001) who, together with other scholars, considers the best authority to be Pytheas of Marseille, who visited Britain *c.* 325 BC. His work does not survive but is reliably quoted by

Diodorus Siculus in the late 1st century BC (ibid 78):

> 'The inhabitants of Britain who live on the promontory of Belerion are especially friendly to strangers….It is they who work the tin, treating the layer which contains it in an ingenious way. This layer, being like rock, contains earthy seams and in them the workers quarry the ore which they then melt down to clean from its impurities. Then they work the tin into pieces the size of knucklebones and convey it to an island which lies off Britain, called Ictis; for at ebb-tide the space between the island and the mainland becomes dry and they can take the tin in large quantities to the island on wagons.'

'Belerion' is generally considered to be the Land's End promontory (Rivet & Smith 1979, 266), but, given the potential for tin production across the whole Southwest peninsula, it can be interpreted as a shorthand for this whole area. 'Ictis' is usually interpreted as St Michael's Mount in West Cornwall, sometimes as Mount Batten at the mouth of the Plym, and may be a conflation of a number of coastal trading places – Herring's (1997, 21) 'Ictis type sites'. There is good evidence for cross-channel contacts from Mount Batten (Cunliffe 1988), and more than is sometimes supposed from St Michael's Mount (Quinnell 1995).

The Tor Royal core indicates tinworking throughout the Roman period and scattered evidence for activity of this period on and around the Moor has been assembled by Greeves (2007) to which can now be added a reference to several coins from the vicinity of the north end of Challacombe Down, probably at Scudley Beam (information T Greeves). A map of 1825 in the Devon Heritage Centre (DRO/36652/P1) has the annotation 'Ancient Tin Mine several Coins of Julius Caesar have been found here (in 1823)'. The full name of 'Julius Caesar' was not used on coins and his coins are rare in Britain but Caesar as a title was used by numerous subsequent rulers of Rome, so these coins cannot be closely dated within the Roman period (Reece 2002).

Three tin ingots from Lewtrenchard Mill just off the northwest side of Dartmoor have been found during metal detecting (Paynter 2003). These are recorded as found 'on top of each other' at a depth of 0.36m, and are of impure tin, containing some lead, the smallest also a little copper. The ingots are considered likely to be of Roman date, based on the type of metal used. These are the first tin ingots from the land in Devon to which a date can be supplied with some certainty. Ingots are much more frequent finds in Cornwall, as are moulds and tinworking detritus, a reminder of the continuance of flourishing tinworking in Cornwall (Penhallurick 1986). However, two conjoining fragments of a granite mould were found in a ditch containing late 3rd/4th century pottery at Springfield, Site 34, on the South–West Gas Reinforcement Pipeline (Mudd & Joyce 2014, 102, *fig 3.27*). The site at Springfield, Ugborough, lies just off the Moor a little to the southeast of Ivybridge (ibid, *fig 1.1*). The mould was part of a nest designed to produce two or more plates (ibid 113, *fig 3.32-33*). X-ray fluorescence analysis of vitreous hearth lining from another context on this site showed some traces of tin, 0.20% and 0.17%, considered to be consistent with the working of pewter on the site, which otherwise had extensive evidence for ironworking (ibid 117).

Moving on into the post-Roman period, evidence for tinworking comes from a core taken from a palaeochannel far down the Erme Valley a little distance upstream from the normal tidal limit (Thorndycraft et al. 2004). The sequence in the core was analysed for its chemistry and a layer of sandy silt, interspersed between two peat deposits, showed heightened tin concentrations (ibid *fig 8*). The beginning and end of this silt deposition was radiocarbon dated between AD 245-366 and AD 440-730. The initial date comes directly from the top of the peat beneath the silt, the later date was estimated, based on the rate of peat growth dated at different points in the core. Both the increase in sandy silt and its heightened tin concentrations were considered consistent with, and therefore potentially dating, tin streaming further up the Erme Valley. This therefore suggests an episode of tinworking at some date in the late Roman to early post-Roman periods. It should be noted that the Tor Royal core discussed above (Meharg et al. 2012) showed an absence of tinworking in this period.

Mothecombe, at the mouth of the Erme, was a coastal settlement with imported amphorae (Agate et al. 2012) as was Bantham, at the mouth of the Avon. Both are late 5th to 6th centuries and both on the estuaries of rivers flowing down from the Moor. Activity at these sites has been linked to the ingot wreck in Bigbury Bay, as this lies in the bay where Mothecombe is situated. The biography of St John of Alexandria, active in the early 7th century, is frequently quoted in connection with post-Roman trade between Britain and the Mediterranean. The text of the biography is published in an Appendix by Penhallurick (1986). This, compiled in the 10th century from drafts by contemporaries, refers to a cargo of tin from the 'islands of Britain'. It should, however, be noted that this work contains elements of miraculous hagiography, more specifically that, once arrived in Alexandria, the cargo of tin was turned into silver: this hagiography calls into question overall reliability of the biography.

There appears to be no current artefactual evidence for the post-Roman period on Dartmoor. However, the work of Peter Crew has reassessed the evidence of ironworking at Kestor, a hut circle excavated by Aileen Fox (1954). This was published as Iron Age, but there is now a radiocarbon date from the iron slag calibrating to AD 428 - 633 (Beta-202300). Crew considers the ironworking as of a trial nature rather than part of an established industry. A summary of this data, together with a review of pottery, which demonstrates the presence of previously unrecognised Middle Bronze Age material, is available in Gerrard (2016). Paradoxically the site, previously considered as a high point of Iron Age activity on Dartmoor, currently provides the sole evidence for early post-Roman activity on Dartmoor! Note, however, the reduction of *Alnus* pollen and charcoal concentrations in the peat of the Walkham catchment radiocarbon dated to the 9th/10th centuries AD which are suggested to be linking with the start of tin streaming at Merrivale (Geary et al. 1997).

This paper has already flagged up several examples of geochemical research which are contributing firm data to the topic of early tinworking on Dartmoor. Here it is relevant to refer to the work carried out at the Trewortha reconstructed round house on Bodmin Moor (Carey et al. 2014). Neil Burridge had carried out replication work here on Bronze Age metals and recorded the positions of his different activities. A fine mesh of samples across the house has been analysed and the results closely reflect the pattern of Burridge's activities which included tinworking. This indicates the potential for geochemical research on sites of all kinds where tinworking may have been carried out.

This paper makes no claim to original research but attempts to gather together the accessible but scattered published data which may be relevant to the production of tin of Dartmoor before the full Medieval period. Any statement in 2016 is only 'work in progress' and we are a long way from establishing the essential facts. These data, drawn together, allow several conclusions to be drawn. The character of early tinworking and its relationships within contemporary societies may have differed in Devon and Cornwall. There is very limited evidence for the working of Dartmoor tin before the full Medieval period but it is highly likely that data for this will be forthcoming in the future. These data are likely to come from the application of the increasingly sophisticated geochemical techniques which may be expected to increase in range and relevance.

Acknowledgements

The author is greatly indebted to Dr T Greeves for supplying details of a number of finds not previously flagged up in the mainstream literature and to all her colleagues who have worked in the field of the prehistory of Southwest Britain through the years and also to F M Griffith for commenting upon this paper in draft.

References

Agate, A, Duggan, M, Roskams, S, Turner, Campbell, E, Hall, A, Kinnaird, T, Luke, Y, McIntosh, F, Neal, C and Young, R 2012 'Early Medieval Settlement at Mothecombe, Devon: The Interaction of Local, Regional and Long-Distance Dynamics' *Archaeol J* **169:1**, 343-94

Allen, M J, Gardiner, J and Sheridan, A (eds) 2012 *Is there a British Chalcolithic? People, place and polity in the later 3rd millennium*. Oxford: Oxbow Books. Prehistoric Society Research Paper 4

Anderson-Whymark, H and Thomas, J 2012. *Regional Perspectives on Neolithic Pit Deposition*. Oxford: Oxbow Books

Bellamy, R 1998 *The Heart of Dartmoor*. Tiverton: Devon Books

Berridge, P 1986 'New Light on the Chuldleigh Rapier Moulds' *Proc Devon Archaeol Soc* **44**,176-180

Bray, P 2012 ' Before 29Cu became Copper; tracing the recognition and invention of metalleity in Britain and Ireland during the third millennium BC' in Allen et al. (eds) 2012, 56-70

Budd, P and Gale, D 1997 *Prehistoric Extractive Metallurgy in Cornwall*. Truro: Cornwall County Council

Carey, C J, Wickstead, H J, Juleff, G, Anderson, J C and Barber, M 2014 'Geochemical survey and metalworking: analysis of chemical residues derived from experimental non-ferrous metallurgical processes in a reconstructed roundhouse' *J Archaeol Science* **49**, 383-397

Cunliffe, B, 1988 *Mount Batten, Plymouth. A Prehistoric and Roman Port*. Oxford: Committee for Archaeology Monograph **26**

Cunliffe, B 2001 *Pytheas the Greek. The man who discovered Britain*. London: Allen Lane, |Penguin Press

Fleming, A 1988 *The Dartmoor Reaves*. London: Batsford

Fox, A 1954 'Excavations at Kestor, an Early Iron Age settlement near Chagford, Devon' *Rep Trans Devonshire Ass* **86**, 21-62

Fox, A, 1957 'Excavations at Dean Moor (1954-6)' *Rep Trans Devon Ass* **98**, 18-77

Fox, A 1995 'Tin Ingots from Bigbury Bay' *Proc Devon Archaeol Soc* **53**, 11-24

Fyfe, R M and Woodbridge, J 2012 'Differences in time and space in vegetation patterning; analysis of pollen data from Dartmoor, UK' *Landscape Ecology* **27**, 745-60

Garrow, D 2012 'Odd deposits and average practice. A critical history of the concept of structured deposition' *Archaeological Dialogues* **19:02**, 85-115. Cambridge Archaeological Journals on-line

Gearey, B R, West, S and Charman, D J 1997 'The Landscape Context of Medieval Settlement on the South-Western Moors of England. Recent Palaeoenvironmental Evidence from Bodmin Moor and Dartmoor' *Medieval Archaeol*, **41**, 195-210

Gerloff, S 1975 *The Early Bronze Age Daggers in Great Britain*. Munich: Prahistorische Bronzefunde **6.2**

Gerrard, S 2000 *The Early British Tin Industry*. Stroud: Tempus

Gerrard, S 2016 'Archaeology and bracken: The Teigncombe prehistoric roundhouse excavation 1999 – 2005' *Proc Devon Archaeol Soc* **74**, 1-64

Greeves, T 2007 'Romans on Dartmoor' [Internet resource] www.dartmoorresource.org.uk/history/ancient/148-the-romans-on-dartmoor-tom-greeves

Greeves, T 2008 'Tinners and Tinworks of the Bovey Tracey area from Prehistory to the Twentieth Century' *Rep Trans Devonshire Ass* **140**, 15- 43

Herring, P 1997 'The prehistoric landscape of Cornwall and west Devon: economic and social contexts for metallurgy' in P Budd and D Gale 1997, 19-22

Jones, A M, 2016 *Preserved in the peat: investigation of a Bronze Age burial on Whitehorse Hill, Dartmoor and its wider context*. Oxford: Oxbow Books

Jones, A M and Quinnell, H 2013 'Daggers in the West: Early Bronze Age Daggers and Knives in the South-west peninsula' *Proc Prehistoric Soc* **79**, 165-92

Jones, A M, Gossip, J and Quinnell, H (eds) 2014 *Settlement and metalworking in the Middle Bronze Age and beyond. New evidence from Tremough, Cornwall*. Leiden: Sidestone Press

Jones, A M, Quinnell, H, Lawson-Jones, A and Tyacke, A 2013 'Landscapes of stone: contextualising greenstone working and lithics from Clodgy Moor, West Penwith, Cornwall' *Archaeol J* **170**, 2-29.

Jones, A M, Quinnell, H, Taylor, R T and Thomas, A C 2015 'Sampling at Viaduct Farm, Polstrong, Cornwall: Identifying the Source of the Group XVI Greenstones' *Lithics* **36**, 55-63

Knight, M, Omerod, T and Pearce, S 2015 *The Bronze Age Metalwork of South West England. A corpus of material found between 1982 and 2014*. Oxford: Brit Arch Rep Brit Ser 6**10**

Malham, A 2009 *The classification and interpretation of tin smelting remains from southwest England*. (Unpublished PhD thesis, University of Bradford)

Meharg, A A, Edwards, K J, Schofield, J E, Raab, A, Feldmann, J, Moran, A, Bryant, C L, Thornton, B, and Dawson, J J C, 2012 'First comprehensive peat depositional records for tin, lead and copper associated with the antiquity of Europe's largest cassiterite deposits' *J Archaeol Sci* **39**, 717-727

Miles, H 1975 'Barrows on the St Austell Granite' *Cornish Archaeol* **14**, 5-82

Mudd, A and Joyce, S 2014 *The Archaeology of the South-West Reinforcement Gas Pipeline, Devon: Investigations 2005-2007*. Cirencester: Cotswold Archaeology Monograph 6

Needham, S, Parham, D and Frieman, C J 2013 *Claimed by the Sea: Salcombe, Langdon Bay, and other marine finds of the Bronze Age*. CBA Research Report **173**

O'Brien, W 2004 *Ross Island: mining, metal and society in early Ireland*. Galway: Galway University Press

O'Brien, W 2010 'Copper Axes, Stone axes: Production and exchange systems in the Chalcolithic of Britain and Ireland', in Prast, M (ed) *Mining in European History*, 255-60. University of Innsbruck

Paynter, S 2003 *Analysis of Ingots from Lew Mill, Devon*. London: Historic England Research Report 68/2003

Peak, R A P and Warren, S E 1979 'The Faience Beads from Shaugh Moor' in G Wainwright, J A Fleming and K Smith 'The Shaugh Moor Project: First Report' *Proc Prehist Soc* **45**, 26-27

Pearce, S 1983 *The Bronze Age Metalwork of South West England*. Oxford: Brit Arch Rep Brit Ser **120**

Penhallurick, R D 1986 *Tin in Antiquity*. London: Institute of Metals

Penhallurick, R D 1997 'The evidence for prehistoric mining in Cornwall, in P Budd and D Gale 1997, 23-34

Quinnell, H 1995 'First Millennium BC and Roman Period Ceramics' in Herring, P *St Michael's Mount: Archaeological Works, 1995-8*. Cornwall County Council, 39-46

Quinnell, H 1999 'Pottery' in Gent, T H and Quinnell, H 'Excavations of a Causewayed Enclosure and Hillfort on Raddon Hill, Stockleigh Pomeroy' *Proc Devon Archaeol Soc* **57**, 38-53

Quinnell, H 2004 *Trethurgy: Excavations at Trethurgy Round, St Austell: Community and Status in Roman and Post-Roman Cornwall*. Truro: Cornwall County Council

Quinnell, H 2012 'Trevisker Pottery: some recent studies', in Britnell, W J and Silvester, R J (eds) *Reflections on the Past. Essays in honour of Frances Lynch*. 146-71. Cambrian Archaeological Association

Reece, R 2002 *The Coinage of Roman Britain*. Stroud: Tempus

Rivet, A L F and Smith, C 1979 *The Place-Names of Roman Britain*. London:Batsford

Rowe, S 1896 *A Perambulation of Dartmoor.* Tiverton: Devon books, 1985 facsimile edition

Salter, C J 1997 'A note on tin slags from Caerloggas Down, Cornwall and the Upper Merrivale blowing house' in P Budd and D Gale 1997, 45-50

Shell, C A 1978 'The Early Exploitation of Tin Deposits in South-West England' in M Ryan (ed) *The Origins of Metallurgy in South-west England.* Dublin: Stationery Office, 251-263

Sheridan, J A, Davis, M, Chambers, S, Anheuser, K, Heron, C and Redvers-Jones, H 2003 'The V-perforated buttons' in L Baker, J A Sheridan and T G Cowie 'An Early Bronze Age 'dagger grave' from Rameldry Farm, near Kingskettle, Fife' *Proc Soc Antiq Scot* **133**, 89-95

Sheridan, J A and Shortland, A 2004. "…beads which have given rise to so much dogmatism, controversy and rash speculation': faience in Early Bronze Age Britain and Ireland' in I A G Shepherd and G J Barclay (eds) *Scotland in Ancient Europe. The Neolithic and Early Bronze Age of Scotland in their European Context.* Edinburgh: Society of Antiquaries of Scotland, 263-9

Silvester, R J 1979 'The Relationship of First Millennium BC Settlement to the Upland Areas of the South-West' *Proc Devon Archaeol Soc* **37**, 176-190

Standish, C D, Bruno, D, Hawkesworth, C J and Pike, A W D 2015 'A Non-Local Source of Irish Chalcolithic and Early Bronze Age Gold' *Proc Prehist Soc* **81**, 149-78

Taylor, S R 2014 *Truro Eastern District Centre, Cornwall. Assessment Reports.* (Archive Report). Truro: Cornwall County Council

Thorndycraft, V R, Pirrie, D and Brown, A G, 2004 'Alluvial Records of Medieval and Prehistoric Tin Mining on Dartmoor, Southwest England' *Geoarchaeology* **19:3**, 219 -236

Wang, Q, Strekopytov, S, Roberts, B W and Wilkin, N 2016 'Tin ingots from a probable Bronze Age shipwreck off the coast of Salcombe, Devon: composition and microstructure' *J Archaeol Science* **67**, 80- 92

Mining for Tin on Dartmoor in the Eighteenth to Twentieth Centuries: The Landscape Legacy

Phil Newman*

Abstract

The landscape legacy for the exploitation of tin reflects some of the most dynamic episodes of human intervention within the moorlands of Dartmoor, manifest mostly through earthwork remains, ruined buildings and long-disused infrastructure. When analysed, these surviving components demonstrate a breadth of chronology, technological advancement, and adaptation to diverse environmental conditions, which although interesting in themselves, can also help throw light on aspects of social and economic variation.

This paper explores the landscape evidence for the mining of tin on Dartmoor, focussing mainly on 19th century examples. It concentrates on what can be learned about extraction and ore dressing through close examination of surface remains and discusses how analysis of this resource, when considered in its historical context, can help us appreciate the extent, complexity and significance of the tin industry on Dartmoor, as well as adding subtle details to the social and economic narrative.

The work also provides a summary of sites where significant field remains survive and includes much new survey data.

1 INTRODUCTION

Compared with 25 years ago, when the DTRG was first formed, the recording and interpretation of tinworking landscapes has expanded massively. Indeed, before that time, Dartmoor's industrial landscapes in general, were rarely considered holistically as we would today, and archaeological research had been aimed mostly at ruined buildings and other structures. More recently, the work has taken several directions, including scientific sampling, documentary research, and excavation, culminating in the works on Crownhill Down (*see* Hughes, *this volume*). However, within this period, the main source of archaeological information has been landscape investigation and earthwork survey, the analysis of which has assisted greatly with our understanding of both the extent and complexity of tinworking remains as well as broader economic, social and technological questions.

In the digital age, earthwork, or topographic survey is often seen as a rather old-fashioned methodology; many archaeologists now prefer to use remote sensing techniques such as LiDAR, digital terrain modelling and aerial survey as their main recording tools, and some dismiss this method as unscientific. There are also those who believe, with some justification, that the landscape remains of mines only represent the surface expression of a much more extensive underground world, and recording this surface evidence alone cannot really be helpful.

But a measured survey should not be seen simply as a means of creating a representation of surface evidence, in the same way we might consider a map, and the preferred term is 'analytical survey'; the outcome should be an interpretation of the site as well as description and graphic record. To most people, and indeed to many archaeologists, a tinwork is an impenetrable jumble of lumps and bumps, which it is the surveyor's job to disentangle and explain. However, the prime purpose of archaeological research is to help us understand the lives of people who lived in the past, not simply to make a record of the 'things' and places they left behind. So, although the origins of these jumbles of earthworks need to be explained, along with their chronology if possible, the human story that might reside within them needs to be addressed as well.

The occasion of this conference offers a good opportunity to share some examples of analytical

*Southwest Landscape Investigations *www.philnew.co.uk*

survey, focussing on the mines of the 18th to 20th centuries, which, for want of a better term, is here referred to as the capitalist period of Dartmoor's mining history.

Following what John Taylor, the famous mining entrepreneur, referred to as 'a period of slumber', in the first part of the 18th century (Taylor 1799, 362), an interest was re-awakened in Devon tin mining from approximately the 1780s onwards. Much capital was required to develop the deeper mines, so most of them were financed on a joint venture basis. The field remains undeniably reflect this step-change in the economic and historical context and an analysis of the surface evidence can offer much more than a descriptive overview.

These later mines do, nevertheless, need to be discussed within their context as components of an evolving mining landscape with much earlier origins, rather than simply examining specific dateable, documented operations in temporal isolation. The miners themselves were very aware of the ancestry of their occupation and decisions they made were often influenced by tradition as well as economics. The environment and the technology required to work with it, were also key agents in the development of the mining landscape.

2 THE DARTMOOR CONTEXT

There are ten major metalliferous mining zones in the southwest peninsula of Britain. The majority of these are in Cornwall, although the Tamar valley is shared with Devon, whose only other tin producing district is Dartmoor.

Devon's tin deposits are configured differently, if compared with some of the very prosperous Cornish districts, which propelled Devon's tin industry on a similar but alternative trajectory. Alluvial tin was plentiful for the medieval tinners in Devon, who harvested great riches from their streamworks, extending, it is often said, along nearly every Dartmoor river valley and sometimes into the hinterland. The place is also well endowed with shallow tin lodes outcropping near the surface. These could be exploited by opencast methods or shallow shafts with access to underground galleries. Deeper tin lodes, of the type that require more advanced underground techniques to exploit them, are fewer in number, especially within the higher altitudes of the granite zone. There are of course notable exceptions, such as Owlacombe mine on the edge of Dartmoor, which, for Devon, was an exceptionally deep tin mine at over 100 fathoms (183m) (Hamilton Jenkin 1981,122).

These subtle nuances in the geology and the consequent scale of the industry, are reflected in the methods employed by miners, and in their landscape legacy, which differs from that of the deep mined zones such as Camborne or St Just. Economically, Dartmoor was very much at the margins of the Cornubian tinfield by the 18th-20th centuries, but what it lacked in output then, it more than makes up for in archaeological legacy today.

Figure 1 shows the distribution of known non-ferrous metal mines, on and surrounding Dartmoor, from which it may be seen that the concentration of copper (green), silver-lead (black) and some tin mines (red), surrounds the upland in places like the Teign valley – which was mostly occupied by lead mines – as well as Ashburton, Plympton and the Tavy Valley. However, tin was the major ore of the district, with a distribution extending over the granite zone of the moorland and its peripheries. The map shows the sites of documented tin mines from the 18th-20th century, where the location is known and/or field remains survive (*see also* Table 1). The full extent of tinworks in Devon, from all ages, awaits a comprehensive map but many of the important locations are represented here by these later mines, if not the earlier detail.

3 EXPLOITING THE 'OLD MEN'S' WORKINGS

Most of the workable Devon tin lodes had been discovered and partly exploited well before the 18th century, but any lack of depth these lodes may have had, did not stop later miners in the 18th and 19th century from assuming that there was still great potential on Dartmoor, especially at locations with evidence of earlier working. In fact, every later tin mine within the granite mass, and many if not all within the metamorphic aureole of Dartmoor (i.e. all tin mines depicted in Fig. 1), were attempts to exploit sources of ore that were evident on the surface by the abandoned workings of earlier tinners, regardless of scale.

It is a common motivation among metal miners the world over, where working in areas of long mining tradition, that their predecessors, or the 'old men', as they are almost universally known, were unable to fully exploit the deposits; an assumption based on the concept that technology and know-how in the past were less developed and, therefore, less effective.

The scene in the Newleycombe Valley (Fig. 2)

is typical of what might have greeted the would-be miners exploring Dartmoor in the 18th and early 19th centuries. There was much evidence that the tin streamers had prospered in the distant past, and that prospecting for lode tin had occurred in the form of many trial pits and shallow shaft workings. There was also massive evidence that tin lodes had been exploited successfully, through the evidence of huge openworks, such as the example to the bottom right of the photo, known as Willabeam. Unless occurring within their own living memory, which is unlikely, these 18th and 19th century miners would be unaware of the date that the long-abandoned sites were last worked.

These later miners believed that the old men had merely scratched the surface, so their own 'modern' techniques of unwatering the mines and hauling ore, as well as the availability of explosives, and advanced forms of ore crushing and dressing, would allow further exploitation of what some claimed were unfathomable and unlimited resources.

This is reflected in the optimistic writings of those who wished to promote tin mining, where old men's workings were often preferred as a prerequisite of assured success. For example, below is a selection of statements made by various mine promoters from the 1790s into the 1880s, all making similar claims.

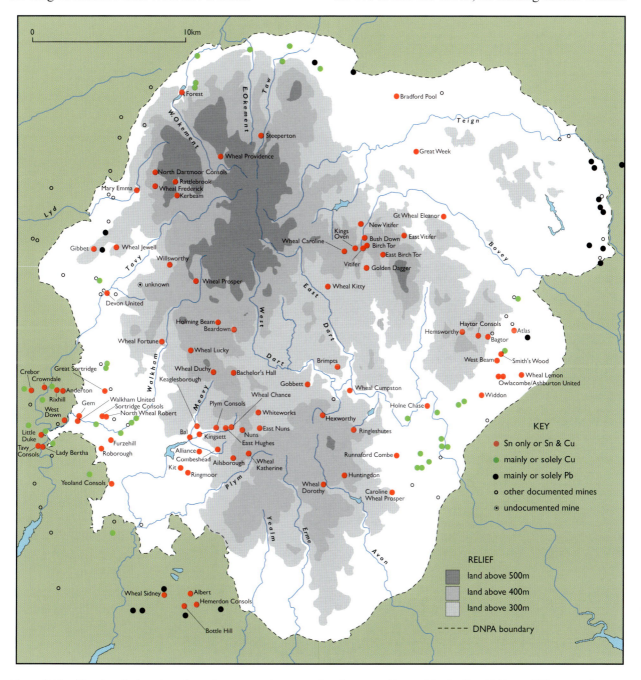

Figure 1 Map Showing the location of non-ferrous metal mines within Dartmoor National Park, Tavy Valley and Plympton district. Only mines where tin was produced or prospected for are annotated, using the most well-known mine name (see also Table 1).

In 1787, William Warren, who was promoting his tin mines near Postbridge, said of the 'old men's' efforts:

> 'where rich ore was not accessible by the simple process then used, the miners had not perseverance or property to pursue or adventure in deeper researches' (Warren 1787, 1)

Prospectuses for several other tin mines tell a similar story:

> .....Wheal Champion, and Wheal Fanny ...., after a lapse of many years, having ceased working in consequence of the then imperfect state of mining science, are to be recommended with all the advantages of modern experiences and machinery. (*EFP* 11.02.1836)

> ...and if this mine proves as successful in depth to the modern miners as it was shallow to the ancients, it will be another proof of their correct judgment as precedents for modern mines in this district....... (*TG* 18.05.1860)

> Some of our best mines in Cornwall were discovered by sinking shafts on the old surface workings and coming upon the magnificent veins of which the men of ancient commerce only possessed means of what is called in mining phraseology "scratching the backs." (*EFP* 10.2.1875)

> History is likely soon to repeat itself in this grand old tin mine. A splendid lode, 10 ft. in width, which has only been operated upon to the depth of 20 ft. by ancient workers, will in a few days be cut at 90 ft. deep, and miners who know the property are willing to work it at a tribute of 6s.8d. in the £." (*MJ* 06.10.1883)

> It is seldom however, that a new mine is opened from the surface.....the reworking of those that are from time to time abandoned being in general sufficient to engage all speculators... (Anon 1851).

It was even asserted that Gobbett Mine, near Hexworthy, had been in production since the time of the prophet Ezekiel (*MJ* 06.10.1883).

3.1 Field Evidence

If we examine the earthwork remains which typically survive at Dartmoor tin mines, we can always witness evidence of earlier episodes, especially within the more extensive and enduring tinworking landscapes such as Hexworthy (Newman 1996), Vitifer (Newman 2004), Ailsborough (Newman

Figure 2 Aerial photograph of the Newleycombe Valley showing old men's workings including streamworks, openworks, pit works, trial pits, leats (Damian Grady © Historic England Archive).

1999, 105-48) and Whiteworks, but three defining examples are Huntingdon Mine, Wheal Prosper and Wheal Mary Emma.

Huntingdon mine (Fig. 3) is in the Western Wella Brook valley, and went by several names in its career (Brooke 1980, 74-6). It is situated on a fairly remote part of south Dartmoor, in a stream valley that was massively affected by earlier working, for both alluvial and lode tin. A large area was taken in for the late 18th and early 19th century mine sett (Greeves 2001, 8-10), but the miners concentrated on sinking a number of shafts into a shallow openwork, which clearly represented remains of an earlier lode working, that extended east to west on both sides of the stream. These separate periods of mining activity have resulted in an alignment of jumbled pits and mounds.

Interpretation of the earthwork survey covering the east side of the brook, has provided a relative chronology for some of the surface remains. Clearly there is also much to be said about the ruined buildings, structures and dressing floors (*see* below) at these mines as well, but for the current purpose the extractive activity is the focus.

Prospecting pits, shown in green, probably represent some of the earliest diggings at this location, their alignment cut through by later features. Orange represents what remains of the earliest extractive phase, or old men's workings, which comprised, probably, a combination of shallow shafts, pits and gullies, working the back of the lode outcrop; they are as yet undated, but perhaps 17th century or earlier. The later shafts were sunk into these old workings and represent the efforts of several mine companies who worked the mine from the mid-18th century. The blue shafts may have been associated with the earlier companies but by the 1860s, an abandoned mine plan (DHC AMR 15314) identifies a number of the shafts viable at that time, some named, whose location coincides with those here depicted in red. The tops of the shafts from all periods have gradually fallen in or have been partly backfilled, leaving wide conical pits, surrounded by spoil.

A similar scenario may be postulated for Wheal Prosper (Fig. 4) in the Walkham valley, where an earlier, comparatively shallow openwork and a number of shallow pits were re-explored by miners in the 19th century. Again, we don't know the date of the old men's workings but we may conjecture 17th century or earlier. Some renewed mining activity is recorded by 1807, but the majority of the underground activity was between 1847 and 1854 (Greeves 1975, 6-7). During that period some tin was sold but the depth of the mine was very limited. At least three

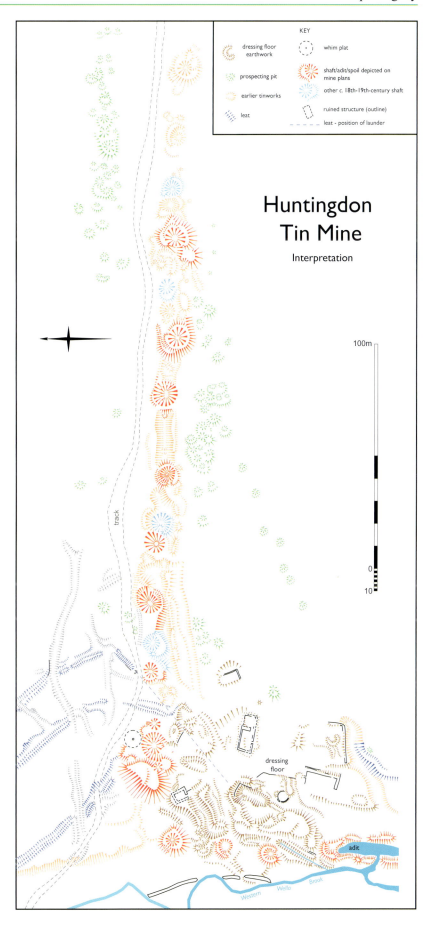

Figure 3 Earthwork survey of Huntingdon Mine, including interpretation.

31

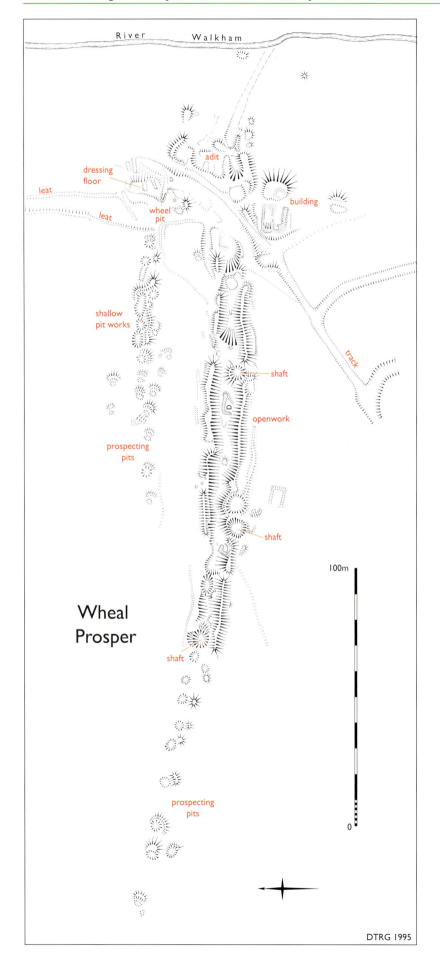

shafts were sunk into the old men's workings and the mine was drained via an adit just above river level.

Wheal Mary Emma is in the Lyd valley on western Dartmoor. The plan (Fig. 6) shows an area of intense activity on the west side of the river, where a deep openwork attracted 19th-century miners to re-develop this mine, sinking a vertical engine shaft (Tindall's) to the west of the openwork (now blocked and levelled) and an adit near the river. A later extension of this sett on the east side of the River Lyd, was inspired by additional old men's workings, in the form of pits, recorded in mine reports (*MJ* 16.12.1868).

None of these three examples were productive mines, and progressed little further than the development stage. They did, however, see repeated attempts to rework them in the 19th century and although some production of tin is known, output was often too small to be recorded in official statistics (*see* Burt et al. 1984).

4 MINES AS JOINT STOCK ENTERPRISES

Although many Dartmoor mine companies of this period represented honest attempts on the part of the adventurers to raise a profit from mining tin, and endured for several decades – albeit intermittently and at the margins of real profitability – others did not. Promoting joint stock mining companies as dubious share dealing schemes was a common practice, usually referred to as 'share jobbing' or 'bal selling'. The geologist De la Beche in 1839 describes the

Figure 4 Earthwork survey of Wheal Prosper, showing the position of shafts within the earlier openwork. Surveyed by members of the DTRG, 1995.

Ore Prices for Tin 1700-1914 (after Schmitz 1979)

Table 2 Tin ore prices between c.1700 and 1914 based on statistics compiled by Chris Schmitz 1979.

practice simply as 'deceiving unwary adventures' (De la Beche 1839, 325).

The usual method of promoting a joint stock mining adventure in Devon and Cornwall, was through a cost book company, typically founded by a small core of adventurers. They were known as 'in adventurers' and they often made money by awarding themselves a proportion of the total shares and selling them on to those, sometimes unwary, 'out' adventurers to whom De la Beche referred. The company would pay a rental to a landowner for the rights to work a defined mine sett, which in the case of tin mines, always contained evidence of earlier workings, as discussed above. However unpromising these workings may have appeared, their potential could be overstated in the share prospectus, to make the investment more attractive.

The 'in adventurers' were often mine agents or local businessmen with a vested interest in the prosperity of mines in their area and it was in everyone's interest to encourage prosperity to come to their district. There was the opportunity for the employment of local men and women, while local businesses could gain by supplying the mines with services, such as buildings and engineering, or supplies like candles, shovels, timber, coal and victuals.

The establishing of these mine companies frequently coincided chronologically with rising tin prices, which climbed steadily up until about 1810, before falling backwards, but were rising again in the 1840-60s and 1870s, with peaks in 1810, 1836, 1857, 1872 and 1888, sometimes doubling in price in just a few years (Table 2), which added an additional appeal and a tinge of excitement to any tin mine investment. The creation of several new mines and the revival of some abandoned mines, can be correlated against these variable tin prices. Some longstanding marginal mines worked intermittently throughout the 19th century and, during periods of rising ore prices, were often re-started in the hope that the better price of tin would compensate for their low grade ores; others had definite origins, or flurries of activity, confined within these price booms only.

Figure 5 A cost book company share certificate of the Dartmoor Consolidated Tin Mines (Ailsborough) issued in 1824 (author's collection).

The landscape evidence relating to the latter of these two, is often easy to recognise in marginal

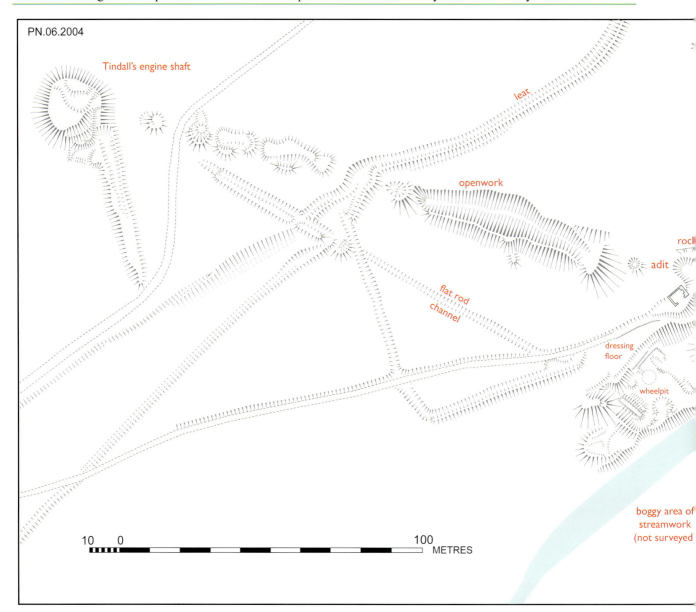

Figure 6 Earthwork survey of Wheal Mary Emma in the Lyd valley showing the openwork and Tindall's (engine) Shaft on the west side of the river and old men's shallow pit workings to the east, also reworked.

mining zones such as Dartmoor because, in terms of mineralisation, many of the sites they chose could never have lived up to the claims of the promoters.

4.1 Field evidence

A lack of waste material, or spoil, at surface is a fairly certain indicator of a mine that was undeveloped underground, for whatever reason. This may be despite the often generous and disproportionate provision of surface infrastructure and ore dressing facilities, which may also survive at some mines (discussed below). Although within developed mines, the waste was often disposed of in exhausted stopes underground, the primary development phase of driving adits, sinking shafts and opening up the stopes, required disposal of waste at surface, resulting in substantial spoil heaps at the head of the shafts or beyond the portals of the adits. If these are lacking, then little work is likely to have occurred underground and little or no tin produced.

Caroline Wheal Prosper near Dean Prior, operated for two years from 1854-6 at a site where an existing, very small, openwork was located beside the Dean Burn. Extensive stamping and dressing facilities were erected, supplied by a well engineered leat. A pumping wheel and flat rods, together with an inclined tramway, were installed to service the main shaft (William's) 680m to the east up a steep gradient (Newman 2004, 3). Altogether, £8000 was expended with only a very small quantity of ore sold, inspiring a correspondent of the *Mining Journal* to comment

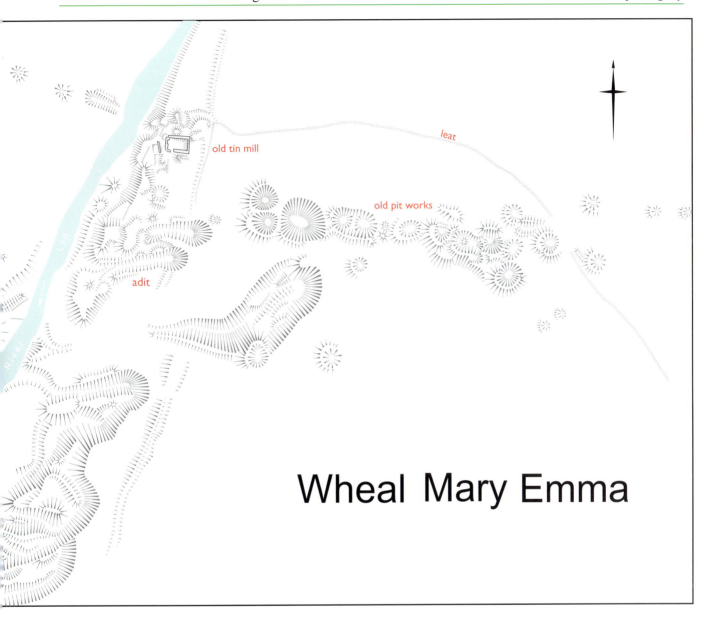

that 'the career of this mine has been remarkable for its recklessness' (*MJ* 22.10.1859). Apart from the extravagant surface infrastructure described above, evidence of underground work is restricted to a short adit. Stony spoil has been dumped below the dressing floor, but not enough to suggest that the adit penetrated the hillside very far. There are also earthworks associated with William's Shaft, where a diminutive spoil heap indicates the depth of the shaft to be only a few metres.

Activity at Holne Chase Mine, Ashburton (Fig. 7) seems to have been exclusive to the 1850s and 1870s, one of several mines on Dartmoor to follow this pattern, including New Vitifer (*see* below). This narrow rock-cut gully has evidence of blasting with explosives, suggesting that the miners first attempted to enlarge an existing small openwork. But there was little else here to encourage a sound investment and

no other evidence of prospecting in the vicinity. Later, a single shaft was sunk to one side, with evidence of a horse whim hauling system, but the moderate spoil heap suggests limited depth. An adit was begun, driving under the openwork but this extended no more than a few metres towards the shaft, evident in this case by a diminutive spoil heap below the portal, and although the mine allegedly sold 4 tons of tin in 1874, progress underground was minimal. Nevertheless, a massive amount of money was invested in an inclined tramway to transport the anticipated riches from the mine to an equally extravagant stamping mill and dressing floor, 420m away and 60m lower down the slope. This all represents capacity that the tin deposits at this location, apparently, failed to fulfil (Newman 2006).

New Vitifer Consols in the valley of the Bovey Combe perhaps epitomises much so far described with regard undeveloped capitalist mines. This valley

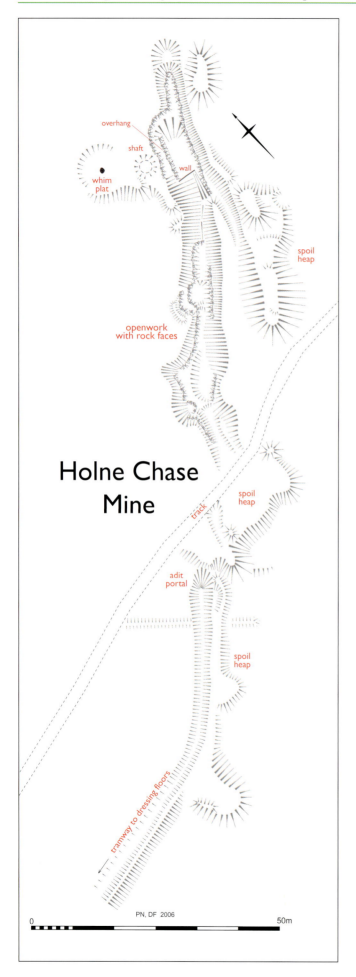

(Fig. 8) was intensely worked by medieval and later tinners and there is a moderate openwork indicative of lode activity. This was sufficient evidence for 19th century adventurers to form mining companies from the 1840s onwards, which would, they claimed, exploit these mines to greater depth. Most of the field evidence for the mine itself can be related to the New Vitifer Consols Company which operated from 1870 (BI Chagford), whose activities coincided with one of the rising tin price episodes described above.

The field evidence is particularly well preserved. A number of very short adits were driven into the hillside, evident by their diminutive spoil heaps, and from which, quite clearly, no tin was ever retrieved. Nevertheless, tramways, which survive as earthworks, were optimistically installed to transport the anticipated ore to the dressing floors. A single shaft was sunk adjacent to the openwork, but more earth was moved to create the platform containing the whim (a horse powered hauling device) than in digging the shaft itself, which is evident by a very small collar of spoil. A 60ft (18m) diameter water wheel was installed to activate underground pumps and power a stamping mill. This is among the largest water wheels used in the Devon mining industry, and considering the diminutive supply of water available in this valley, and lack of water storage, there must be doubt that it was ever fit for purpose.

The adventurers also installed a state of the art stamping mill and dressing floor with circular centre head buddles (*see* below). Apart from the wheelpit, which was later backfilled, nearly all of this installation survives today in an earthwork form.

At Great Wheal Eleanor near North Bovey, a mining company was formed in 1874, attracted by the prospects of re-working a large openwork, dug by the 'old men', and encouraged by the rapidly rising tin price in the early 1870s, reaching £150 per ton in 1872, a price not seen since 1810 and not repeated again until 1910 (Schmitz 1979). Underground development of this mine progressed a little further than some of the mines in this category, judging

Figure 7 Earthwork survey of Holne Chase Mine. An open cutting has been partly re-worked via a shaft and adit.

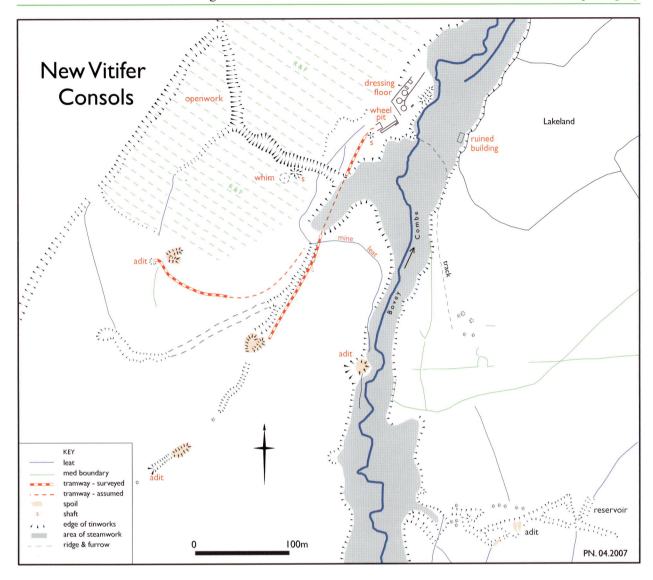

Figure 8 Map of Bovey Combe showing mining and other evidence, including New (or West) Vitifer Consols. Features associated with this mine are annotated in red.

by a moderate heap of spoil deposited outside the adit mouth, but the extravagant surface equipment, including one of only two steam-powered stamping engines in the Dartmoor district, and a large water wheel (Fig. 9), went far beyond what was required at this unpromising site, which closed following five years of intermittent operations, with a recorded value of tin output of £682 (Burt et al. 1984). Founded and sold to investors on the idea that the old men's working would prove profitable while tin prices were high, sadly the output fell short, whilst tin prices plummeted by approximately 50% in the period this mine operated.

Other examples of this type of mine, where surface indicators suggest that little was achieved below ground, might include Gobbett Mine, Great Week Consols, Wheal Frederick, Smith's Wood Mine, Sigford Consols, Great Sortridge and East Vitifer. The last was the subject of an unusually well reported court case of 1876 in which a shareholder tried to prosecute a Torquay stockbroker for fraud after losing her money invested in this mine (*WDP* 10.04.1876), claiming the agent who sold them had overstated their worth.

5 Technology

In recent years industrial archaeologists have debated the academic legitimacy of technology as a topic of study; some claiming, with good reason, that an obsession with machinery and steam engines should never be an end in itself, without linking the artefacts to their social and economic implications, and assessing what the technology meant for the people who operated it and invested in it.

For the landscape archaeologist interested in the impact of metal mines, this is less of a dilemma

The Tinworking Landscape of Dartmoor in a European Context: Prehistory to 20th Century

Figure 9 View of the large wheelhouse at Great Wheal Eleanor Mine, North Bovey, which powered both pump rods and stamps. 1m scale (Phil Newman).

because the machines rarely survive. The main task is to piece together the subtle earthworks and extensively ruined structures that are the main form of evidence available, to reconstruct what existed on the surface. Then we may establish how the miners used technology to overcome some of the problems they encountered, above and below ground, or to increase the mine's efficiency.

As mentioned above, Devon's tin mineralization, and the techniques used to exploit it, were different from the more prosperous areas of Cornwall, particularly in terms of scale; the variation in technology is one manifestation of those differences. The development of three aspects of technology are particularly significant – pumping, hoisting and dressing – and evidence for each collectively contributes to the narrative of Dartmoor as a mining district, beyond form and function.

5.1 Pumping

Water power totally dominated the mechanised pumping of 19th-century mines in Devon, particularly in tin mines. Only the deepest mines required the use of steam engines, and in Devon, these are almost always found around the peripheries of the moor[1], in places such as the Tavy, Tamar and Teign valleys, and with only a few exceptions, were at copper and lead mines.

But the environmental paradox of Dartmoor was, that although flooding was a problem below ground in non free-draining mines, the high rainfall and abundance of water on the surface, made water power the most economical choice for pumping it out. Typically, as at Huntingdon Mine (Fig. 10), a water wheel was installed some distance from the pumping shaft, located to maximize advantage from the available water supply, which was usually from small streams or rivers. A system of reciprocating flat

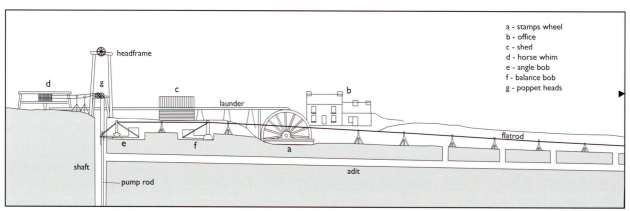

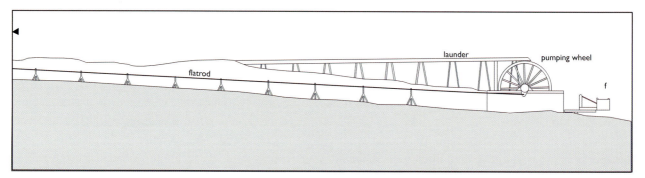

Figure 10 Huntingdon Mine sectional view in two pieces, showing extent of the flat rod system from the large water wheel (lower), which extended for 520m south to north to the engine shaft (upper), and details of the horse whim and stamping mill (redrawn from DHC AMP 15314).

Figure 11 Ailsborough Mine, Sheepstor: view along the stone flatrods from above the large engine water wheel. 1m scale (Phil Newman).

rods, with counterbalances, known as balance bobs, and angle bobs, which changed direction of the rod's movement, would then transmit the power to the shaft and pitwork.

Field evidence for the water wheels and the leats that supplied them, along with the flat rod systems, is plentiful on Dartmoor, particularly on the uplands. Of 38 flatrod systems recorded, 26 were used at tin mines and of those, the majority are on the open moorland (Newman 2010, *table 7.2*).

Ailsborough is probably the best known of these, thanks to the unique survival of the upright stone posts that supported the rods (Fig. 11), and the two 'engine' wheelpits that contained the large water wheels to supply the power (Fig. 12). The longest flatrod system at Ailsborough was a staggering 1.2km long (Newman 1999).

Elsewhere, straight V-profile gullies, provide telltale evidence of former flat rods, which traversed all that went before in a dead straight line. In the West Webburn valley, the gully may be noted running up the valley from a ruined wheelpit and possibly serving several of the shafts (Fig. 13).

Some of the mines discussed above have clear evidence of flatrod systems, including Huntingdon (Fig. 9) and Wheal Mary Emma (Fig. 6). Hexworthy Mines, had two flatrods serving separate shafts. The Hensroost section survives as a channel, but also an alignment of small earthen mounds, which we may assume supported metal or timber posts.

Over twenty, very large water wheels have been recorded at Dartmoor tin mines (Newman 2010, *table 7.1*), installed to drive these flatrod systems;

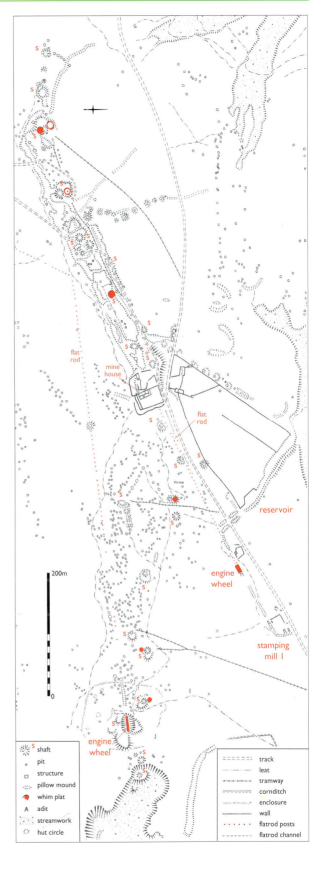

Figure 12 1:2500 scale earthwork plan (part of) of surface evidence along the main lodes at Ailsborough Mine (after Newman 1999).

Figure 13 Aerial view of the West Webburn valley looking south including East Birch Tor Mine and its flat rod channel (Damian Grady © Historic England Archive).

Figure 14 A bob pit to house the counterweights at the head of Low's Shaft, Hexworthy Mine. 1m scale (Phil Newman).

the wheels could be up to 18m in diameter. At Ailsborough, Hexworthy, Huntingdon, Brimpts and Great Wheal Eleanor (Fig. 9), remains of substantial stone wheelpits or wheel houses survive, though sadly, many others were demolished or backfilled as a safety measure for livestock.

At the shaft end of the flatrod, counterweights and balance bobs were housed in sunken stone structures (bob pits) adjacent to the shaft to transfer the horizontal movement of the rods vertically down the shaft via the spear rods, to power the pumping equipment in the shafts (pitwork). Low's shaft at Hexworthy Mine offers a fine example of a stone-lined bob pit (Fig. 14), but others survive in good condition at Huntingdon and East Birch Tor.

Large water wheels required plentiful water supplies. Leats were dug to divert the water from river sources, in some cases quite distant, and at some mines, water storage capacity was required in the form of large reservoirs. These survive as dried up earthworks, with fine examples at Hooten Wheals, Ailsborough Mine (Fig. 12), Steeperton Mine, Great Wheal Eleanor and North Wheal Robert, which still contains water.

The silted, earthwork remains of dried up leats provide important evidence of this aspect of mining infrastructure. Accurately surveying or tracing the course of a leat can help identify the locations of wheelpits that were demolished long ago, as well as help with the interpretation of complex water management systems at sites where multiple wheelpits and other water consuming processes are present. At Ailsborough Mine (Newman 1999), Vitifer Mine (Newman 1999), and Whiteworks Mine, such complicated systems have been surveyed, but equally impressive systems remain to be examined associated with mines on western Dartmoor around the Mary Tavy area.

5.2 Hoisting/hauling

The methods used for hoisting ore and waste material up shafts, also offer clues as to the depth of a mine. For the period under discussion there were four systems available.

The windlass, or jackroll, was powered by human operators and obviously very limited in its capacity. Although probably an extremely common sight at the head of many shallow shafts from the 17th to the 20th century, field evidence at surface for the apparatus itself is extremely difficult to recognise. However, much of the spoil surrounding the majority of early shafts and small later shafts at surface, serves to indicate their former presence (Fig. 15).

Figure 15 The surface evidence of an 18th or early 19th-century shaft at Holming Beam; the spoil, now collapsing back into the shaft, was probably raised using a windlass (Phil Newman).

Figure 16 A mellior stone part buried at the centre of a whim plat at Whiteworks. 1m scale (Phil Newman).

The horse whim was a more robust piece of apparatus, and capable of raising moderate loads from a reasonable depth. These may have been introduced to Westcountry mining by the 16th century (Earl 1968, 68) but were certainly in use by the 18th century and remained so for much of the 19th.

For deeper mines, requiring stronger and more efficient hauling, water powered whims were available, with examples surviving at Gem mine in the Walkham valley, and at Golden Dagger. Later, steam whims were attached to specially designed engine houses.

In an admittedly non-exhaustive field investigation (Newman 2010, 139-53)[2], only five water whims associated with Dartmoor tin mines were identified, three of which were at Vitifer/Golden Dagger. So far, no steam whims are known on or around Dartmoor, other than at copper and lead mines (Newman 2010, 148).

However, the landscape supports the earthwork remains of at least 50 horse whims, 30 of which survive at tin mines (Newman 2010, *table 7.4*) confirming that the majority of Dartmoor's tin mines relied on these devices as their major means of hauling. The dominance of horse whims, with their limited capacity compared to the water and steam devices required for greater depths, provides further insight into the limited operational depth and below-ground development of the industry here as a whole. They are among the more subtle earthworks associated with mines, surviving as circular, level platforms, either sunken or raised, often with the central mellior stone surviving (Fig. 16), and sited close by the head of the shaft. Ailsborough Mine (Fig. 12) has six earthwork whim plats distributed along the alignment of its shafts.

5.3 Tin stamping and dressing

Once raised to surface, metallic ores need to undergo a series of refining processes, before being of suitable purity for smelting. For tin there are essentially four main processes:

Crushing and Classifying – reducing the ore to a suitable size for refining

Concentrating – removing impurities by settling out gangue in water using a variety of apparatus

Calcining removing impurities in a furnace

These processes took place on the surface, therefore all surviving evidence should be accessible to the field archaeologist, within the limitations of safety. However, some, including several described by writers of the past, involved the use of portable apparatus or timber structures and machinery, most of which have left an imperceivable archaeological record; therefore only evidence of processes that survive as structures or earthworks are discussed here[3]. Even in these cases the timber and iron components of the apparatus have been removed and the evidence today comprises primarily just the groundwork created to accommodate them. Buried aspects and residues of tin dressing are yet to be investigated archaeologically on Dartmoor and will be an important focus for future investigations. Nevertheless, close examination of individual stamping mills and dressing floors can tell us much about their date, technology and capacity which, when combined with other evidence of the associated mine, can illuminate additional aspects of their use as well.

The Tinworking Landscape of Dartmoor in a European Context: Prehistory to 20th Century

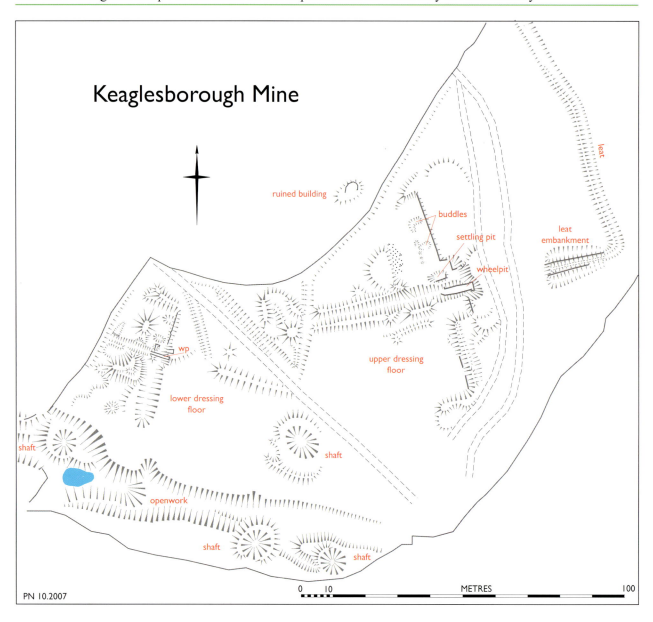

Figure 17 Earthwork survey of Keaglesborough tin mine, Walkhampton, stamping mills and dressing floors.

5.3.1 The stamping mill

The stamping mill as a means of crushing tin has origins in the medieval period (*see* Greeves *this volume*); specific examples were first documented in Cornwall in 1402 and in Devon in 1504, though in both counties their probable introduction is likely to have been earlier (Gerrard 2000, 104). The basic principle behind the stamping mill changed scarcely at all from then until the 1920s, when the last set of water-powered tin stamps ceased work on Dartmoor. The main developments were that of scale and layout, as the number of stamps increased with bigger water wheels, and refinements to secondary elements of the machinery.

During fieldwork in 2008-10 (Newman 2010), seventy-eight water-powered stamping mills/ dressing floors were recorded, associated with 53 tin mines (Table 3). Others may exist at sites which it was not possible to visit in the course of fieldwork, while some documented examples have been effaced; others exist at copper and silver/lead mines[4]. Several mines have more than one stamping mill, with associated dressing floors; Keaglesborough (Fig. 18) and Haytor Consols both have two mills, Bachelor's Hall has four, but they are most numerous at Ailsborough Mine, which has six.

In some cases, isolated operational dates can be known with precision, if recorded, but for some undocumented examples, no date of any type is available. For some, however, an outline chronology can be established through a combination of documentation and field evidence, such as the six

Figure 18 View looking across the Keaglesborough Mine lower mill, showing wheelpit in the foreground, and the stone revetment at the rear of the dressing floor. 1m scale (Phil Newman).

Figure 19 The robust revetments above the Haytor Consols (Crownley) stamping mill. The wheelpit sits just below the lower terrace. 1m scale (Phil Newman).

mills at Ailsborough Mine which were installed between 1805 and 1814 (Newman 1999, 126-39).

The layout for the more developed tin stamping mill, comprised a level terrace cut into the hillslope with a stone revetment built to retain the slope, often with short return walls at one or both ends, defining the dressing floor area. The stone wheelpits were sunk at right angles against or cut into the revetment, projecting into the level area, sited either at one end or centrally on the terrace, with stamps frames mounted on one or both sides of the wheel. In many cases these revetments survive *in situ*, as at Keaglesborough upper mill (Fig. 17), where a robust, 1m-high wall defines an area of approximately 62m long by 9m wide. Several of the Ailsborough mills survive in good condition, as does that at Wheal Katherine (Newman 1999, *fig. 15*) and Brimpts. A particularly well-built revetment is at Haytor Consols (Crownley section, Fig. 19).

The water wheels, which provided the power for the stamps, were accommodated in wheelpits sunk into the ground and lined with stone. The size, where they can be measured, varies between the largest example at New Vitifer of 18.5m long, which housed a wheel of 60ft diameter (18.4m) that served also to power pumps in a nearby shaft (Fig. 20), and the smallest, which were about 4.5 – 5m with wheels of approximately 15ft –16ft (4.5 – 4.8m). The width of the structures is between 3.7m at Golden Dagger and 0.8m at Wheal Chance. Wheelpits were often slighted after abandonment by backfilling with stone, leaving just a hollow with traces of the wheelpit outline, as at Gobbett, Keaglesborough lower (Fig. 18) and New Vitifer (Fig. 20). However, several survive in better condition including at East Hughes, Kit Mine (Fig. 21), Gem Mine, Great Wheal Eleanor (Fig. 9) and several of the Ailsborough examples.

Like the pumping wheels, these mills required reliable sources of water to power them, diverted to the water wheel via a leat system, drawing water from streams and rivers. Often the leats would serve both stamping wheels and pumping wheels, and occasionally hoisting wheels too.

5.3.2 Dressing floors

The tin ore was fed wet into a coffer from behind the stamps, and once crushed, the product, known as 'pulp', passed through a perforated grate into (usually two) rectangular settling pits just below the stamps, as described by contemporary technical writers, such as Henwood (1832, 148).

The working principle of the settling pit was that the heavier tin ('best work') would settle in the first pit, while the lighter portion ('slimes') would come to rest in the second. Once full, and the water had drained away, the two grades could be separated for further processing. The pits usually survive as rectangular, masonry-lined, earthwork depressions. Brimpts north mill, installed 1852-3 (Bird & Hirst 1996, 18) is a key exemplar, having two distinctly separate elongated pits sited just below the stamps area. At Keaglesborough upper mill, which may have been installed as late as 1830 (Fig. 17), there is one large pit with masonry lining still visible and at the lower mill of probable earlier date, the pit survives only as a silted earthwork.

By the mid-19th century the settling pits were being replaced by pairs of long parallel troughs

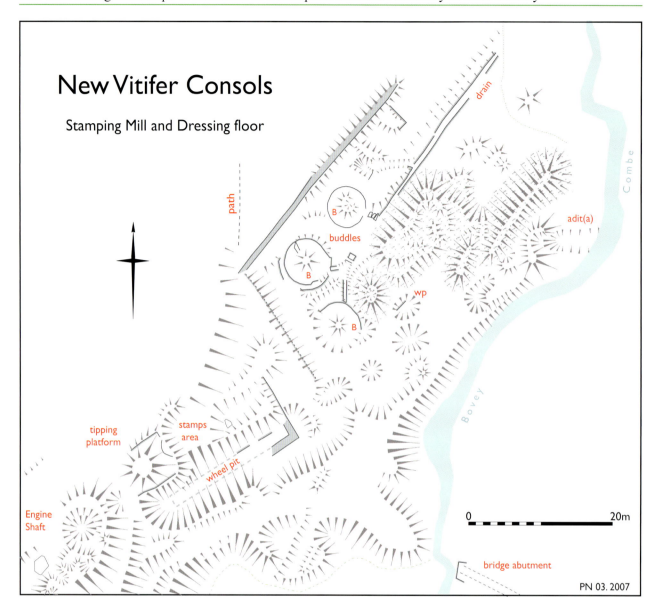

Figure 20 Earthwork survey of New Vitifer Consols dressing floors, showing the location of the backfilled wheelpit and the circular buddles. The large heaps are likely to be material removed during creation of the wheelpit.

known as strips, a transition that was described by Henderson (1858, 195-220. Evidence for the strip system is rarer on Dartmoor. Holne Chase Mine has a likely example where the probable 1870s date of the mine makes this very likely (Newman 2006). Another probable example may be seen at Gobbett Mine where the stamping mill was recorded in the early 1830s (Greeves 2006, 12-13) but the mine was also working in the 1860s – 70s. Just below the stone reinforced stamps platform a silted linear earthwork channel, representing probable evidence of the strips, leads down to two larger rectangular pits to receive the tailings.

Placed along the remaining areas of the terrace, or dressing floor, was a series of additional pits used in the concentrating processes known as 'buddles', either rectangular or circular in plan. Buddles represent the main field evidence for the concentration of tin ore and although the remains are sometimes rather subtle, they frequently survive. Early buddles consisted of an elongated rectangular pit or a trough, with an inclined timber or slate floor (Fig. 21). Crushed ore, which had received an initial sorting in the settling pits, was introduced to the upper end of the buddle in a stream of water that ran down the incline, using the same principle as the settling pits and strips, the heavier tin would sink near the head while the waste was washed to the tail. When full, and the water was drained away, the product was dug out and separated into three grades of purity, before undergoing additional processes.

Rectangular buddles remained standard well

Figure 21 An intact stone wheelpit survives at Kit Mine, Sheepstor (on private land), which once powered a stamping mill. 1m scale (Phil Newman).

into the later 19th century, but by the 1830s, a new circular version, known as the convex or centre-head buddle was gaining popularity, and examples were being installed on Dartmoor from *c*.1840 (Newman 2010, 186), although rectangular buddles were still being installed, notably at Brimpts Mine in 1853 (Bird & Hirst 1996, 18). The centre-head buddle was a variation whereby the buddle pit is circular with a central cone and inclined surface radiating from the centre. The tin stuff and water were released onto the central cone to flow outwards and become separated by the same settling principles as the previous processes discussed. Rotating sweeps or brushes agitated the mixture in the buddle to aid the separation. The latter were powered by small water wheels located amidst the dressing floors, each wheel powering several buddles via line-shafts. These features are clear on photographs of Golden Dagger Mine (Greeves 1986, 51) and Lady Bertha (Hamilton Jenkin 1974, 74) whilst still operational in the early 20th century.

Earthwork evidence for rectangular buddles survives at 30 of the recorded dressing floors (Table 3). The majority survive only as silted and turf-covered, approximately rectangular, hollows of various depths, as at East Hughes, Wheal Fortune and Brimpts but some clearer examples exists at Ailsborough, Wheal Cumpston and Wheal Katherine, with stone linings still visible along the edges of the buddles.

Typically a circular buddle will survive as a flat-bottomed hollow, often with evidence of a stone kerb lining the circumference. On early examples, such as that at Huntingdon Mine (Fig. 24), the interior details, including the dome, would have been constructed from timber, hence the earthwork is all that survives. As the 19th century progressed it became common for the domes to be made from stone and concrete, and they often survive *in situ* as a result as at Golden Dagger Mine, Kit Mine (Fig.24), North Wheal Robert and Yeoland Consols.

In Cornwall, it was not unusual for tin dressing floors to contain 50 or more circular buddles but at Dartmoor mines, with more modest output, the number was always much smaller. At Lady Bertha Mine and North Wheal Robert, six buddles are depicted on Ordnance Survey maps of 1905, many of which survive, but often two or three is the norm as at New Vitifer Consols (Fig.10), Wheal Frederick, Hexworthy Mine, Kit Mine, Gem Mine and Bagtor Mine.

5.4 The over-capacity of stamping mills and dressing floors

It is notable that for a number of tin mines, the capacity to process the ore using the dressing techniques described, is many times greater than would have been required, judging by the evidence for underground development at these sites. Some clear examples survive, and their names are familiar from the discussions above. Holne Chase had a large capacity dressing floor, stamping mill and inclined tramway to cart the ore to it, associated with a mine whose surface remains indicate that it fell short of even the early stages of development underground (Newman 2006). Caroline Wheal Prosper had a large dressing floor but had scarcely any development underground (Newman 2004). New Vitifer Consols (Figs 7 & 19), which was worked between 1867 and 1875 (BI, Chagford), had a 60ft waterwheel and a dressing floor with three centre head buddles, though evidence of underground development is also minimal.

Great Wheal Eleanor was in work between 1874 and 1881, where a 40ft water wheel powering 16 heads of stamps was augmented by a steam-powered stamping mill with a further 16 stamps. This information is known from the auction details following closure of the mine in 1881 (BI, North Bovey). At that time it is also recorded that the maximum depth of Great Wheal Eleanor's shafts was 20 fathoms, and the mine had sold only 18.7 tons of ore between 1876 and 1880 (Burt et al. 1984, 48). Claims by the management in newspaper reports of further small sales are not verified in the

The Tinworking Landscape of Dartmoor in a European Context: Prehistory to 20th Century

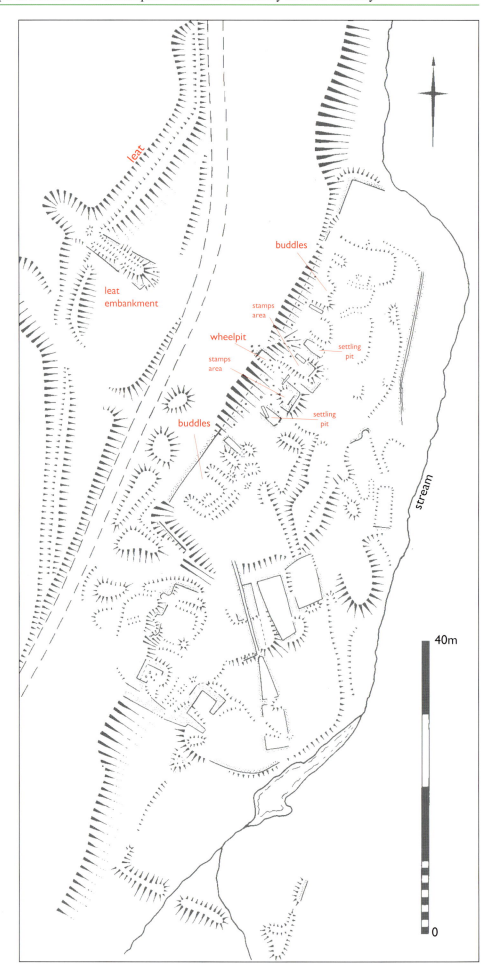

Figure 22 Earthwork plan of the lower mill and dressing floors at Ailsborough Mine, built possibly as early as 1805, showing a centrally placed water wheel pit, with a stamps area, settling pits and buddles on either side of the wheel. A range of other, mostly rectangular, pits which contained additional elements of the concentrating process have also survived (after Newman 1999).

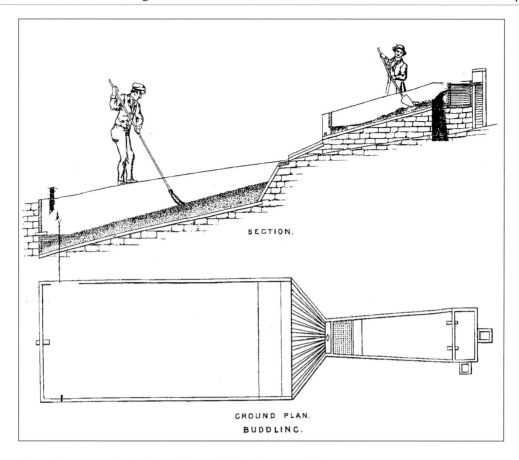

Figure 23 A rectangular buddle as depicted by Henderson in 1858.

mineral statistics.

At Haytor Consols are the remains of a particularly impressive stamping mill (Fig. 19) and a dressing floor, which it is recorded housed 32 heads of stamps when installed in 1851; a second mill not far away brought this number up to 48 (Hamilton Jenkin 1981, 133). Although 16 tons of tin were sold between 1853-5 (Collins 1912, 506) and 14 tons between 1863-5 (Burt et al. 1984, 4), evidence of underground working at this mine is minimal, comprising a few short adits and shafts equipped with horse whims and, although one shaft (Prosper) has a moderate spoil heap, generally there is very little spoil associated with this mine; indeed nothing commensurate with this level of dressing capacity.

Extensive dressing floors and remains of a large water wheel pit also survive at East Vitifer Mine representing a period of activity after 1870 (BI, North Bovey) during which minimal quantities of tin were sold, often little over one ton for a whole year (Burt et al. 1984, 114).

Finally, at Ailsborough Mine, five stamping mills are known to have been either operational or under construction in 1814 and a sixth added in about 1822 (Newman 1999, 126). Although this mine was at times productive, particularly in the 1820s (Cook et al. 1974, appendix B), these five mills almost certainly represent dressing capacity far beyond likely output of ore. Although it has been suggested that this over capacity could have been employed to stamp the ore from neighbouring mines (Cook et al. 1974, 190), this is unlikely given that most known mines in the vicinity had their own dressing capacity.

Although it was essential to have some capacity to stamp ore during and following the development stage of a mine when production began, archaeological and documentary evidence confirms that many of these examples were installed long before the mines were even partly proven underground. These cases all indicate either over-capacity or premature investment in unnecessary ore dressing machinery, which might be explained in a number of ways.

Over-optimism or a genuine miscalculation as to the future prospects for the mine, based on a failure to grasp the limitations of Dartmoor's tin lodes, is one possibility although in a carefully budgeted and genuine enterprise this would be unlikely. Broughton (1971, 1-25), who cited the case of Haytor Consols in particular, quoting much (unreferenced) supporting documentation, explained the situation as the result

Figure 24 Round buddles: Kit Mine, Sheepstor (left) with masonry walls and concrete dome in place; Huntingdon (right) probably constructed from timber where only an earthwork now survives. 1m scale (Phil Newman).

of reckless or inexperienced management and malpractice. Indeed this common scenario may also represent material evidence for 'share jobbing' or 'bal selling' described above, where mine companies were set up solely as a means of profiting from dealing in shares. The apparent existence of a large capacity to process ore on the surface could be part of a ruse aimed at reassuring investors as to the credibility and value of a mine; the installation of this machinery implying to those 'unwary adventurers' mentioned by De la Beche (1839, 325), that the production of tin was either already taking place, about to commence, or so overwhelming that extra capacity was needed. Of the examples cited, the companies that promoted Great Wheal Eleanor, Caroline Wheal Prosper, New Vitifer, East Vitifer and Holne Chase all went into liquidation having produced insufficient ore to cover costs.

The expense of these installations of questionable necessity, must have contributed to the demise of these mines to no small extent, although under the circumstances of their origins, their viability has to be questioned more broadly. Any correlation between the existence of one or more stamping mills at a mine, and its stage of underground development at abandonment, or its output, should be applied with caution.

Conclusion

The renowned, though somewhat inward-looking, Cornish mining writer, R Bradford Barton, was dismissive and quite scathing as to the usefulness of archaeological fieldwork in the world of mine research. He once wrote that 'a square yard' of documents will 'reveal far more of substance' than a 'square mile' of 'old ruins' (Bradford Barton 1968,10). Research carried out in both Cornwall and Devon since Barton's time would suggest otherwise. Indeed, there is much to be learned through close investigation of mine landscapes, that often cannot be found in documents, especially where no documents survive; a factor that Barton failed to recognise. The intimate knowledge of the remains, which can be achieved through structured field observation and survey, can assist in understanding how the component parts and infrastructure functioned at individual mines, and how productive or enduring they might have been. Collectively, and within their historical context, the study of these mines greatly enhances the industrial, economic and social narrative for Dartmoor. For this writer, the insights gained into human behaviours that lie behind the landscape evidence, be it the contribution of capitalism, tradition, technology, or as a response to the environment, are the big rewards of mining archaeological study.

The later period of tin mining on Dartmoor offers great examples of continuity and change, for which archaeologists are always on the lookout; whilst there was a centuries-long tradition of digging for tin in Devon, the later miners of the 18th to 20th century brought not only technological change, but also economic and social variation in the way they perceived and exploited the same environment as their predecessors.

Dartmoor's tin mines may have been mostly shallow but a few had a reasonable if intermittent output. Most, however, clung on within the margins of economical viability, and some others were no-hopers. This narrative in itself, I think, has great value, particularly given the landscape legacy that survives for us to explore.

But like the 'old men', I have only scratched the surface with this paper. The diversion and storage of water to power water wheels and dressing processes is a huge topic, which lends itself to topographic study using these techniques. And there are other forms of infrastructure such as the movement of materials to, from and around the mines, including cart tracks, tramways and inclines, all of which I have mentioned only briefly, but they must have impacted greatly on the viability of the mine. Away from the technology and the extractive activity, the miners resided in nearby villages and hamlets on or around the moor, or sometimes at the mines themselves, and this too needs research, as does their cross-moorland routes, places of entertainment and any other aspect of their lives for which material evidence may survive.

Notes

1. A single and anomalous exception is at Ringleshutes tin mine on Holne Moor, where a very ruined engine house sits at the top of a shaft amidst the earlier openworks.
2. This investigation did not include Owlacombe Mine, Ashburton which, if examined, would alter these statistics.
3. With the exception of calciners, which are not covered in this paper.
4. *see* Newman 2010 for copper mine data.

Abbreviations

BI (parish) – Justin Brooke Index of Devon Mines. Devon Heritage Centre, Exeter
CRO – Cornwall Record Office
DHC – Devon Heritage Centre, Exeter
EFP – Exeter Flying Post
MJ – Mining Journal and Railway Gazette
SYM – Sherborne and Yeovil Mercury
TG – Tavistock Gazette
WDP – Western Daily Press
WDRO – West Devon Record Office

Bibliography

Barton, D Bradford 1968 *Essays in Cornish Mining History 1*. Truro: Bradford Barton

Brooke, J 1980 *Stannary Tales - The Shady Side of Mining*. Truro: Twelveheads

Broughton, D G 1971 'The Land Half Made' *Kingston Geological Review* (Research Seminar **2.1.6**), 1-25

Brown, M nd. *Walkhampton Parish History*. Dartmoor Press

Bruce, B 2001 'Over Tor Brook survey completed' *DTRG Newsletter* **22**, 5-9

Bruce, B 2003 'Greena Ball Streamwork: another survey completed' *DTRG Newsletter* **24**, 5-7

Burt, R, Waite, P and Burnley, R 1984 *Devon and Somerset Mines*. Exeter: University Press

Collins, J H 1912 Observations on the West of England Mining Region. Plymouth: Brendon

Cook, R, Greeves, T and Kilvington, C 1974 'Eylesbarrow (1814-1852) - a study of a Dartmoor tin mine' *Rep Trans Devonshire Ass* **106**, 161-214

De La Beche, H 1839 Report on the Geology of Cornwall, Devon and West Somerset. London: Longman

Earl, B 1968 *Cornish Mining: The Techniques of Metal Mining in the West of England, Past and Present*. Truro: Bradford Barton

Gerrard, S 1992 The Beckamoor Combe Streamwork Survey' *DTRG Newsletter* **3**, 6-8

Gerrard, S 2000 *The Early British Tin Industry*. Stroud: Tempus

Greeves, T 1975 'Wheal Prosper - a little-known Dartmoor tin mine' *Plymouth Mineral and Mining Club J* **6.1**, 6-7 and 15

Greeves, T 1981 *The Devon Tin Industry 1450-1750: an Archaeological and Historical Survey*. Unpublished PhD, thesis, University of Exeter

Greeves, T 1986 *Tin Mines and Miners of Dartmoor*. Exeter: Devon Books

Greeves, T 2001 'Huntingdon Mine and tinworking on the moorland Avon' *Dartmoor Magazine* **63**, 8-10

Greeves, T 2006 'J W Colenso's Report on Dartmoor Mines, 1836' *Plymouth Mineral and Mining Club J* **35.3**, 12-13

Greeves, T 2016 *Called Home: The Dartmoor Tin Miner 1860-1940*. Truro: Twelveheads

Hamilton Jenkin, A K 1974 *Mines of Devon Volume 1: The Southern Area*. Newton Abbot: David and Charles

Hamilton Jenkin, A K 1981 *Mines of Devon: North and East of Dartmoor*. Exeter: Devon Library Services

Henderson, J 1858 'On the Methods Generally Adopted in Cornwall in Dressing Tin and Copper Ores' *Proc Inst Civil Engineers* **17**, 195-220

Henwood, W J 1832 'On the Manipulation to which the Ores of Tin and Copper are subjected in the central mining district of Cornwall' *Trans Royal Geological Soc Cornwall* **4**, 145-162

Lysons, D and Lysons, S *Magna Britannia Vol 6: Devonshire*. London: Cadell

Newman, P 1996 *Tinworking in the O Brook Valley, Dartmoor, Devonshire*. RCHME AI report

Newman, P 1999 'Eylesbarrow (Ailsborough) Tin Mine' *Proc Devon Archaeol Soc* **58**, 105-48

Newman, P 2002 *Headland Warren and the Birch Tor and Vitifer Tin Mines*. EHAI Report Series **AI/34/2004**

Newman, P 2004 *Caroline Wheal Prosper: a Tin Mine at Buckfastleigh in Devon*. EHAI Report Series **AI/29/2004**

Newman, P 2006 *Holne Chase Tin Mine, Holne, Devon: an Archaeological Survey*. EHAI Report Series **AI/50/2006**

Newman, P 2010 *Environment, Antecedent and Adventure: Tin and Copper Mining on Dartmoor, Devon*. Unpublished PhD thesis, University of Leicester

Richardson, P H G 1992 *Mines of Dartmoor and the Tamar Valley after 1913*. British Mining **44**

Schmitz, C J 1979 *World non-ferrous metal production and prices, 1700 – 1976*. London: Frank Cass

Taylor, J 1799 'Sketch of the mining history of Devon and Cornwall' *Philosophical Magazine* **5**, 357-65

Warren, W 1787 *A State of the Tin Mines, on Dartmoor, in the County of Devon*. (Pamphlet)

The Tinworking Landscape of Dartmoor in a European Context: Prehistory to 20th Century

Table 1 Named tin mines of known location included on Fig. 1, which were worked or prospected for tin between the 18th and 20th centuries and possess field evidence

Name	NGR (SX)	Alternative and Associated Name(s)	Parish	Old Men's Workings
Ailsborough	5980 6825	Dartmoor Consolidated; Dartmoor Consols; Aylesborough; Wheal Ruth; Eylesbarrow	Sheepstor	PW; OW; SW
Albert, Wheal	5680 5955	Wheal Florence	Plympton	PW; SW
Anderton	4851 7234	Anderton United, Old Anderton, Rixhill, New Anderton, Tavistock United	Whitchurch	U
Alliance	5761 6878	Roughtor	Sheepstor	PW
Atlas	7810 7655	Albion, South Devon Iron and General Mining Co	Ilsington	PW; SW
Bachelors Hall	5975 7330		FoD	PW
Bagtor	7668 7584	Haytor Consols, Great Central, Crownley, Cranstoun	Ilsington	PW; OW; SW
Bal	5682 6917		Walkhampton	PW; OW
Beardown	5975 7630	Wheal Virgin	FoD	PW
Bertha, Lady	4710 6890	Bertha United, Lady	Buck Mon	U
Birch Tor and Vitifer	6850 8150	Birch Tor, New Birch Tor etc, Birch Tor Consols, Vitifer	FoD; Manaton	PW; OW
Birch Tor, East	6935 8100	East Burch Tor, Headland Mine, Devon Great Tincroft, New East Birch Tor, East Birch Tor Tin	North Bovey; Manaton	PW: OW
Bottle Hill	5624 5870	Bottlehill, Wheal Mace	Plympton	OW
Bradford Pool	7000 9100	Wheal St Ann	Drewsteignton	OW
Brimpts	6600 7400	Devon Tin, Duke of Cornwall Consolidated, Brempts, Brent's	FoD	PW; OW
Bush Down	6820 8190		Chagford	PW; OW; SW
Caroline, Wheal	6680 8117		FoD	PW; OW
Chance, Wheal	5950 7000	Wheal Chance and Nuns	Walkhampton	PW; OW; SW
Combeshead	5849 6840	Eylesbarrow, Ailsbarrow	Sheepstor	PW; OW; SW
Crebor	4623 7234		Gulworthy	OW
Crowndale, Wheal	4713 7254		Tavistock	PW; OW
Cumpston, Wheal	6720 7210	Dartmoor Consols, Dartmoor United	FoD	PW
Devon United	5155 7875	North Devon United, South Devon United, Wheal Ann, South Wheal Friendship, East Wheal Freindship	Peter Tavy	PW
Dorothy, Wheal	6552 6640		FoD	PW
Duchy, Wheal	5850 7359		FoD	PW
Eleanor, Great Wheal	7350 8340		North Bovey	OW
Fortune, Wheal	5500 7550	Merrifield Bridge, Merrivale Bridge, Morefield Bridge	Walkhampton	PW
Frederick, Wheal	5458 8538	Foxhole		SW
Furzehill	5180 6920		Horrabridge/ Walkhampton	PW; OW
Gem	7055 4948	West Sortridge Consols	Whitchurch	U
Gibbet (Hill)	5030 8090		Mary Tavy	PW
Gobbett	6470 7280	Dartmoor Consols, Dartmoor United, Swincombe Vale, Gobbets	FoD	OW; SW
Golden Dagger	6830 8020		Manaton	PW; OW; SW
Haytor Consols	7530 7550	Bagtor, Great Central, Crownley, Hemsworthy, Cranstoun	Ilsington	PW; OW; SW
Hemerdon Consols	5717 5868		Plympton St M	U
Hemsworthy	7440 7609		Ilsington	OW
Hexworthy	6560 7090	Hooten Wheals, Henroost, Wheal Unity, Wheal Princetown, Holme Moor	FoD	PW; OW
Holming Beam	5880 7680	Wheal Mist Tor, Omen Beam	FoD	PW
Holne Chase	7230 7145	Chase	Holne	OW
Hughes, East	5931 6995		Walkhampton	PW; OW
Huntingdon	6680 6700	Avon Consols, Devon Wheal Vor, Devon Consols Tin, New Huntingdon, Dartmoor Forest, East Wheal Rose	FoD	PW
Jewell, Wheal (Huel)	5230 8140	Jewel, Wheal Budlar, Wheal Freindship, Budlake, Budleybeer	Mary Tavy	PW
Katherine, Wheal	6070 6830	Crane Lake, Eylesbarrow, Ailsborough	FoD	OW
Keaglesborough	5731 7003	Keagle Borough, Keaglesburrow	Walkhampton	OW
Kerbeam	5610 8452	Curbeam, North Dartmoor, Curr Beam	FoD	OW
King's Oven	6750 8130	Water Hill, West Vitifer	Chagford	OW
Kingsett	5776 6980		Walkhampton	PW; OW; SW
Kit	5628 6745	Sheepstor	Sheepstor	U
Kitty, Wheal	65-- 79--		FoD	U
Lemon, Wheal	7820 7350	East Ashburton	Ashburton	PW
Little Duke	4702 6946	Raven Rock, North Tavy	Gulworthy	PW
Lucky, Wheal	5720 7487	Luckey	Walkhampton	PW; OW

Name	NGR (SX)	Alternative and Associated Name(s)	Parish	Old Men's Workings
Mary Emma, Wheal	5325 8316	Wheal Mary(?)	FoD	PW; OW; SW
Nuns	6033 6987		FoD	PW; SW
Nuns, East	6150 7010		FoD	PW
Owlacombe	7700 7350	Ashburton United, Union, Stormsdown, Owlacombe Beam & Union,	Ashburton	OW
Plym Consols	5850 6984		Walkhampton	PW; OW; SW
Prosper, Caroline Wheal	7015 6586	Caroline	Buckfastleigh	OW
Prosper, Wheal	5740 7930		FoD	PW; OW
Providence, Wheal	5885 8730		FoD	SW
Rattlebrook	5585 8570	Ammicombe (Wheal), North Dartmoor Consols, Wellington Consols	FoD	PW; OW
Ringleshutes	6750 6980	Holne (Holme) Moor	Holne	PW; OW
Ringmoor Down	5679 6719	Ringmoor and Sheepstor	Sheepstor	PW
Rixhill	4820 7233		Whitchurch	U
Robert, North Wheal	5130 7080	East Wheal Robert, Sortridge Consols	Whitchurch	OW
Roborough Down, North	5131 6856	Wheal Champion	Buck Mon	PW; OW
Runnaford Combe	7015 6811	Combe	Buckfastleigh	OW
Smith's Wood	7730 7480		Ilsington	U
Sortridge Consols	5094 7074	East Sortridge, West Sortridge, West Wheal Robert	Whitchurch	PW
Sortridge, Great	5091 7235	Sortridge Consols	Whitchurch	PW
Steeperton	6130 8820	Wheal Virgin, Knock	FoD	OW
Tavy Consols			Tavistock	PW; OW
Vitifer Consols, New	6790 6280	West Vitifer	Chagford	OW
Vitifer, East	7088 7238	Agnes	North Bovey	OW
Walkham United	4896 7067	Devon Poldice, Walkham and Poldice, Old Poldice	Buck Mon	AD
Week Consols, Great	7132 8750	Greatweek, Teign Valley Mining Company	Chagford	OW
West Beam	7655 7335	Ashburton Consols, Ashburton United, Owlacombe, Stormsdown	Ashburton	OW
West Down	4871 7055	Sortridge and Bedford	Whitchurch	U
Whiddon	7560 7215	Whiddon Down, Wheal Widdon, Widdon Smelting House Tin and Copper, Widdon and Brownshill	Ashburton	PW
White Works (Great)	6140 7100	Wheal Industry	FoD	PW; OW
Willsworthy	5485 8091	Baggator	Mary Tavy	PW
Yeoland Consols	5140 6630	South Yeoland, East Yeoland, Plymouth Yeoland	Buck Mon	PW

OW - openwork; PW - pit working; SW - streamwork; U - unknown

The Tinworking Landscape of Dartmoor in a European Context: Prehistory to 20th Century

Table 3 Dartmoor tin stamping mills and dressing floors of the 18th to 20th centuries where archaeological evidence has been recorded

Name of Mine	NGR (SX)	A	Date	Date Reference	B	C	D	E	F	G	H	I	J	K
Ailsborough 1	5944 6797	ID	1814	WDRO 874/50/2	S	6	0.9	E	S	✓			G	✓
Ailsborough 2	5939 6785	ID	1814	WDRO 874/50/2	S	6.1	1.1	E	S	✓			G	✓
Ailsborough 3	5934 6776	ID	1814	WDRO 874/50/2	S	5.5	1	E	S	✓			G	✓
Ailsborough 4	5929 6770	ID	1804	EFP 08.11.1804	S	5.7	1	S	S	✓			G	✓
Ailsborough 5	5916 6763	ID	1822	Cook et al. 1974	S	6.8	1	E	S	✓			F	✓
Ailsborough 6	5915 6747	ID	1804	EFP 08.11.1804	S	8.8	1.1	S	D	✓			G	✓
Anderton	4880 7233	OD	1845	BI, Tavistock	-	-	-	-	-		✓		D	-
Atlas	7810 7652	OD	1889-1914	OS 1st & 2nd ed 25"	S	-	-	S	S		✓		G	✓
Ausewell *	7269 7120	E	18th c		S	5	1	S	S	✓			F	✓
Ausewell *	7269 7123	E	18th c		S	5	0.9	S	S				F	✓
Ausewell *	7269 7125	E	18th c		S	8	2	S	S				F	✓
Ausewell *	7270 7129	E	18th c		S	6	1	S	S				F	✓
Bachelor's Hall (Bullpark)	6015 7344	E	early 19th c		PS	4.2	2.3	S	S				P	✓
Bachelor's Hall (lower)	5986 7341	E	1800-1845		E	0	0	E	D				F	✓
Bachelor's Hall (riverside)	6016 7345	OD	1790s	Hamilton Jenkin 1974, 94	E	4.2	2.3	E	S				P	✓
Bachelor's Hall (upper)	5982 7342	E	1800-1845		E	0	0	E	D				F	✓
Bal	5690 6931	E	1800		S	6.8	1.7	S	S				F	✓
Beam, West	7652 7358	ID	1836-47	DRO 1164B/11/8	S	13	1.8	S	S	✓			G	✓
Beardown	5974 7626	ID	1801	SYM 09.02.1801	E	5	0	E	S				P	✓
Bertha, Lady	4712 6891	ID	1886-1906	not present on 1886 OS 25"	S	10.8	1.5	S	S		✓	6	G	✓
Birch Tor and Vitifer	6819 8091	OD	1845-58	MJ 23.01.1858		-	-	S	n/k	✓	✓			✓
Birch Tor and Vitifer	6833 8072	ID	1903	Greeves 1986	E	-	-	E	S		✓		P	✓
Birch Tor, East (lower)	6946 7999	OD	1836-1852	Broughton 1968-9; BI, North Bovey	E	-	-	E	S					✓
Birch Tor, East (upper)	6944 8065	OD	1836-1852	Broughton 1968-9; BI, North Bovey	S	6.5	0.95	S	S	✓				✓
Brimpts (lower)	6701 7384	ID	1798	Bird & Hirst 1996	-	0	0	S	S				P	-
Brimpts (North)	6530 7478	ID	1853	Bird & Hirst 1996	S	7.7	1.5	S	S	✓			G	✓
Brimpts (Plantation)	6658 7393	ID	1850	Bird & Hirst 1996	S	8.8	1.4	E	S	✓			G	✓
Caroline, Wheal	6663 8082	OD	1826	DHC 3665Z	E	0	1.5	E	S				P	✓
Chance, Wheal	5951 7002	ID	1806	DHC 1311M/deeds/4/6	S	6.5	0.8	S	S	✓			F	✓
Combeshead	5850 6838	OD	1830	Greeves 1969	S	10	1.1	E	S	✓			F	✓
Cumpston, Wheal	6727 7233	OD	1840 pre-	Greeves 1978	S	6.2	1.2	S	S	✓			G	✓
Devon United	5121 7857	E	late 19th c	marked on 1905 OS 25" not on 1884	S	0	0	S	S		✓	4	G	✓
Dorothy, Wheal	6656 6647	-	n/k		E	5	2	S	S	✓			F	✓
East Hughes	5929 6995	E	1800-1830		S	8	1.3	E	S	✓			G	✓
East Lady Bertha	4780 6903	OD	1856-61	MJ 18.10.1856; MJ 13.07.1861	-	0	0	E	n/k		✓	2	P	-
Eleanor, Gt Wheal	7351 8342	ID	1876	EFP 23.08.1876	S	12.8	2	S	S			3	P	-
Fortune, Wheal (lower)	5520 7529	OD	1806	Greeves 1976, 3-5	S	-	-	S	S	✓			P	✓
Fortune, Wheal (middle)	5493 7538	OD	1806	Greeves 1976, 3-5	E	6	2.7	E	S	✓			F	✓
Fortune, Wheal (upper)	5495 7567	OD	1806 - c.1860	Greeves 1976, 3-5	S	5.5	0.8	S	S				F	✓
Frederick, Wheal	5458 8537	OD	1853	MJ 5.02.1853	S	7.6	1.3	S	S		✓	2	E	✓

Name of Mine	NGR (SX)	A	Date	Date Reference	B	C	D	E	F	G	H	I	J	K
Furzehill Wood	5159 6915	OD	1860-76	BI, Buck Mon	D	-	-	E	n/k		✓	2	P	✓
Gem	4945 7057	E	after 1850		S	6.5	2.3	S	S		✓	3	E	✓
Gobbett	6465 7277	ID	1831-2	Greeves 2006	E	14	1.8	E	S		✓	2	F	✓
Golden Dagger (1)	6837 8024	OD	1870-80s	Greeves 2016; OS 1885		5	1.7	-	S		✓		D	✓
Golden Dagger (2)	6834 8012	OD	1906-1914	absent OS 1906; Richardson 1992		7.5	3.4	E	S				G	✓
Golden Dagger (3)	6846 8005	OD	1809	Greeves 1986; OS 1809	S	13	1.5	-	S					✓
Golden Dagger (Walla Brook)	6729 7991	E	1800-1830		S	6	1.1	S	S	✓			G	✓
Great Week	7157 8743	ID	1887	MJ 06.08.1887	D	-	-	-	n/k				D	?
Haytor Consols (Crownley)	7667 7587	ID	1853	MJ 20.08.1853; BI, Ilsington	S	9.8	1.5	S	S		✓	5	G	-
Haytor Consols (Sig)	7619 7531	ID	1853	MJ 20.08.1853; BI, Ilsington	E	10.3	1.7	S	S				F	-
Hexworthy (Henroost)	6605 7108	OD	1880s	Burt et al. 1984	S	15.5	2	S	D	✓	✓	4	G	✓
Hexworthy (Hooten Wheals)	6567 7084	ID	1905	Greeves 1986	-	-	-	S	n/a		✓	2	F	-
Holne Chase	7143 7100	ID	1874	BI, Holne	S	4.5	4.2	E	S	✓	✓	6	G	✓
Huntingdon	6677 6693	ID	1859	CRO STA/1/136/1	E	15.5	5.5	E	S		✓	1	F	✓
Katherine, Wheal	6075 6829	E	1808 pre-	Newman 1999	S	8.8	0.9	S	D	✓			G	✓
Keaglesborough (lower)	5728 7009	ID	1801	DHC 924B/B2/1	S	6.2	0.9	S	D	✓			F	✓
Keaglesborough (upper)	5738 7011	OD	1830	Brown (nd)	S	9	2.2	S	D	✓			G	✓
Kingsett	5784 6972	E	early 19th c		E	7.5	-	E	S				P	-
Kit	5627 6744	ID	1900	BI, Sheepstor	S	7.1	1.2	E	S		✓	3	E	-
Kitty, Wheal	6601 7913		1887	Greeves pers com	S			S			✓			-
Mary Emma, Wheal	5323 8515	ID	1850	MJ 12.01.1850	E	13.5	1.3	S	S		✓	1	F	✓
Nuns, East	6145 6999	E	1800-1830	Woods Map 1850	S	4.8	0.7	S	S	✓			F	✓
Prosper, Caroline Wheal	7013 6585	ID	1854	Hamilton Jenkin 1981	S	9.1	5.5	S	S	✓			G	✓
Prosper, Wheal	5737 7935	OD	1848	Greeves 1975, 6	PS	5	0.9	E	S	✓			P	✓
Rattlebrook	5589 8565	E	c.1845	Greeves 2003, 22-4	PS	5.4	1.3	S	S	✓	✓	1	F	✓
Ringleshutes	6785 7032	ID	1854	MJ 21.01.1854	PS	4	-	-	S	✓			P	-
Ringmoor	5679 6719		1809 pre-	Lysons 1822	E	5	-	E	S				P	-
Roborough Down North	5131 6856	ID	1863	BI, Buck Mon		-	-	E	n/k		✓	2	P	-
Sortridge Consols	5085 7075	OD	1850s-		D	-	-	-	n/k		✓	3	F	✓
Steeperton	6143 8840	ID	1877	Greeves 1986	S	9.9	3	S	S		✓	1	G	✓
Virtuous Lady*	4722 6969	E	early 19th c		E	5	1.4	S	S				F	✓
Vitifer, East	7088 8236	ID	1846	MJ 16.05.1846	E	14	4	S	S		✓	2	G	✓
Vitifer, New	6789 8275	ID	1870	BI, Chagford	S	18.5	8	S	S		✓	3	G	✓
Walkham United	4949 7050		n/k		S	9.2	3.3	S	D	✓	✓	2	G	✓
Whiteworks (eastern)	6144 7108	ID	1808 pre-	Greeves 1980	E	6	-	E	S	✓			P	✓
Whiteworks (lower)	6153 7078	OD	1840 pre-	DHC AMP R43C	E	-	-	E	S		✓	2	P	✓
Whiteworks (upper)	6131 7083	ID	1869	Greeves 2002	PS	9	-	E	S				F	✓
Willsworthy (Baggator)	5489 8090	OD	1925	Richardson 1992							✓	1	E	✓
Yeoland Consols	5216 6635		n/k			-	-	-	n/k		✓		G	-

A = Date status (OD = operational date; ID = installation date; E = estimated date)
B = Wheelpit status (E = earthwork; S = structure; PS = part structure; D = destroyed)
C = Length of wheelpit if known
D = Width of wheelpit if known
E = Dressing floor revetment (E = earthwork; S = structure)
F = Dressing floor type (S = single; D = double)
G = Rectangular buddles
H = Round buddles
I = Number of round buddles in situ
J = General condition (D = destroyed; P = poor; F = fair; G = good; E = excellent)
K = leat present
* = better known as a copper mine

Lodges and Mills: The Field Archaeology of Tin Accommodation, Stamping and Smelting on Dartmoor

Tom Greeves

Abstract

This paper is intended as a summary of the state of our knowledge relating to some of the key structures associated with the Dartmoor tin industry and their surviving field remains. It is also a celebration of the rich archaeological and metallurgical evidence of tinworking represented within the Dartmoor landscape. Particular attention is paid to tinners' lodges and mills (for stamping and smelting) before about AD 1750. Previous works of synthesis include those by Worth (1953); Greeves (1981a; 1981b; 1991; 1996; 1997); Newman (1998; 2010; 2011); and Gerrard (2000).

Lodges

The generic term for an accommodation building used by the tinners (and others) before about 1750 was 'lodge'. A 'Tynlogge' at 'Shullake' is mentioned in 1456 on the East Quarter of the Forest of Dartmoor (TNA/SC2/166/46). In 1586 the Bailiff of Blackmore Stannary in Cornwall (corresponding to the St Austell region) wrote of 'litle lodges made up with turf' having 'handsome benches to sit upon' and we can assume there were equivalent structures on Dartmoor (Greeves 1993). Many visible structures are marked on Ordnance Survey maps of Dartmoor as 'Tinner's Hut', though some are now known to be the sites of mills. Some may have had a primary function for storage. Those that have been identified in the field on Dartmoor are usually rectangular structures, invariably walled with stone and earth (Fig.1).

Most have a visible entrance gap for a doorway and many include obvious signs of fireplaces. A pioneer survey on northern Dartmoor was carried out in 1979 (Le Messurier 1979), which included some buildings more certainly connected with peat cutters or stockmen. Recent fieldwork by Murray Oates has identified approximately 200 structures other than mills, associated with tinworks on moorland Dartmoor, evenly spread between north and south Dartmoor (Map 1).

Only one Dartmoor tinners' lodge has been excavated – at Greyhound Marsh, Postbridge on the left (east) bank of the East Dart River, at SX 64607910 (Baring-Gould 1902, 164-5). The structure measured internally approx. 12ft x 7ft (3.7 x 2.1m). Pottery, claimed to be of 13th/14th century date, was found, but this has not been located and assessed in

Figure 1 Lodge on left bank of Duck's Pool Stream SX 62956765. 1m scale (Tom Greeves).

Figure 2 Dated inscription inside left bank lodge on River Swincombe (Tom Greeves).

The Tinworking Landscape of Dartmoor in a European Context: Prehistory to 20th Century

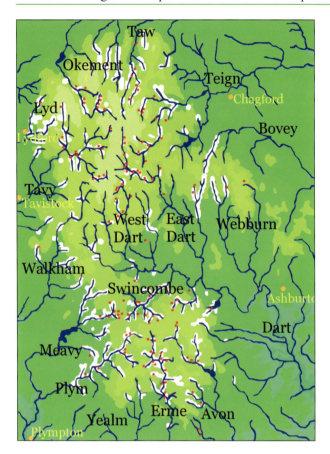

Figure 3 (above) Accommodation building for miners at Vitifer Mine c.1900 (detail) (Chapman and Son).

Map 1 (left) Map of tinners' lodges on Dartmoor by Murray Oates 2015.

recent times and its actual date might be somewhat later. Some ironwork was also found and a layer of fibrous material was suggested as having once been a roof of 'vags' (surface peat). A hearthstone, charcoal, and a covered drain were also uncovered.

Within about five metres of a tinners' lodge on the Blackbrook at SX 614740, surface finds of pottery, identified by John Allan, have been dated to the 13th or 14th century AD (Greeves 1998). A sherd of probable 17th-century pottery, also identified by John Allan, was found within the tinners' lodge by Skir Ford at SX 6510 7132 (Greeves 1981a, 170). One mid-18th-century lodge has, uniquely, a carved date and initials (I C 1753) on an internal face of a stone, on the left bank of the River Swincombe at SX 625712 (Fig. 2).

From an incident in 1640 we know that some of these moorland structures apparently had doors that could be locked and, within, ceramic vessels for the storage of preserved (salted) meat etc. (Greeves 1992).

In modern times, after *c.* 1750, some tinners on larger mines would be accommodated in 'barracks' for the working week, as at Ailsborough, Hexworthy

Figure 4 Miners' accommodation built 1872-3, New London, Princetown (Tom Greeves).

Figure 5 Interior of cache, right bank of River Meavy below Black Tor Falls (Tom Greeves).

Figure 6 Clash mill at Broad Falls, River Avon; newly built in 1599 (Tom Greeves).

and Vitifer (Greeves 2016; Newman 1999) (Fig. 3). Cottages specifically for miners were built at Whiteworks in 1871 and at New London, Princetown in 1872-3 (Greeves 1999) (Fig. 4).

Caches

A poorly studied category of structure associated with tinworking is the *cache* (Fig. 5). These are underground or semi-underground structures, using lintels or natural boulders as roofs, often with several well-built courses of drystone walling inside. Floors are usually of subsoil (growan). The sites are scattered among tinworks (especially streamworks) and must primarily have been for hidden or secure storage of tools and tin itself (in sacks as 'black' unsmelted tin, or as ingots). No comprehensive survey of them has been undertaken and scores must remain to be recorded.

Mills

Table 1 lists the sites of all known Dartmoor water-powered tin mills, with locations of slag and stone artefacts associated with stamping and smelting, before about AD 1750 – these comprise 177 named places altogether. The generic contemporary term for a water-powered mill associated with tinworking is 'tin mill'. A mill which had the function of crushing tin ore and preparing unsmelted black tin was variously known as a Clash Mill (one was built at Broad Falls on the R. Avon in 1599 – TNA/SC2/167/11 – Fig. 6), a Knocking/Knacking Mill, or a Stamping Mill. A mill where there was a blast furnace for smelting tin (and which sometimes incorporated a crushing mill) was variously known as a Blowing Mill/House, a Smithy, a Tin Smith(y), a Melting House or Smelting House. In 1479 'a blawyngsmyth' at Weleford (unidentified location) is the term used (TNA/SC2/166/48). A mill structure which included horizontal millstones for grinding tin ore was described as a Crazing Mill (though documentary evidence of this term has so far only been found in Cornwall).

Documentary references have been found for a

Figure 7 Upper Merrivale Mill A under excavation. 2m scales (DTRG).

Figure 8 Teignhead Farm or Fayrecombe tin mill 1457, with furnace structure and moulds. 1m scale (Tom Greeves).

minimum of 66 mills predating about AD 1750, but it is expected that more will be revealed (especially in manorial court rolls).

In terms of archaeological field evidence, we now know of a minimum of 79 of these 'early' mills which have visible structural remains surviving (Fig. 7). Those mills that combined stamping and smelting can often be about 10m x 5m internally, while those that were only for crushing ores can be significantly smaller (e.g. Outcombe which is internally 4.5 x 4.2m). More than 40 sites have produced tin slag (*see* Fig. 27), much of which has been analysed in great detail by Albertine Malham (2010). At two mills (Blacktor Falls Left Bank and Gnatham/Horrabridge) Roman numerals have been found cut into stones, which may represent registration numbers, though no documentary evidence yet supports this.

The earliest documented tin mill on Dartmoor, with structural remains surviving, is at Teignhead Farm/Fayrecombe, recorded in 1457 as a 'Tynsmyth' (Greeves 2013; TNA/SC2/166/46) (Figs 8-9).

Earthwork evidence of *leats* is visible at most mills though no comprehensive survey of them has yet been made. It is not uncommon to find that leats were several hundred metres in length. For example, those associated with the three Merrivale mill complexes, on the R. Walkham upstream of Merrivale Bridge, are 610m (Lower), 500m (Middle) and 490m (Upper) long. Exceptionally, the Southill Leat which is documented in the 1490s and which seems to have served two mills near Chagford was

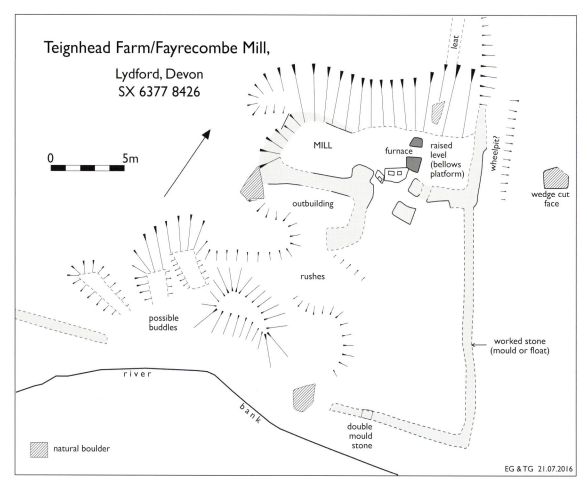

Figure 9 Plan of Teignhead Farm/Fayrecombe Mill 1457.

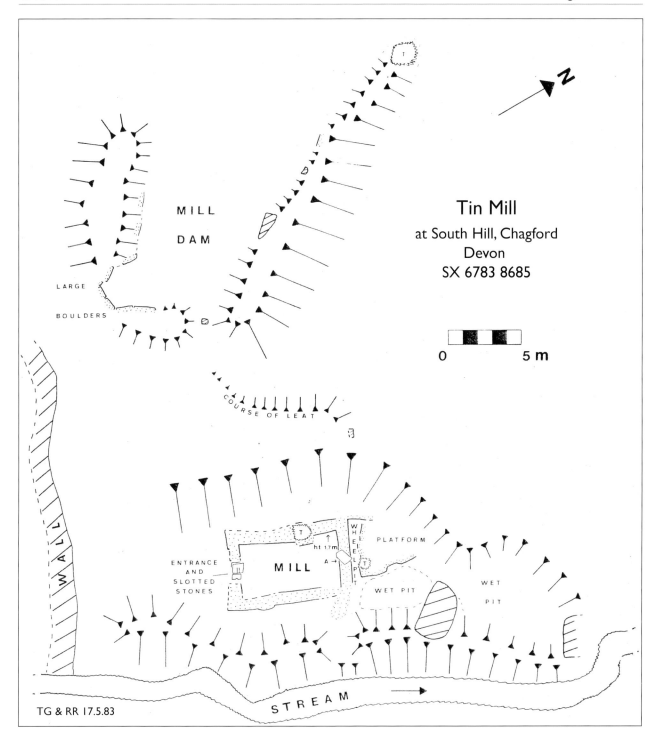

Figure 10 Plan of South Hill tin mill and reservoir.

some 5 miles (8 km) in length (Bodman 2015, 70). The longest known leat serving both a tinwork and probable mills was the Bradford Leat, perhaps dating from the early 16th century, which was 12 miles (19 km) long (Moss 2015). Much fieldwork remains to be done in identifying the headweirs of these leats and plotting their courses precisely.

Ponds or *reservoirs* serving mills have only occasionally been identified – that at South Hill A (Fig. 10) is exceptionally clear as is the one that probably served the early 16th century blowing and knocking mill at Dartmeet (Fig. 11). Upper Merrivale had a distinct reservoir above Mill A and Lower Merrivale is likely to have had an elongated pond formed by the widening of the leat as it approached the mill (Greeves & Newman 1994, *fig.* 5). It is likely that several other mill reservoirs remain to be identified.

The most distinctive stone artefact associated with tin mills is the *mortarstone* (Fig. 12) on which ore was crushed, in the great majority of cases mechanically by stamps (iron hammers or stones bound with iron) powered by a waterwheel. We now know of a minimum of 235 of these mortarstones within the Devon landscape, but forty-four per cent of these (104) come from just four sites – Gnatham/Horrabridge, Upper Merrivale, Nosworthy Left Bank and Outcombe. Surviving stones indicate that two or three stamps (hammers) were used. Those with three mortars (Fig. 13) are, for some reason, commoner on the east side of Dartmoor. Stones of granite were very carefully selected (the finer the grain the more long-lasting) and many were used on different faces or were adjusted for the stamps to fall in a different position on the exposed face. Two mortarstones (Bagtor and Deep Adit, Ailsborough) may well be the product of manual rather than mechanical crushing (Newman 2003; Greeves 2002)

We know from documentary sources (Greeves 1981a, 212-4) that there was a transition, probably in the 16th century, from dry to wet stamping, but we do not yet know whether mortarstones reflect this difference in any way.

At Upper Merrivale tin mill a double mortarstone (used on opposing faces) was found during excavations, still *in situ* in a stamps pit (Figs 14-15), unexpectedly with its long axis parallel to the wheelpit.

Only six horizontal *crazing millstones* (Figs 16-17) have been recorded from just five sites and only four are extant now (Bowden Mill, Gobbett (2), Gnatham/Little Horrabridge), the whereabouts of those from Outcombe and Yellowmead being no longer known. However, the presence of stones with long narrow slots at Yellowmead Farm, Sheepstor mill and at four additional tin mill sites (Glazemeet, Longstone, Nosworthy Left Bank, Ruddycleave), suggest that these may also have once had crazing millstones, as the slotted stones are likely to be supports for horizontal millstones, as such stones are found not infrequently at the site of corn mills (as at the early 14th century site at Babeny). A fifth mill

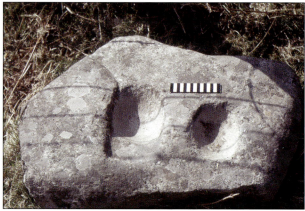

Figure 11 (top left) Probable reservoir for Dartmeet tin mill 1514, SX 67167392; Figure 12 (top right) Double mortarstone at Riddipit. 15cm scale; Figure 13 (bottom left) Triple mortarstone (incomplete) at Golden Dagger Mine, now at Stone, Widecombe. 30cm scale; Figure 14 (bottom right) Double mortar in situ with packing stones, Upper Merrivale Mill B. 30cm scale (Tom Greeves).

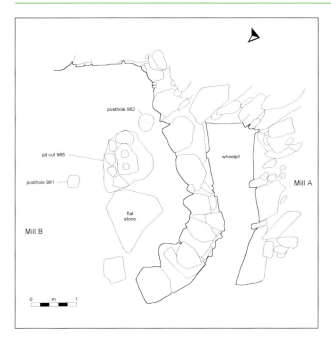

Figure 15 Wheelpit and stamps pit with mortarstone still in situ, Mill B Upper Merrivale (Passmore 2000).

site, Hook Lake, has a slotted stone (30cm in length) that must also be considered a possible indicator of the existence of a crazing mill.

At least 49 *mouldstones* (many of them incomplete) are known from Dartmoor. The moulds in which ingots were formed are neat cavities often with top measurements of about 40 x 30 cm, with bevelled sides, set within a proportionally large block of granite. Some have slight ridges projecting into the base of the mould from its short sides (this would create a groove which would be helpful when roping an ingot to the side of a packhorse) (Fig. 18). The recently excavated example from Brownie Cross may date to the late 13th century (Taylor et al. 2014). Some of the mouldstones have a second smaller mould cavity as at Fayrecombe and Bowden Mill (Figs 19-20), and some have additional very small rectilinear hollows, interpreted as sample moulds, which have been recorded from about fourteen sites. These 'sample' moulds often measure about 85 x 60 x 25 mm (depth), but there is some variation. Exceptionally large moulds from three sites (Bradford, Longstone, Postbridge) probably date between the late 17th century and the end of the 18th century (Greeves 1981a, 223).

Nine visible *furnace structures* have been identified at early (pre-1750) mills (Fig. 21; Figs 8 & 9 above). These are not attached to side walls of the mills but archaeologically appear as three-sided narrow (internally approx. 0.5-0.6m in width) stone structures, with an 'open' side where the furnace would be tapped, freestanding or set against the scarp defining the edge of a raised bellows platform. That at Upper Merrivale is the only one to have been excavated so far (Fig. 22). It was set against a massive boulder which itself had been trigged up within a specially dug pit (Figs 23-24; Passmore 2000). The lower part of the furnace, which included clay lining, was set within the upper fill of the pit. Furnaces were powered by a pair of bellows which, with the exception of Brownie Cross, seem to have been water-powered and set on a raised portion of the interior of mill structures, in order for their nozzles to feed into the back of the furnace at a height significantly above that of the taphole. Albertine Malham's simplified drawing shows the likely form of a blowing mill furnace in use in Devon and Cornwall between about AD 1300-1750 (Fig. 25; Malham 2010). These raised platforms can be identified at several mills e.g. Lower Merrivale, Upper Merrivale, Week Ford Lower, Teignhead Farm/Fayrecombe.

Documentary sources tell us that peat charcoal

Figure 16 Probable crazing mill stone (incomplete) at Bowden Mill, North Bovey. 30cm scale (Tom Greeves).

Figure 17 Probable crazing mill fragment at Gnatham/Little Horrabridge. 15cm scale (Tom Greeves).

Figure 18 Mouldstone at Upper Yealm Steps, showing ridge. 15cm scale (Tom Greeves).

Figure 19 Small mould with sample mould at Bowden Mill, North Bovey. 15cm scale (Tom Greeves).

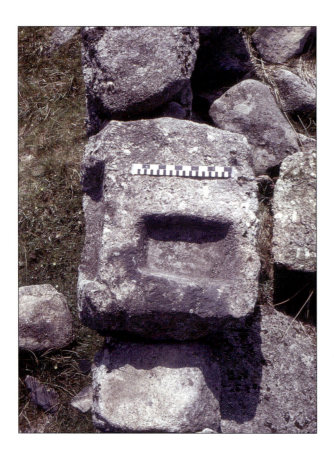

Figure 20 Small moulds at Teignhead Farm/Fayrecombe tin mill. 30cm scale (Tom Greeves) (see also Figs 8 and 9).

was a favoured fuel but that wood charcoal, or a mixture of the two, was also used, depending on the quality of ore being smelted (Greeves 1981a, 254-8). Briquettes of peat charcoal were found in excavations at Upper Merrivale.

Extensive archaeological remains of both a blast furnace and a reverberatory furnace survive at Ailsborough Mine, Sheepstor (Fig. 26). These were in operation 1822-1831 (Greeves 1996; Newman 1999) and were the last tin furnaces to operate on moorland Dartmoor. Other tin smelting houses in operation in Devon *c.*1750-*c.*1890 are listed in Table 2.

Tin *slag* is commonly found (Fig. 27) and occasionally *furnace lining* in the form of partially vitrified stone and clay fragments with a slagged face.

An enigmatic artefact mentioned in contemporary documentary and published sources is the *float* or *floatstone*. This appears to have been a shallow granite trough into which tin metal was first tapped from the furnace and which presumably would allow the removal of lighter slag by scraping it from the surface. Several stones with very shallow rectilinear troughs are alleged to be floatstones. One is directly associated with the furnace remains at Lower Merrivale as one end of it is lying at an angle within

Figure 21 Gobbett tin mill showing furnace remains on the left and scattered artefacts (Tom Greeves).

the base of the furnace (Worth 1953, Plate 68B). Similar stones, or possible fragments, have been found at three other sites (including four possible examples from Upper Merrivale).

Wheelpits are visible at a minimum of 51 sites and 39 *bearing stones* which supported axles have been recorded. These sometimes have concentric polish marks below the open bearing itself (Fig. 28).

All mills must have had *dressing floors* with shallow settling pits known as buddles, and a variety of wooden equipment such as kieves (tubs). These floors are not easy to identify in the field owing to encroachment by bog or vegetation, but terraced or level areas adjoining mills are likely candidates, especially if two or three small roughly rectilinear pits are visible. Probable floors are known at about twenty sites (pre-1750) so far.

Conclusion

The remarkable survival of so many structures within the Dartmoor landscape that relate to tinworking accommodation, storage and milling before AD 1750 represents an unparalleled resource for the study of so-called 'pre-industrial' society. Where smelting occurred the metallurgical resource is

Figure 22 Back edge of furnace structure with side walls visible and sectioned clays, Mill A, Upper Merrivale. 50cm scale (Tom Greeves).

The Tinworking Landscape of Dartmoor in a European Context: Prehistory to 20th Century

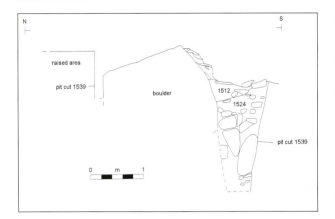

Figure 23 Section of furnace structure, Mill A Upper Merrivale. Context 1512 consists of basal clays of the furnace (Passmore 2000).

Figure 26 Collapsed blast furnace of 1820s, Ailsborough Mine, Sheepstor (Tom Greeves).

Figure 24 Sectional view of basal clays of the furnace (context 1512), Mill A Upper Merrivale. 30cm scale (DTRG).

Figure 27 Tin slag from Middle Merrivale tin mill. 15cm scale (Tom Greeves).

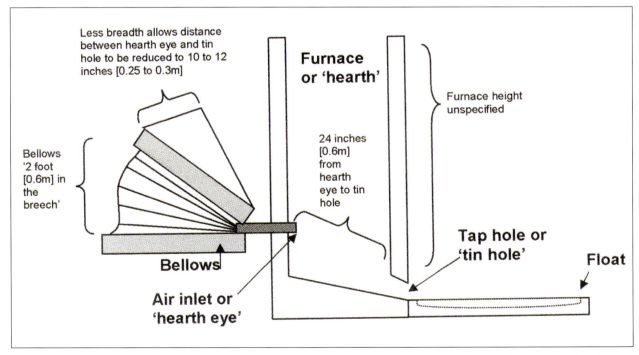

Figure 25 Simplified diagram of the type of blowing mill furnace used on Dartmoor and in Cornwall c.1300-c.1700 (Malham 2010).

64

Figure 28 Bearing stone with concentric wear marks on vertical face, Upper Merrivale. 30cm scale (DTRG).

of exceptional interest and reminds us of the high level of metallurgical skill that must once have been relatively commonplace on Dartmoor. Numerous structures also survive for the period between *c*.1750 and *c*.1930 (*see* Newman *this volume*). Linking all these features was a supreme culture of water management.

Bibliography

Baring-Gould, S (ed) 1902 'Eighth Report of the Dartmoor Exploration Committee' *Rep Trans Devonshire Ass* **34**, 160-5

Bodman, M 2015 *Mills on the Teign – a gazetteer of water-powered sites on the Teign and Bovey and their tributaries.* Cullompton: Leat Press

Gerrard, Sandy 2000 *The Early British Tin Industry.* Stroud: Tempus Publishing Ltd

Greeves, T 1981a *The Devon Tin Industry 1450-1750; an archaeological and historical survey.* Unpub Phd thesis, University of Exeter

Greeves, T 1981b 'The Archaeological Potential of the Devon Tin Industry' in D W Crossley (ed) *Medieval Industry*. Council for British Archaeology Research Report **40**, 85-95

Greeves, T 1991 'Blowing and Knocking – the Dartmoor Tin Mill Before 1750' *Dartmoor Magazine* **23**, Summer 1991, 18-20

Greeves, T 1992 '"Almost a Whole Sheep Salted..." – Tinners and Walkhampton in the Early 17th Century' *Dartmoor Magazine* **29**, Winter1992, 6-8

Greeves, T 1993 'The Good Life? – The Westcountry Tinner AD *c*.1500 - *c*.1700' *Journal of the Trevithick Society* **20**, 39-47

Greeves, T 1996 'Tin Smelting in Devon in the 18th and 19th Centuries in Newman, P (ed) *The Archaeology of Mining & Metallurgy in South-West Britain*. Bulletin Peak District Mines Historical Society **13.2**, 84-90

Greeves, T 1997 'Tin Stamping Mills of Dartmoor After AD 1750' *Dartmoor Magazine* **49**, Winter 1997, 6-8

Greeves, T 1998 'Medieval Pottery and Tinworking' *DTRG Newsletter* **14**, January 1998, 4-5

Greeves, T 1999 'An Unrecognised Building Heritage at Risk' *Dartmoor Magazine* **54**, Spring 1999, 20-21

Greeves, T 2002 'Unusual Mortarstone Discovered at Ailsborough, Sheepstor' *DTRG Newsletter* **23**, Summer 2002, 5

Greeves, T 2013 'Fayrecombe – A 15th Century Record for 'Blacksmith's Shop' Tin Blowing Mill (Teignhead)' *DTRG Newsletter* **44**, January 2013, 9

Greeves, T 2016 *Called Home – The Dartmoor Tin Miner 1860-1940.* Truro: Twelveheads Press

Greeves, T and Newman, P 1994 'Tin-working and Land-Use in the Walkham Valley: A Preliminary Analysis' *Proc Devon Archaeol Soc* **52**, 199-219

Le Messurier, B 1979 'The Post-Prehistoric Structures of Central North Dartmoor' *Rep Trans Devonshire Ass* **111**, 59-73

Malham, A 2010 *The Classification and Interpretation of Tin Smelting Remains from South West England*. Unpub PhD thesis, University of Bradford

Moss, M 2015 'The Bradford Tinwork Leat and Its Route: Through Enclosed Ground' *Rep Trans Devonshire Ass* **147**, 155- 184

Newman, P 1998 *The Dartmoor Tin Industry – A Field Guide.* Newton Abbot: Chercombe Press

Newman, P 1999 'Eylesbarrow (Ailsborough) Tin Mine' *Proc Devon Archaeol Soc* **57**, 105-148

Newman, P 2003 'A Mortarstone on Pinchaford Ball' *DTRG Newsletter* **25**, 6

Newman, P 2010 *Environment, Antecedent and Adventure: Tin and Copper Mining on Dartmoor, Devon c.1700-1914.* Unpub PhD, University of Leicester

Newman, P 2011 *The Field Archaeology of Dartmoor.* Swindon: English Heritage

Passmore, A 1998 'Finds at Upper Merrivale: The Larger Stone Artefacts' *DTRG Newsletter* **14**, January 1998, 10-11

Passmore, A 2000 Upper Merrivale Tin Mills – Summary Report on the Mill A Furnace and Mill B Stamping Area. Unpub typescript

Taylor, S R, Jones, A M, Young, T 2014 'Smelting Point: Archaeological Investigation along the route of the Avon Water Main Renewal, Plympton, Devon 2009' *Proc Devon Archaeol Soc* **72**, 187-276

Worth, R H 1953 (ed Spooner G M & Russell F) *Dartmoor.*

Abbreviations

DTRG – Dartmoor Tinworking Research Group
TNA – The National Archives, Kew, London

Table 1: Early Tin Mills (see also Map 2)

No	Pre-1750 Site Name (date) and NGR	Type (documented)	Structure present	Wheelpit visible	Bearing stone	Leat Embankment	Leat and length (metres)	Reservoir	Furnace structure	Mouldstone	Float stone	Slag	Mortarstone	Crazing millstone	Slotted stone	Fireplace	Trough	Dressing floor/buddles	Ancillary lodge/ building	Documentary evidence
1	Aller Brook (Holne) SX 6753 7181		?										?							
2*	Ashburton (1504)	T																		•
3	Avon Dam SX 6722 6553		•	•	•	•	•		•	4		•	7					•	•	
4	Bag Park (see also Pitton) SX 722783												1							
5	Bagtor SX 7612 7625												1							
6	Bal Mine/Whitemoor Mead SX 5683 6928				•				?				1							
7	Barramoor SX 7140 8388 (findspot)												1							
8	Belstone SX 6212 9337 & SX 6213 9332									1			1							
9	Blacka Brook SX 564 644												1							
10	Blackaller (1527) SX 7377 8377	B/T				•					•									•
11	Blackaton (pre-1566) SX 700 779 & 6986 7782	B		•			•													
12	Blackaton Ball Moor SX 6884 7812		•	•		•												•		
13	Blackaton Brook/ Lovebrook* (1530-1590)	B				•														•
14	Blacklane Brook/ Wollake (1532, 1538-9) SX 6290 6690		•			•										•				•
15	Blackm[ore] (1582) SX 698 770 (?)	T																		•
16	Black Tor Falls A (left bank) SX 5749 7161	T	•	•	•								2							
17	Black Tor Falls B (right bank) SX 5748 7162	T	•	•	2	•							7			•			•	
18	Black Tor Falls C (lower) SX 5743 7157	T	•	•									1							
19	Blacktor(Middleworth) (1693) SX 5760 6915		•	•		•														•
20	Bowden (Buckland) SX 7277 7356		•	•		•														
21	Bowden Mill (N.Bovey) SX 7252 8407									1			5	1						
22	Bradford* (1687-1697)	B/K/S				•				1										•
23	Brisworthy (1560) SX 56026469	B	•		•					1			3							•

No	Pre-1750 Site Name (date) and NGR	Type (documented)	Structure present	Wheelpit visible	Bearing stone	Leat Embankment	Leat and length (metres)	Reservoir	Furnace structure	Mouldstone	Float stone	Slag	Mortarstone	Crazing millstone	Slotted stone	Fireplace	Trough	Dressing floor/buddles	Ancillary lodge/ building	Documentary evidence
24	Broad Falls (1599) SX 6545 6692	C	•	•		•	•						2							•
25	Brockhill Stream SX 6783 6609			?														?		
26	Brownie Cross SX 5452 6090		•							1		•								
27	Burrator Lodge SX 5520 6859												3							
28	Butterbrook SX 6422 5920		•		•		•			?		•	3							
29	Caseleigh (1599, 1613) SX 7877 8216	B/Sm	•									•								•
30	Chagford Bridge SX 6950 8778												1							
31	Challacombe A SX 6933 7941			•						1										
32	Challacombe B SX 6940 7961												1							
33	Challacombe C (16th cent.) SX 6922 7915	T	•	•	•															•
34	Chance, Wheal SX 5955 7000												1							
35	Chittleford (mill names on tithe apptmt) SX 7215 7577																				•
36	Cholwell Brook SX 5095 8076												1							
37	Claziwell SX 5824 7035			•														•		
38	Colesmills SX 5935 6676	S	•	•	•	•	• 625						6							•
39	Colleytown SX 5668 6748		•				•			1			7							
40	Collihole SX 6863 8558												2							
41	Colly Brook SX 5423 7782		•	•	2		•						1			•		•		
42	Combeshead/Harthill (1571, 1582, 1584) SX 5850 6838	B/K	•	•			•						6					•		•
43	Cornish Adventure (1690) SX 69 89	S																		•
44	Cowsic Combe* (1602)	C																		•
45	Crane Lake SX 6077 6818		•				•											?		
46	Creason (1606, 1607, 1609, 1716) SX 5300 8034			•	?															•

The Tinworking Landscape of Dartmoor in a European Context: Prehistory to 20th Century

No	Pre-1750 Site Name (date) and NGR	Type (documented)	Structure present	Wheelpit visible	Bearing stone	Leat Embankment	Leat and length (metres)	Reservoir	Furnace structure	Mouldstone	Float stone	Slag	Mortarstone	Crazing millstone	Slotted stone	Fireplace	Trough	Dressing floor/buddles	Ancillary lodge/building	Documentary evidence
47	Criptor SX 5564 7266		•	•																
48	Dartmeet (1514) SX 672 735	B/K					• 500	•												•
49	Dean Moor SX 678 653										•									
50	Deep Adit/Deepwork, South (Ailsborough) SX 5915 6820												1							
51	Deepwork, North SX 5886 6846		•	•			•													
52	Devon United (Central) SX 5155 7879		•	•		•														
53	Ditsworthy* (findspot unknown)												•							
54	Doetor Green/Mary Emma (1594, 1627, 1694, 1732, 1740) SX 5333 8524		•	•		•	•						•		•		•			•
55	Dorothy, Wheal SX 6552 6650		•				•											•		
56	Drakeford Bridge SX 7878 8015						• 500						•							
57	Dry Lake, Lower SX 6400 6337		•				• 340													
58	Dry Lake, Upper SX 6336 6636		•	•		•	•											•		
59	Ducks Pool Stream SX 6293 6766		•	•	•	•	•													
60	East Okement Farm SX 6062 9181		•				•						•							
61	Eggworthy A (1583) SX 5435 7183		•	•					1				•				•			•
62	Eggworthy B SX 5425 7183		•	•																
63	Elfordleigh SX 545 586												•							
64	Fardel SX 6118 5743												1							
65	Fernhill/Portworthy (1545-8, 1550, 1552, 1562, 1570, 1594) SX 5565 6018	B																		•
66	Fishlake Foot SX 6490 6834		•	•		•	• 300													
67	Glazemeet A SX 6683 6031		•	•	•	•						?	•	3		•		•	•	
68	Glazemeet B SX 6682 6017		•	?			?											?		

No	Pre-1750 Site Name (date) and NGR	Type (documented)	Structure present	Wheelpit visible	Bearing stone	Leat Embankment	Leat and length (metres)	Reservoir	Furnace structure	Mouldstone	Float stone	Slag	Mortarstone	Crazing millstone	Slotted stone	Fireplace	Trough	Dressing floor/buddles	Ancillary lodge/ building	Documentary evidence
69	Gnatham/Fillace/Furze-hill/Little Horrabridge (1521, 1528, 1538, 1569, 1576-1588, 1596) SX 5149 6962	B/K/T			•					1			38	•			•			•
70	Gobbett SX 6453 7280		•			•			•	3		•	3	2					•	
71	Golden Dagger SX 685 800 – one m/s now at SX 7209 7940												2							
72	Goodameavy/Doubts House (1616, 1815) SX 5295 6460	T																		•
73	Gratnar/Everly SX 7201 8362		•				•						2							
74	Hartor Tor, Lower SX 6748 6743	S	•	•			• 75						2							
75	Hatchwood, Little (1743, 1748) SX 443 719 (?)	S																		•
76	Heckwood SX 5445 7347		•	•																
77	Hemerdon Ball* (1706)	K																		•
78	High Down SX 5315 8559		•		2		• 450							•						
79	Hole & Collaton* (1617)	T																		•
80	Hook Lake SX 6393 6509			•	•	•	• 370		?						•					
81	Horrabridge (Franco) SX 5109 7010 now at SX 5088 7860									1										
82	Horridge* (1631)	T																		•
83	Huntingdon SX 6658 6653		?																	
84	Ilsington* (1557)	B																		•
85	Impham A* (1724, 1726, 1728-9) SX 4398 7055	M/ S/ SH	•								•									•
86	Impham B* SX 4405 7130	S	•	•																
87	Ivybridge/Meyes/ Lewes Burys* Blowing Mill (c.1550,1555)	B/K/T																		•
88	Keaglesborough A* (1565, 1577, 1584)	B/K																		•
89	Keaglesborough B SX 5750 7002													1						
90	Lady/Louder Brook SX 6285 9175		•	•		•	•											•		

The Tinworking Landscape of Dartmoor in a European Context: Prehistory to 20th Century

No	Pre-1750 Site Name (date) and NGR	Type (documented)	Structure present	Wheelpit visible	Bearing stone	Leat Embankment	Leat and length (metres)	Reservoir	Furnace structure	Mouldstone	Float stone	Slag	Mortarstone	Crazing millstone	Slotted stone	Fireplace	Trough	Dressing floor/buddles	Ancillary lodge/building	Documentary evidence
91	Langcombe SX 6037 6723		•	•									1					•		
92	Leather Tor Farm SX 5668 6981 & 5672 6981 (slag)											•	1							
93	Leftlake, below SX 6413 6273												1							
94	Lingcombe SX 6883 8440											•								
95	Liverton (1566) SX 823 743 (?)	B/K																		•
96	Longstone A SX 5600 6876		•										•		•					
97	Longstone B (1623) SX 5607 6880	T	•	•						2			•	1						•
98	Longstone C SX 5575 6828												•							
99	Lovaton, Meavy* (c.1550)	B/K																		•
100	Lumburn (1560) SX 4590 7310	B																		•
101	Lumburn Meadow (1579) SX 463 720	K																		•
102	Manga Left Bank SX 6399 8467												1							
103	Manga Right Bank SX 6409 8478		•			?														
104	Merrivale, Lower SX 5527 7535		•				• 610	•	•	1	•	•								
105	Merrivale, Middle SX 5527 7624		•	•			• 500			1			•	1						
106	Merrivale, Upper SX 5519 7640		•	2	10	•	• 490	•	•	6	4?	•	24			•	•	•		
107	Metherel SX 6682 8402 & SX 6697 8412												•							
108	Michelcombe (Dodbrooke) SX 6983 6877												1							
109	Middlecott (Ilsington) SX 7820 7693									1										
110	Middleworth SX 5709 6923												?							
111	Newleycombe (Blacksmith's Shop) SX 5893 6986		•	•			•	?										•		
112	Newleycombe (Nosworthy) SX 5713 6952		•	•		•	•										•			
113	Newleycombe (Plym Consols) SX 5858 6990			?			•						1							

No	Pre-1750 Site Name (date) and NGR	Type (documented)	Structure present	Wheelpit visible	Bearing stone	Leat Embankment	Leat and length (metres)	Reservoir	Furnace structure	Mouldstone	Float stone	Slag	Mortarstone	Crazing millstone	Slotted stone	Fireplace	Trough	Dressing floor/buddles	Ancillary lodge/ building	Documentary evidence
114	Newleycombe Right Bank SX 5820 6991																	•	•	
115	Nosworthy Bridge SX 5678 6940 & SX 5673 6938 (mouldstone)		•							1								•		
116	Nosworthy (Cook's) SX 5687 6942												1							
117	Nosworthy Left Bank SX 5678 6958		•	•	•		• 100					•	14	•				•		
118	Nosworthy Right Bank (1511) SX 5674 6954 & SX 5675 6943 (1 x m/s)	K	•	•			• 150						2							•
119	Nuns Cross Ford SX 6105 6988		•	•		•	•											•		
120	Outcombe SX 5801 6860 & SX 5795 6861		•	•	2	•	•						28	•		•		?		
121	Outer Down (1617) SX 682 866	T	•	•					?	2		•	?							•
122	Owlacombe Cottage SX 7658 7317												2							
123	Parktown SX 547 732									1										
124	Pitton (1526, 1574, 1581, 17th cent.) SX 7210 7852	S/T	•	•			•						4							•
125	Pizwell (1521, c.1538, 1578, 1599) SX 6656 7849	Sm					•			1										•
126	Plaster Down (pre-c.1750) SX 5168 7225	S/T					•													•
127	Plym Steps (1499) SX 6026 6724		•	•	2		•													•
128	Plympton St Mary (parish)* (1680, 1719, 1730, 1751)	B/SH																		•
129	Ramsley SX 6480 9327	B																		•
130	Rattlebrook Combe* (1602)	C																		•
131	Red Brook SX 6694 6279		•	•														•		
132	Redlakecombe* (1609)	C																		•
133	Riddipit (1565, 1584) SX 5702 7016	K	•										4							•
134	Riddon SX 6741 7668						•			1		•	1							
135	Roborough Down (1600, 1603) SX 52 66	C/K/T																		•
136	Rudford next Churlbroke* (1451-2)	B																		•

No	Pre-1750 Site Name (date) and NGR	Type (documented)	Structure present	Wheelpit visible	Bearing stone	Leat Embankment	Leat and length (metres)	Reservoir	Furnace structure	Mouldstone	Float stone	Slag	Mortarstone	Crazing millstone	Slotted stone	Fireplace	Trough	Dressing floor/buddles	Ancillary lodge/ building	Documentary evidence
137	Ruddycleave SX 7308 7407		•	•									•							
138	Runnaford Combe (1619, 1622-3, 1630, 1651, 1652) SX 700 682 (approx)	B/K/S																		•
139	Rushford Wood SX 7024 9002		•	•	•															
140	Sandsgate SX 6989 9019		•	?																
141	Seven Stone, Holne* (1685)	T																		•
142	Sheepstor A* (1530)	K																		•
143	Sheepstor B* (1680, 1719, 1730, 1751)	B																		•
144	Shipley Cottage SX 682 628									1	?									
145	South Hill A SX 6783 8685		•	•			•	•				•						?		
146	South Hill B SX 6801 8710		•		•							•								
147	Stannon Brook SX 6483 7956		•		•		•			1		•							•	
148	Stennan* (1601)																			•
149	Swincombe River SX 6239 7113		•	?			•											?		
150	Taw River (1538-9, 1608) SX 6205 9197	B/K	•	•		•	• 450	?	•			•	?					?		•
151	Teignhead Farm/Fayrecombe/ Blacksmith's Shop (1457) SX 6377 8426	TS	•	?			• 500		•	3		•						•		•
152	Thorn/Smutty Park SX 685 869																			•
153	Thornworthy SX 6723 8443		•										•							
154	Throwleigh (? Ford)* (1558, 1560)	B/T																		•
155	Topsham (38 Elm Grove Rd)* SX 969 881												1							
156	Venford Brook SX 6859 7118 and SX 685 708 (findspot)												1							
157	Wallabrook Clapper SX 6720 7489												•							
158	Wallabrook Soussons SX 6716 7957												2							

No	Pre-1750 Site Name (date) and NGR	Type (documented)	Structure present	Wheelpit visible	Bearing stone	Leat Embankment	Leat and length (metres)	Reservoir	Furnace structure	Mouldstone	Float stone	Slag	Mortarstone	Crazing millstone	Slotted stone	Fireplace	Trough	Dressing floor/buddles	Ancillary lodge/ building	Documentary evidence
159	Wapsworthy SX 5450 7980											•								
160	Week Ford Lower/ Oakbrookfoot (1521?, 1608, 1609, 1730, 1737) SX 6619 7234		•	•					•	3		•	7							•
161	Week Ford Upper/ Oakbrookfoot (1521?, 1608, 1609, 1730, 1737) SX 6618 7232		•	•	•	•							7							•
162	Week, Great SX 7145 8760												1							
163	West Cleave SX 6077 9397		•	•		•														
164	Westhill, Torquay* (1680, c.1695) SX 91 65 (?)	S																		•
165	Whiddon (1757, pre-1765) SX 7545 7217	S/SH	•																	•
166	Whittenknowles SX 5859 6696												•							
167	Widecombe North Hall (pre-1669) SX 7184 7690 & 7194 7683 & 7185 7679	Sm							•?				4							•
168	Will SX 5332 8145								1											
169	Willaford Mills* (1479, 1578, 1609, 1614)	B / K/ Sm/T																		•
170	Woodtown SX 5398 7164												1							
171	Yadsworthy SX 6250 6070								1											
172	Yealm Steps Lower SX 6179 6352		•						•	2			1							
173	Yealm Steps Upper SX 6172 6385		•	•	•		•	•	•	2			•					•		
174	Yelland (Chagford) (1755) SX 69 85 (?)	S																		•
175	Yellowmead /Oldmede (1502, 1727) SX 5742 6755	B	•	•					1			•	1	?	•					•
176	Yeo (Sheepstor) SX 5512 6696 & 5509 6697												3							
177	Yes Tor Bottom SX 5669 7295												•							

Type (documented): B - Blowing mill; C - Clash mill; K - Knacking/Knocking mill; M - Melting house; S - Stamping mill; SH - Smelting house; Sm - Smithy; T - Tin mill; TS - Tinsmith.

* sites not depicted on Map 2 (below).

One of the mortarstones from Burrator Lodge is now at the Museum of Dartmoor Life, Okehampton.

The Tinworking Landscape of Dartmoor in a European Context: Prehistory to 20th Century

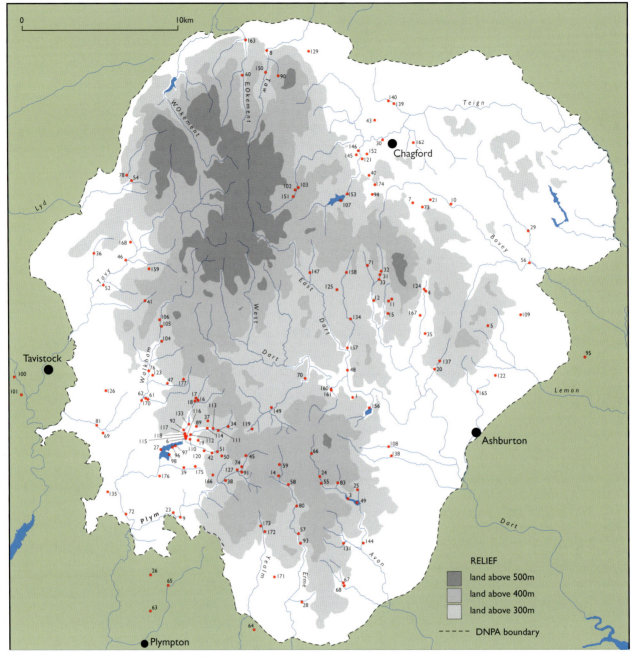

Map 2 Distribution map of located tin mills pre-AD 1750.

Additional documentary references, Table 1

Most sources for dated documented references to the mills in Table 1 can be found in Greeves (1981a) Appendix 2 and Appendix 3. Additional references are given below:

24. Broad Falls – TNA/SC2/167/11
33. Challacombe C – DHC/1508M/16TH cent. survey (inf. Harold Fox)
44. Cowsic Combe – TNA/SC2/167/13
46. Creason – PWDRO/407/1863; 407/3/11(8)
61. Eggworthy A – PWDRO/745/122
65. Fernhill/Portworthy – PWDRO/72/345a; 72/346
69. Gnatham etc – TNA/STAC 2/15/152; PWDRO/70/313; 70/266; 1196/7
97. Longstone B – PWDRO/407
100. Lumburn – DHC/W1528M/D49/2
101. Lumburn Meadow – DHC/L1258/2/66/1
124. Pizwell – TNA/SC2/167/5; 167/11
125. Plaster Down – DHC/maps of *c.*1750 (inf. Helen Harris)
126. Plym Steps – TNA/Court Roll 1499, in Rowe (1848) *Perambulation of Dartmoor*. p.273
129. Rattlebrook Combe – TNA/SC2/167/13
135. Rudford next Churlbroke – TNA/SC6/829/9
140. Seven Stone – Spitchwick Manor MSS
141. Sheepstor A - TNA/STAC 2/14/47-50
147. Stennan – TNA/SC2/167/13
150. Teignhead Farm – TNA/SC2/166/46
159. Week Ford – TNA/SC2/167/16
163. Westhill – Ellis (1930) *An Historical Survey of Torquay*, p.264
164. Whiddon – Chester RO/DBC 1/17/2
166. Widecombe North Hall – DHC/ 74/9/9/2
168. Willaford Mills – TNA/SC2/167/5; 167/16; 166/48
173. Yelland – *Devon Min & Mining Club Journal*, **3.2**, June 2002, 21
174. Yellowmead – churchwardens' accounts (inf. Brad Scott)

Table 2: Tin smelting houses on Devon c. 1750-c.1890

DATE	COMPANY	SITE
1751		Plympton (blowing)
1751		Sheepstor
1757		Whiddon, Ashburton
c. 1760		Whiddon, Ashburton
1786	Dartmoor Mining & Smelting Co	Postbridge (blowing & smelting)
1787/8	Devon Tin Mining & Smelting Co	
1793	Dartmoor Mining & Smelting Co	
1795-7		R. Tamar
1796	Mr Lane, Proprietor	near Tavistock
1798-1807		Bachelors Hall
1804	Devon Metal Co	Tavistock
1806-8		Tuckersmarsh
1812	Gill, Bray & Hornbrook	Tavistock
1815	Tavistock Smelting Co	Tavistock
1815-1837	Devon Smelting Co (Gill & Co)	Tavistock
1816	Tavistock Tin Smelting Co	Tavistock
1817-?	Tavistock Smelting Co	Tavistock
1822-1831	J H Deacon & Co	Ailsborough (blowing & smelting)
1830	Tavistock Smelting Co	Crowndale, Tavistock
1833	Devon Stannary Mining & Smelting Co	
1834	Devon Smelting Co	Crowndale, Tavistock
1849-1863	Union Tin Smelting Co	Weir Quay
1850		Crowndale
1850		South Brent
1871-1876	Tamar Tin Smelting Co	Weir Quay
1884-1890	Tamar Tin Smelting Co	Weir Quay
1891-1898	The West of England Smelting & Refining Co Ltd	

The Hemerdon Project

*Simon Hughes**

Introduction

In 2008, Wolf Minerals UK Ltd. took on the mineral rights for the working of tungsten, china clay and tin at Drakelands Mine - formerly Hemerdon Mine – at Plympton near Plymouth, Devon. The planning permission for extraction, granted by Devon County Council in 1986, was rekindled and the tradition of mineral working in south Devon was extended into the 21st century. This provided the stimulus for archaeological investigations throughout this mineral-rich landscape, an overview of which is set out below.

Site Conditions

The Drakelands Mine site lies 1km to the northeast of the village of Hemerdon, some 2km northeast of Plympton and 2km southwest of the Dartmoor National Park boundary.

It covered a total area of 264ha, bounded to the west by the Tory Brook valley and the Newnham Park estate, to the north and northeast by the china clay works of Lee Moor and Headon, and by Bottle Hill and farmland surrounding Hemerdon and Sparkwell villages to the south.

The mine site spanned three principal landscape character types; open moorland and woodland comprising Crownhill Down to the north, disused industrial land extending between Hemerdon Ball and Drakeland Corner to the south, with enclosed agricultural fields and paddocks present elsewhere.

Crownhill Down encompassed the majority of the mine site and was bisected by the B3417 Plympton to Lee Moor road and the Lee Moor and Sparkwell parish boundary. From just below an elevated ridge, which extended along the east boundary of the mine site towards Bottle Hill, the ground sloped down broadly to the west, towards the Tory Brook valley. Its slope was divided by an east-west valley, which in the lower slopes contained a watercourse that formed the Hooksbury Stream flowing to the west of the Plympton to Lee Moor road. This valley, which follows the alignment of a tin lode, was extensively accentuated between the Tory Brook and the top of the ridge by medieval and post-medieval tin workings. The activity here formed the focus of much of the fieldwork undertaken.

Hemerdon Ball was the highest point within the mine site at 210m above OD and formed the southern extent of a ridge that was separated from Crownhill Down by a valley occupied by the Smallhanger Brook. This part of the site contains the fourth largest tungsten reserve in the world, which is now being extracted. Hemerdon Ball was already dominated by former industrial land that comprised the open cast extraction pits, tips and building complex of the derelict Hemerdon Mine, while on its lower slopes lay the former Smallhanger China Clay Works.

Previous work

Previous archaeological surveys and assessment had taken place across the site since 1979 when the first planning application for extraction was submitted by Amax Exploration. These included desk based assessments, detailed earthwork surveys, interpretation and plotting of aerial photographs,

Renewed interest in the mine from Wolf Minerals Ltd. in 2008 instigated an archaeological framework agreement, endorsed by Devon County Council, which guided further evaluation of the site's archaeological potential, commencing with a review of previous surveys and contemporary data and continuing with a programme of assessing LiDAR survey data, geophysical survey, building survey and trial trench evaluation. Through this work new monuments were identified along with the reclassification of many previously identified archaeological features as natural, though the overall picture was of an area of liminal moorland rich in complex archaeological

---

*Project manager AC Archaeology, Bradninch, Exeter, Devon. Email: *shughes@acarchaeology.co.uk*

The Tinworking Landscape of Dartmoor in a European Context: Prehistory to 20th Century

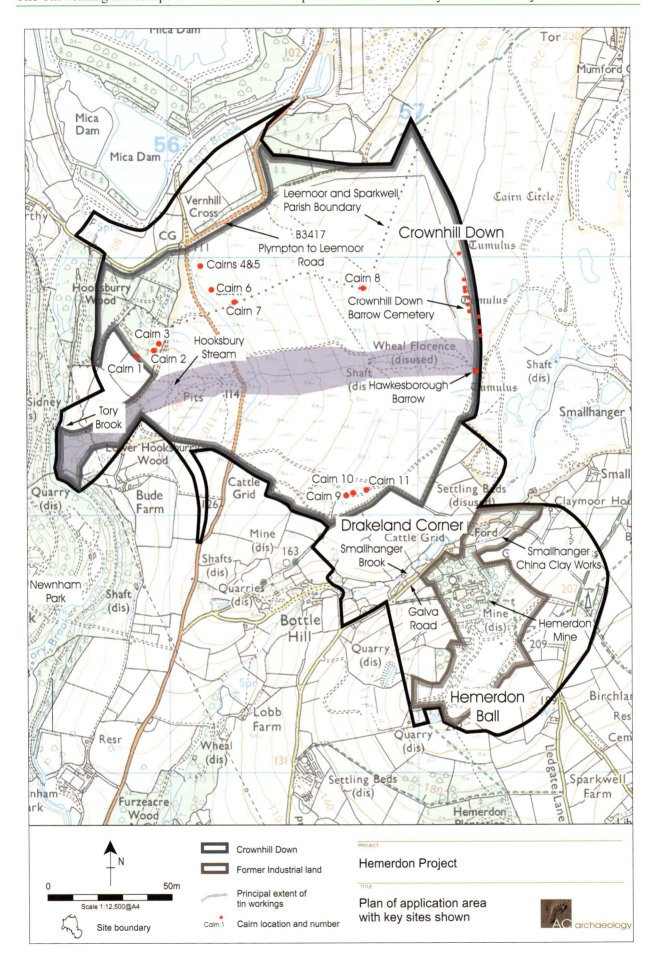

remains of many periods, commencing in at least the early Bronze Age.

Fieldwork overview

This comprehensive programme of evaluation allowed for a targeted and detailed project design to be created for the investigation and recording of the significant monuments across the site. In the four year period between 2011 and 2014 the fieldwork project principally covered:

- The excavation of 11 prehistoric cairns on Crownhill Down;
- The detailed survey and investigations of earthwork systems on Crownhill Down. These consisted of a series of medieval and post medieval field systems that comprised 100 targeted trench investigations;
- The detailed survey of over 1.8km of complex tinworkings on Crownhill Down followed by the excavation of around 120 targeted excavations;
- The detailed survey and targeted trenches investigating a small tin streamwork in the Smallhanger Valley;
- Site wide evaluative trial trenching. This provided a sample coverage of the enclosed land surrounding Crownhill Down and comprised the excavation of around 140 trenches measuring a total of nearly 8km in length;
- The survey and excavation of The Smallhanger China Clay Works; and
- A detailed mine building survey of the derelict Hemerdon Mine complex.

Crownhill Down Cairns

The open upland environment of Crownhill Down contained numerous visible earthworks, the earliest of which consisted of a number of prehistoric barrows. Many of these were located just below the ridge forming the eastern boundary to the site, with the majority of these making up The Crownhill Down barrow cemetery (Historic England Scheduled Monument ref. 1004572). This group comprises 12 barrows/cairns of various forms and positioned in a linear alignment. On the ridge to the south of this group, lies a further round barrow, known as the Hawkesborough Barrow (1002597). This and the Crownhill Down barrow cemetery, whilst within the application area, were excluded from areas of proposed development and therefore not investigated.

Figure 1 (left) Map showing the limit of the project area and the location of main points of investigation.

Figure 2 Showing scheduled cairn 1003201 (cairn 8) with trial trench scar in foreground.

A third scheduled area was located on the western slopes of Crownhill Down (1003201). This area contained a kerbed cairn, Cairn 8, which comprised an 11m diameter annular stone ring. This fell within the application boundary and was investigated under scheduled monument consent granted by Historic England. On the lower slopes, was another cairn, Cairn 7, which along with the Cairn 8, as well as a natural periglacial feature, formed a node on the line of the Shaugh Prior parish boundary with Plympton St Mary.

Close to this were three further cairns on the lower slopes; an earthen ring cairn set in a prepared terrace, with adjacent simple stone ring cairn (Cairns 4 and 5); and latterly, a small stone cairn positioned nearby (Cairn 6).

Hooksbury Wood occupied the western side of Crownhill Down and contained three cairns (1 to 3), one of which contained evidence for Beaker burials. The final group of cairns (9 to 11), were positioned in a line extending along the elevated ground towards the southern extent of Crownhill Down. These consisted of kerbed cairns with mounds formed of cut turfs: two of which had conjoined arrangements, forming a 'figure of eight' shape.

The excavations of the 11 cairns established that Crownhill Down was utilised for the siting of ritual / burial monuments from the Beaker period and Early Bronze Age, with activity potentially continuing as late as the Late Bronze Age. The finds assemblage recovered from the group was varied, including pottery of Beaker and later dates, Middle Bronze Age palstaves, worked stone, flint and faience. The majority of the finds appeared to have been deliberately placed.

The siting of the monuments in different locations poses questions about their role in the perception of

The Tinworking Landscape of Dartmoor in a European Context: Prehistory to 20th Century

Figure 3 Crownhill Down tin workings looking west.

the landscape and ideas of territoriality and ownership. The monuments appear to surround the tinwork, running east-west across the Down and into the Tory Brook Valley. This may indicate the importance of the tin resource during the Bronze Age and presents the possibility of comparable relationships across the tin-rich uplands.

Analysis of the group of cairns will look at a range of factors, including: variations in siting; date; construction and finds assemblages; and will look at the potential for comparisons to be drawn between the individual monuments within the group as well as parallels from other excavated examples locally, from sites such as Shaugh Moor, and on the Dartmoor uplands more generally.

Tinworking remains

The tinworking remains formed a major part of the investigations and related to the exploitation of the tin resource during the medieval and post-medieval periods.

These remains were principally concentrated within the Hooksbury Stream valley along the line of an eluvial and lode tin deposit that extended from between the Tory Brook to just below the ridge adjacent to the Hawkesborough Barrow. However, associated features also radiated out across the down. Within the core of the workings was a highly-complex sequence of intercutting and overlapping earthworks that included streamworking channels, lode back pits, tailings ponds and dumps. These features represented activity that was consistent with medieval and post-medieval methods of extraction; while later techniques were also represented, including the establishment of shafts in the 19th century. In the wider area on Crownhill Down was an extensive network of leat channels that would have supplied the water required for the streamworks and subterranean works, as well as for the Bottle Hill Mine (located just beyond the application area to the south). Other features included a possible tinners' lodge and numerous tin prospecting pits and hushes that littered the slopes of Crownhill Down.

Aerial photographs of the site demonstrated the complexity of the earthworks and recording such a large resource presented a challenging task. Indeed, no other investigations of tinworkings on this scale had been previously undertaken. The essential first stage was the survey of the entire Crownhill Down landscape. These were initially plotted by Cotswold Archaeology and then enhanced by Sandy Gerrard (Gerrard 2012a and 2012b) while additional areas

Figure 4 Crownhill Down tinworkings with investigation in progress. View looking south

were surveyed by Phil Newman and provided the basis for setting out the objectives for enhancing the survey interpretations through targeted excavations.

For each of the 120 excavations undertaken within the core of the Crownhill Down tinworkings, as well numerous further trenches looking at the network of leats and a sample of the many prospecting pits, specific questions were set for each trench to work towards achieving an overall understanding of the remains. This work exposed the range of activities that were associated with tinworking throughout its medieval to 19th century operation. A series of features that were associated with the prospection, extraction and processing of tin ore were investigated, with these including streamworking channels, lode back pits, buddles and the anti-pollution methods employed to prevent the tailings from entering watercourses.

Smallhanger Clay Works and Hemerdon Tungsten Mine

Although there was some evidence for further tin streaming to have taken place within the Smallhanger valley, industrial activity in the southern portion of the application area was chiefly concerned with the Smallhanger China Clay Works and the adjacent Hemerdon Tungsten Mine.

The Smallhanger China Clay Works were found to be remarkably well preserved since abandonment some 60 years ago, due largely to it having become hidden and entangled by the growth of rhododendron and trees. It represented a rare, if not unique, example of the traditional nineteenth-century method of china clay processing with extensive use of settling tanks, sun pans and air drys. China clay was first worked on southwest Dartmoor at Lee Moor in 1830. The Smallhanger property is within sight of Lee Moor, and china clay was also perhaps first investigated here in the 1830s. Smallhanger Works produced around 2,000 tons of china clay annually between 1892 and 1926 and was very small scale compared with Lee Moor. The processing operation on site closed in 1951 following its sale to the English China Clays.

Fieldwork here, directed by Peter Stanier, comprised the survey and cataloguing of the remains of the china clay works, while detailed survey and targeted excavations of a sun pan were undertaken in order to understand its phasing and technology.

Mine buildings survey

A key feature within the mine site was the ruin of the main dressing mill positioned downhill from

The Tinworking Landscape of Dartmoor in a European Context: Prehistory to 20th Century

Figure 5 Smallhanger china clay works. View southwest alongside pan kiln showing exposed tramway.

Figure 6 Hemerdon Mine dressing mill surge bins. View to northeast.

the opencast tungsten workings on Hemerdon Ball. Tungsten was extracted on the site in four main periods; during the First World War, in the inter-war years, the Second World War and the late 20th century.

The site was historically important because wolfram is a relatively rare mineral and the mill complex of the mid-20th century period is said to have been the largest of its kind in the UK. Following over 60 years of neglect, many of the structures had deteriorated to the point of collapse. These were recorded by Peter Stanier and a phasing of the site's development established.

A low-grade stockwork of wolfram (tungsten) and cassiterite at Hemerdon Ball had been known from at least the mid-nineteenth century and attempts to exploit this large reserve had taken place on several occasions. There was limited prospecting in 1898 and 1907 but the two most serious periods of development at the site were related to shortages of the strategic metal tungsten during the First and Second World Wars. The workings were mainly opencast, with limited underground activity, but the dressing mills for processing the ore were built late in each conflict and were closed before fully achieving their potential. Subsequent interest in the site has been at times of high metal prices, first in the 1970s and 1980s, and from 2008 for the current development.

The First World War period at the mine is of special interest, being the first full-scale mill to be built for exploiting the Hemerdon ore body and it covered a surprisingly large part of the site. Despite demolition, substantially-built brick walls survived. However, the Second World War period workings were the most important and had left the most impressive structures. There are good plans of the mill which could be matched with the physical evidence. Its significance was enhanced by the fact that after more than 60 years, evidence for the complete mining operation had survived in some form, from the open pit to the state-of-the-art dressing mill of 1943 with its accompanying ore storage bins, conveyors and waste handling hopper, and settling tanks, to the pylon foundations of a once impressive aerial ropeway system.

Bibliography

Gerrard, S 2012a Crownhill Down - project design for tin streamworks and adjacent features west of the public highway (B3417)

Gerrard, S 2012b Crownhill Down - project design for tinworks and associated features east of the public highway (B3417)

Tinworking in the Cornish landscape

Peter Herring*

Abstract
Dartmoor's wealth of well-preserved historic tinworkings has been made richer by the improvement in understanding gained from their close investigation by, among others, the Dartmoor Tinworking Research Group.

Tinworking (including early working) on the lower Cornish granite uplands and in their hinterlands had greater intensity and variety, and its impact on Cornwall physically, topographically, economically and socially was heavier and longer-lasting. Those impacts of tinworking have affected so many places and have affected the meanings and values that people give them that a substantial part of Cornwall may be regarded by some as an industrial landscape, or a post-industrial one, with mining (principally for tin and copper) being the main industry involved. Of course that over-simplifies an especially complex history and region, whose landscape and identity might equally be regarded as maritime, rural, recreational, artistic and non-conformist, but which has industry, mainly extractive and mainly tin threaded through all those and many other aspects.

This paper will attempt to meld the particular with the general by considering how the study of historic landscape, a place perceived by people in the past and now by people in the present, is informed by the archaeological investigation and historical study of leats, streamworks, pits, shafts and heaps, mills, dressing floors, shelters, engine houses, tramways and blowing houses and of workers' housing, mine-owners' mansions and field systems.

Cornwall and Dartmoor share many aspects of their industrial histories: the practices and technologies that were employed by streamworkers and miners as well as the methods of historical and archaeological research that have been employed in developing our current understanding of them. This paper touches on these and on how tinworking has affected place, landscape and identity in Cornwall, and by extension or implication how it may have done likewise on Dartmoor and in west Devon.

Landscape is at the same time a physical thing and a mental construct, with people central to its creation and its perception (Fairclough 2006; Council of Europe 2000). Places and landscape are always changing, both materially and in the ways individuals and groups perceive them. Raising the profile of an aspect of a place, such as when improving understanding of the history of tinworking on Dartmoor, will change the way a place is regarded and valued. So the work of the DTRG, and the effects of its May 2016 Tavistock conference, have changed Dartmoor, just as the work on the Bronze Age boundary patterns known as reave systems changed it a generation ago (Fleming 1988) and reading Conan Doyle's *The Hound of the Baskervilles* did a century ago. As an understood and perceived landscape Dartmoor will never be the same again.

In Cornwall (and a part of west Devon) the nomination of ten separate areas as a UNESCO World Heritage Site that acknowledges the universal significance and value of the mining landscape of the early modern period, the age when technological advances enabled highly capitalised industrialisation, has substantially affected perceptions of Cornwall (World Heritage Site Bid Partnership 2005). Some may now regard Cornwall as an industrial landscape, or a post-industrial one (Brayshay 2006; Fig. 1).

Others, however, see instead a 'quintessentially

---

*Historic England; Head of Historic Places Investigation, South & West. Email: *peter.herring@historicengland.org.uk*

The Tinworking Landscape of Dartmoor in a European Context: Prehistory to 20th Century

Figure 1 Geevor mine (which closed in the late 20th century) and, in the distance, Lower Boscaswell medieval hamlet, swollen in the post-medieval period by homes for mining families. The mine is now protected by scheduling and celebrated by being within the Cornwall and West Devon Mining Landscape World Heritage Site (Phoebe Herring).

maritime region', with fishing, importing and exporting, defence, victualling and ship and boat building important (Payton et al. 2014), and the sea as 'an active moulding element' (Deacon 2014, 276).

And many more people, and especially those who visit Cornwall as various forms of tourist (around five million each year), see and treat Cornwall as primarily a place of recreation and pleasure, populating it more through various fictions than through understanding of historical or modern realities (Harvey 2006; Brace 2006). This sits uncomfortably with appreciation that Cornwall is and long has been a land of stark contrasts in terms of wealth and opportunity, with extremely wealthy people living or staying close to zones that are amongst the most deprived in Britain (Cornwall Council 2012).

Cornwall is not unusual in being complex, with overlapping uses, and inconsistent and contested narratives; most places are like this (Howard et al. 2013). But Cornwall does have a stronger than normal sense of identity, reflected most simply in the range of uses of the adjective 'Cornish' compared with, say Devonian or Devonish. That identity is tied to the place by narrative and custom, and by nationalism, under the now familiar flag with its white cross on a black ground 'formerly the banner of St Perran, and the standard of Cornwall; probably with some allusion to the black ore and the white metal of tin', first so described in 1838 (Davies Gilbert 1838, vol 3, 332). The extent of this nationalism was also recorded in the latest census, of 2011, when 73,200, or 13.8%, identified their nationality as Cornish (Cornwall Council 2013, 5). Cornishness is also symbolised by named items like the pasty, the shovel and most formally in the coat of arms, created in 1939, which includes the Cornish chough, the Cornish fisherman and of course the Cornish miner (holding a sledgehammer). Another symbol, to some an icon, is the tall strong stone-built structure, usually with arched windows and brick detailing and with a tall tapering chimney stack, that housed the Cornish beam engine (Barton 1969; Fig. 2). These engine houses make instantly visible the industrial strand in Cornish history and in the present-day Cornish landscape, and when encountered in Ireland, Mexico or Australia, still turn corners of distant lands Cornish (Payton 2007).

Farmers and landowners might suggest that industry, the coast, tourism and post-industrial poverty all intrude only slightly upon the appreciation that Cornwall is fundamentally rural with a rural landscape. Over 80% of its surface is enclosed farmland (Herring 1998) and agriculture is the most enduring land use, with most fields having medieval-derived forms and most commons having been in place since prehistory (Herring 2006; 2008; 2013). Most farmland is now worked from fairly isolated farmsteads, though their fields have patterns that indicate origins in different, more communal, ways of arranging land and drawing food from it. Those indications, when pursued, confirm that medieval and earlier farming society in Cornwall was closely cooperative and that its commons (especially the rough grazings of Bodmin Moor and the other uplands) were administered well (Herring 2006).

The historic landscape characterisations of

Figure 2 Engine house and spoil heaps at Unity Wood, near Chacewater (Phoebe Herring).

Cornwall and Devon emphasise how rural the land that was once the Iron Age territory of Dumnonia is; land whose character is predominantly industrial covers a tiny proportion of Cornwall (less than 2%, and that includes the extensive china-clay workings) and even less of Devon (Herring 1998; Turner 2007). But the impact of industry, visually and through the strength of its historical and communal meanings, and thus the ways that it is valued, is considerably greater. The head gear, engine house and the darkly vegetated spoil dump catch the eye and industrialise the most rural scene (Fig. 3), and this paper will illustrate how the agricultural backdrop has itself been altered by the effects of industry.

Cornish historical writing is also dominated by industry. There are hundreds of books on mining (see for example the bibliography of the WHS Nomination document; World Heritage Site Bid Partnership 2005, 206-219), but just dozens on maritime Cornwall and only handfuls on Cornish rural history. A K Hamilton Jenkin (Fig. 4), whose bardic name was Lef Stenoryan ('Voice of the Tinners'), the doyen of Cornish mining

Figure 3 A ruined 19th-century engine house (Carn Galver Mine) in rural Zennor, where the fields and commons have prehistoric origins (Peter Herring).

The Tinworking Landscape of Dartmoor in a European Context: Prehistory to 20th Century

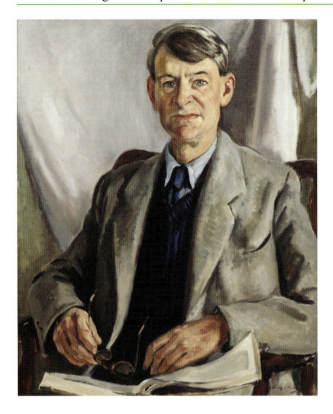

Figure 4 Cornwall has had many fine mining historians, but perhaps the greatest was Arthur Kenneth Hamilton Jenkin. He kept in mind always the link between the life of a mine and the lives of those who worked in and around it (Portrait painted by Leonard Fuller and part of the Cornish Studies Library's collection).

historians, established in his *The Cornish Miner* (1927) an authority, tone and seriousness that few have matched, and he did that by concentrating as much in his writing on place and people as on engines and shafts. Other influential writers include George Randall Lewis who, before Jenkin's time, gathered together documentation for and an understanding of the stannaries, the administrative bodies established in each of the main tinning areas, and their relationship with ultimate authority in the form of the Crown (Lewis 1908).

As long ago as 1935 the Cornish Engines Preservation Committee, precursor of The Trevithick Society (named from Cornwall's premier mining engineer and inventor), was established in order to save the Levant whim engine from loss. In addition to the successful protection and conservation of several important steam engines and waterwheels, The Trevithick Society has encouraged much detailed historical research and archaeological recording and interpretation. The fine granularity of research reflects the complexity of Cornwall's mining history, with each mining area, from Hingston Down west to St Just, having its own peculiarities of geology and geomorphology and its own ways of exploiting those. Each mining area thereby developed its own character and qualities. Those in the east of Cornwall, with extensive streamworks and surface workings, and considerable use of water power, have much in common with Dartmoor.

In the last few decades of the twentieth century each Cornish mining area was subjected to close historical and archaeological study, mostly through projects undertaken by the Cornwall Archaeological Unit. These surveys were stimulated by different needs and their scale and detail also varied accordingly. For example, Kit Hill on Hingston Down, near the River Tamar, was the subject of a detailed record (in which every pit was carefully plotted) in order to guide management of a newly created country park (Herring and Thomas 1990). Bodmin Moor, formerly the Foweymore Stannary, was studied in part to obtain the understanding required to address the effects of various threats to this poorly recorded upland area, especially afforestation, reservoir construction, agricultural change and road construction (Herring et al. 2008). The survey led to the identification of candidate sites for statutory protection through Scheduling (Rose and Herring 1990). Also on Bodmin Moor, the Minions area, intensively mined in the last two centuries and now heavily visited, was subjected to more detailed study through a community programme that led to conservation works on selected significant structures (Sharpe 1989).

A third strand of the study of Bodmin Moor's medieval tinworking was in part inspired and influenced by the work on Dartmoor undertaken by the DTRG silver jubilee conference's principal organiser, Dr Tom Greeves (1981). Dr Sandy Gerrard had worked with Greeves on the important complete and closely recorded excavation of a later medieval and early post-medieval tin stamping mill at West Colliford (in St Neot parish) (Austin et al. 1988). Gerrard realised that there were significant gaps in the knowledge and understanding of the practical methods of early tinworking, and tin streamworking in particular, and in the social and economic impacts of the industry on later medieval Cornwall. His doctoral research in St Neot parish involved single-handed plane-table survey and close critical observation of the complex earthworks of valley-bottom alluvial streamworks and hillside eluvial streamworks. These were done in order to establish, by analysis of the patterns of spoil tips (and thus their contiguous

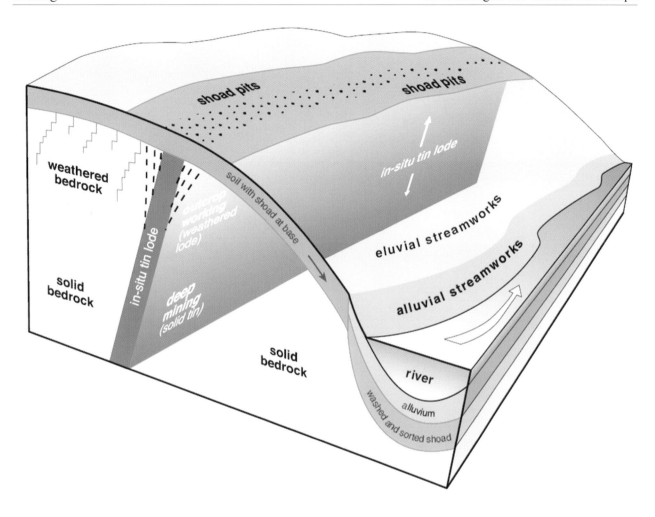

Figure 5 This model, developed by Adam Sharpe, shows how tin workers have exploited the lode by outcrop and deep mining and the shode (or shoad) weathered from the lode by shode pits and by eluvial and alluvial streamworks. (From Sharpe 2008, fig 25; image copyright Rosemary Robertson)

working areas, the tyes), the mechanics of digging through the shode and preparing dressing areas for the separation of stones containing the heavy tin ore from lighter waste (Gerrard 1986; 1987; 2000; Austin et al. 1988).

Gerrard and his later co-worker Adam Sharpe prepared explanatory models of the ways that geomorphological processes had dislocated ore from the roughly vertical lodes and carried it downslope as 'shode' or 'shoad', and then how tinworkers had used ingenious hydraulic engineering to exploit it; engineering that left distinctively patterned archaeological remains (Gerrard 2000; Sharpe 2008; Fig. 5). The explanatory models that Gerrard and Sharpe developed owed much to earlier accounts from the likes of William Pryce (1778), Thomas Beare in 1586 (Buckley 1994), and an anonymous writer of 1671 (cited in Lewis 1908, 5). Some shode was sorted by alluvial action and deposited in valley floors where it was dug over in pits known as hatches or in long narrow pits, the forms and locations of which are signalled by either patterns of ramped dumps emanating from the sub-circular hatches (and up which barrows of spoil may be expected to have been pushed) or parallel linear dumps along the sides of the trenches. A major constraint on working alluvial deposits was the continued flowing in the valley bottoms of the streams. Tinners diverted these into channels running parallel to one side of the natural stream-course to allow easier access to the tin-bearing ground. Alluvial streamworking was best suited to the summer months when streams were running at their lowest volume.

Conversely the winter was the better season for working the mid-slope eluvial deposits of shode, to which water had to be brought for dressing, to separate the tin-bearing stones from the waste. Long contour-following leats caught run-off rain water and drew it into banked reservoirs ready for careful diversion into the working tyes set within the

Figure 6 Eluvial streamworks in the dry valley between Leskernick Hill and Bray Down on West Moor, Bodmin Moor. Reservoirs on the far side of the cutting stored water for use in the tyes, on the nearer uphill sides of the parallel dumps that lie each side of the central drain. Leats brought water to the tyes on the nearer side. Three tinners' lodges or shelters survive at the sheltered far end. See Sharpe 2008, fig 32 for a survey and interpretation of this site (top right) (Peter Herring).

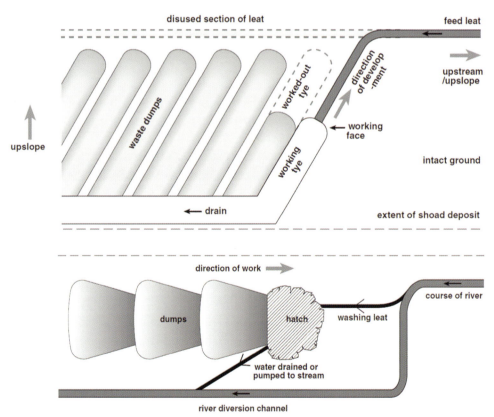

Figure 7 Schematic models of how eluvial (top) and hatch-based alluvial streamworks were typically operated. Both used a carefully directed flow of water to assist the separation of relatively light waste material from the heavier tin ore. In eluvial works this water was usually obtained from run-off water taken by leats into earth-banked reservoirs and then drawn from them along another leat to the working areas within the streamworks, the tyes. In alluvial streamworks the water was obtained from the river that still flowed down the valley, most of whose water was diverted around the working area in an excavated channel. In both types of streamwork the subsoil, stones and shoad were largely shifted by muscle-power, using shovels, picks and barrows. (From Sharpe 2008, fig 27; image copyright Rosemary Robertson)

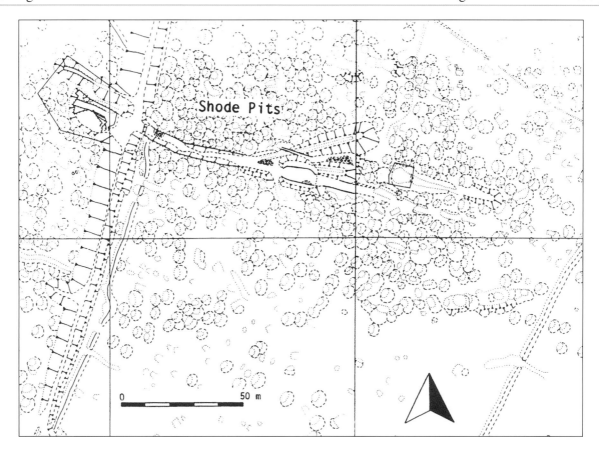

Figure 8 Measured survey of a shamble of shode pits on the high eastern side of Kit Hill. The hundreds of pits are oval with heaps on their downhill sides. Tinners worked uphill in rough lines often throwing their spoil into pits immediately downhill to reduce the area of ground sterilised by dumps. (From Herring and Thomas 1990, fig 60.)

cuttings dug into the linear spreads of shode (Figs 6 and 7). The tinners calculated how to draw the water through the dressing areas within their tyes at the optimal velocity to remove the lighter waste (the average specific gravity of quartz, feldspar and mica being 2.65, 2.53-2.60 and 2.94 respectively) while leaving the heavier tin-bearing ore (specific gravity of cassiterite varying from 6.8 to 7.1)(Gerrard 1987, 7).

Shode found on the highest parts of hills, where water could not be brought to it for dressing purposes, was dug over by small pits and the material collected taken downhill to sources of water for dressing. Complex patterns, or 'shambles', of shode pits have been recorded in several places, notably on Goonzion Downs on the flat-topped downland west of St Neot (Gerrard 2000, *fig. 33*), and further east on the summit plateau of Kit Hill. These detailed surveys indicate that these apparently random scatters of pits were dug systematically, the tinners working up hill and casting the spoil from the small sub-rectangular pits downhill into the earlier pits behind them (Herring and Thomas 1990, 106-7, *fig. 60*; Fig. 8).

The Bodmin Moor Survey showed that this upland area was thoroughly worked over – most valley bottoms have alluvial works and most dry side valleys have eluvial works (Sharpe 2008, *fig. 39*; Fig. 9). Many streamworks were re-worked several times, each revisiting deepening the cutting to leave some as much as 15m deep (as between Leskernick and Buttern Hills on West Moor; Fig. 10). Much of the material removed from such streamworks was taken in suspension down river to be dropped where the waters slowed in the middle and tidal reaches of the Fowey, Lynher, Tamar and Camel, silting up formerly navigable channels at great cost to trading towns and leading to complaints against tinners as early as 1357, when Abraham the Tinner was imprisoned for his role in the clogging up of Lostwithiel (Gerrard 1987, 8).

Abraham appears to have been in charge of a large enterprise involving 300 people (men, women and children) in seven named works, including four streamworks (Gerrard 2000, 40). He was not a small-scale, semi-subsistence miner, but a proto-capitalist whose principal resource would have been the skill and the muscle-power of those 300 people. Where might such people have lived and were they themselves like Abraham, full-time tinners?

The Tinworking Landscape of Dartmoor in a European Context: Prehistory to 20th Century

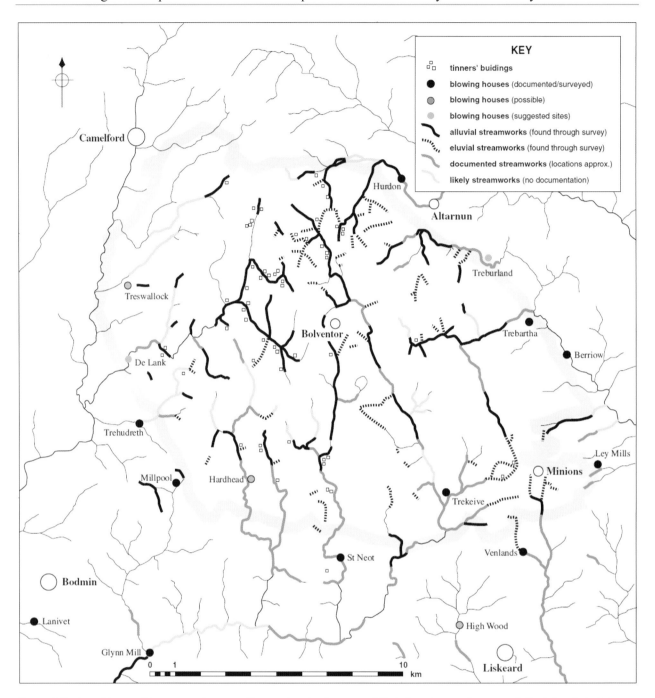

Figure 9 Bodmin Moor, or Foweymore Stannary district, showing known and likely locations and extents of alluvial and eluvial streamworks etc. Known and possible blowing houses, all near the edge of the Moor, are also shown, as are tinners' huts, or lodges, largely distant from farming hamlets. (From Sharpe 2008, fig 39; image copyright Rosemary Robertson)

Streamworking's seasonality (alluvial summer works and eluvial winter works) suggests the possibility that some or many fitted tinworking within a farming calendar and formed parts of households living in the hamlets of longhouses whose remains survive in many places on Bodmin Moor (and Dartmoor). There is also archaeological evidence for the accommodation of tinners both near and within streamworks; nearly 50 ruined buildings have been recorded on Bodmin Moor, small rectangular structures, mostly of earth or turf with single entrances in one long side and some with small stone fireplaces in end walls (Fig. 11). These appear to be equivalents of the 'lodges… made up with turves covered with straw' in which dinner was taken, described in 1586 by Thomas Beare the bailiff of Blackmore (the Stannary of central Cornwall) (Buckley 1994, 57). Most lodges recorded on Bodmin Moor are in the more remote central areas distant from permanently occupied farming settlements (Sharpe 2008, *fig. 39*; Fig. 9), strengthening the argument that other tinners walked to work from their permanent homes, probably within

Figure 10 People indicate the scale of the probably later medieval eluvial streamwork between Buttern and Leskernick Hills, most of the material dug being washed down to the lower Fowey where it silted up ports like Lostwithiel (Peter Herring).

Figure 11 Lodge immediately adjacent to the cutting (foreground) of an eluvial streamwork on Buttern Hill. To its right is a ditched rectangular platform, a turf stead on which the locally cut fuel used in the lodge's stone fireplace was stored (Peter Herring).

farming settlements.

West Colliford stamping mill, the one whose excavation set Sandy Gerrard on to his tinworking studies, appears to have been used over a period of 300 years, probably sporadically and probably largely for crushing ore-bearing material excavated from an adjacent openwork, a linear excavation opened on the back of a lode (Austin et al. 1988, 62-66). Openworks continued to be created as late as the first half of the 20th century in some parts of Cornwall, but may generally have been supposed to have been old-fashioned by the 18th (Sharpe 2008, 51). Broadly similar in form to openworks were stockworks in which swarms of closely spaced lodes or veins were removed *en masse* with the rock in which they lay, before the material was broken and dressed to abstract the ore, as in the great Carclaze Pit (in Blackmore) (Bristow 2008), at the remarkable site, an enormous pseudo-openwork, at Treveddoe in Warleggan (Sharpe 2008, 50-55, *figs 44 and 45*) and on the high western slopes of Kit Hill (Herring and Thomas 1990, 111-112, *fig. 62*).

Adam Sharpe sets out the various ways that miners turned their attention directly onto lodes through pits, proto-shafts, adits and shafts proper, using, broadly successively, muscle, horse, water and steam power to pump workings dry enough to work and to hoist ore and materials (Sharpe 2008, 50-68). In most of Cornwall's mining fields individual lodes can be found that retain evidence of each (e.g. Fig. 12), but they are most easily seen on Rillaton Common, on the seven broadly parallel lodes lying between Stowe's Hill and Minions (Sharpe 1989; 2008, *figs 50 and 51*).

A once-common feature, now much less visible in Cornwall's mining grounds than it is on Dartmoor, is the blowing house. Here waterwheel-driven bellows raised a kiln's temperature to the level where dressed black tin melted, around 1,100 degrees centigrade. Sandy Gerrard estimated that there would have been around 120 blowing houses in Cornwall in the early sixteenth century alone (to meet the local needs of numerous tinworking areas), but the sites of only 15 are known, and those mostly through documentary sources (cited in Sharpe 2008, 82). On Dartmoor, however, blowing houses are found in large numbers beside its fast-running streams, close to the tin grounds (Greeves this volume). In Cornwall the relatively short distances from moorland mines to optimal mill sites on or beyond the edges of the granite uplands, where small streams fell faster and so generated greater power, meant that few blowing houses were established on the granite itself. Most lay downslope and their sites either lie undiscovered in the woodlands of gorges or have been lost to change, either of function (becoming grist or fulling mills) or of land use (to agricultural improvement). One surviving ruined blowing house is the small building at Coombe in the valley east of Millpool, Cardinham (SX 1229 7070), found during the Bodmin Moor survey. The waterwheel, whose pit is still detectable beside the remains of the building, appears to have powered stamps (probably for reprocessing slag) as well as the blowing house's bellows, as there is a

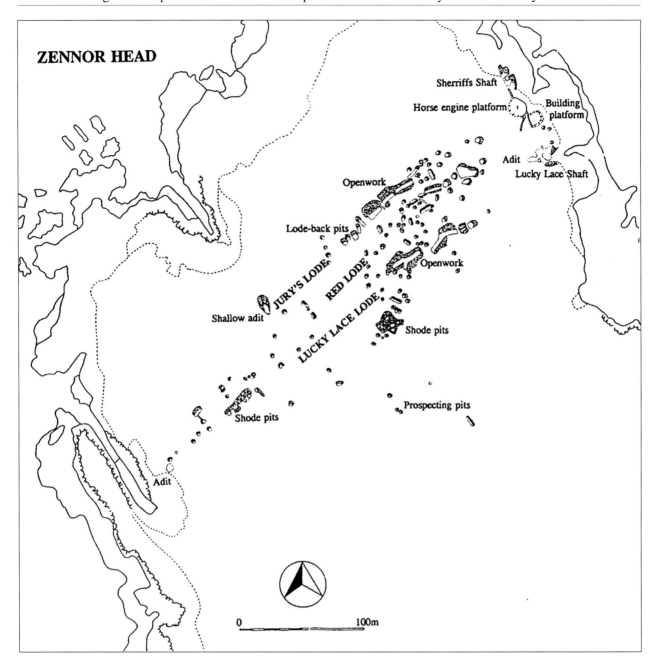

Figure 12 Three closely spaced lodes on cliffs at Zennor Head: prospecting pits searched for shode, worked in a small shambles, and then lodes worked by openworks, lode-back pits, adits and finally shafts. Records are poor, so this archaeological survey, coupled with later 19th century descriptions (from which the names are drawn) provides the clearest evidence of a superficially simple mine's complicated story. (From Herring 1986, fig 3)

four-head mortar stone alongside the building and tiny fragments of crushed slag in the nearby stream (Herring & Rose 1990, 470; Sharpe 2008, 82 and *fig. 63*).

It is not certain when Cornish tinworkers first turned their attention from shode to lode, from streamworks and shode-pits to openworks and lode-back pits. Lewis followed Pryce in thinking it might have been in the 15th century, but Gerrard suggested that there was lode mining in western Cornwall by the 13th century. He saw the shift westwards of higher levels of tin coinage (and thus production) away from Cornwall's richest streamworkings and towards areas where tin remained largely in lodes in the preceding centuries as confirmation of fleeting documentary hints. Archaeological evidence for early working of the lodes can now support that interpretation. Two lines of closely spaced lode-back pits on the eastern and southern slopes of Godolphin Hill (in Breage parish in west Cornwall) appear to have been dug before a lane was run from the Godolphin settlement to the common. This was most likely in the 13th century (Herring 1997, 179 and 297) and before a large deer

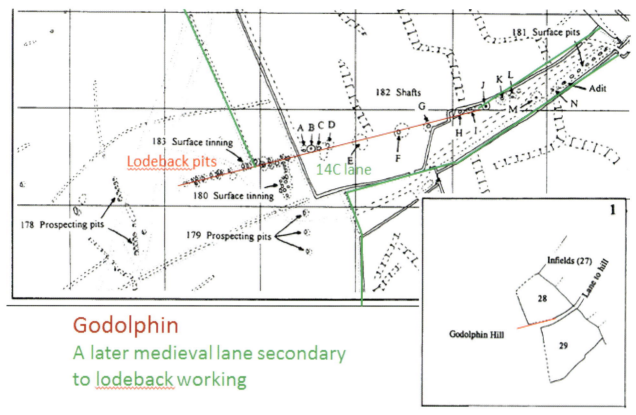

Figure 13 Analytical survey of a medieval lane from Godolphin house to the pastures on Godolphin Hill (left). Its sides were largely banks or built hedges, but in one stretch (shown in red) re-used a line of contiguous lode-back pits, indicating that lodes were being exploited here by the 13th century. (From Herring 1997, figs 55 and 97)

park was established, probably by the 15th century and possibly by the 14th century respectively (Herring 1997, 293; Herring 2001, 17-21; Figs 13 and 14).

Godolphin is the place *par excellence* in Cornwall for illustrating the effect of the wealth created by tinworking on later medieval, early post-medieval and early modern society. In the late 13th and early 14th centuries Alexander de Godolghan, named from the hamlet on poor farmland on the cold northern slopes of the granite hill now called Godolphin, began acquiring land around his ancestral home, land that was astutely selected as all of it seems to have borne rich tin lodes, at Sparnon, Trescowe, Herland, Carsluick and Nanjenkin, among other places. By the late 14th century the tin-based wealth of the family had increased to such an extent that a chapel was licenced at the 'manor' of Godolghan and in the 1470s mention is made of a former 'castle' there, probably a fortified house set within a large rectangular precinct (Herring 1997). In a few more decades the Godolghans were providing sheriffs for Cornwall, were being knighted and were acting directly for King Henry VIII in suppressing local uprisings. John Leland visiting at this time (the late 1530s) noted that there were 'no greater Tynne Workes yn al Cornwall than be on Sir Wyllyam Godolcan's Ground'. By now the family were Members of Parliament, were marrying into Cornwall's greatest families, and were being made Governors of Scilly.

Their wealth and influence continued to grow so that by the turn of the seventeenth century Sir Richard Carew in his *Survey of Cornwall* noted first the accomplished personal qualities of Sir Francis Godolphin and then, to give him, and them, context, stated that:

> by his labours and inventions in tin matters, not only the whole country hath felt a general benefit, …but her Majesty hath also received increase… by the same at least to the value of £10,000. Moreover, in those works which are of his own particular inheritance, he continually keepeth at work three hundred persons or thereabouts, and the yearly benefit that out of those his works accrueth to her Majesty amounteth, on a yearly average, to £1000 at the least, and sometimes to much more… not to be matched again by any of his sort and condition in the whole realm. (Carew 1602, 153r).

Godolphin's wealth was indeed phenomenal, with the proportion of his tin-based earnings paid as a form of tax, £1000 per annum, worth many millions

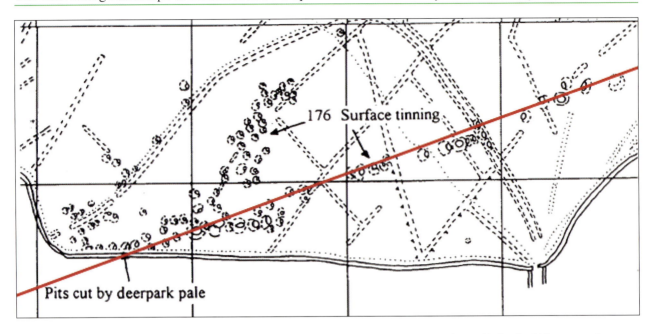

Figure 14 The deer park on Godolphin Hill was probably established by the 15th century and possibly by the 14th century. Its southern side clearly slices through lode-back workings, again indicating an early date. (From Herring 1997, fig 54)

of pounds today. Indeed, at around the same time, John Norden stated that 'Godolphyn Ball ... hath bene to Sir Francis and his auncestors manie yeares as a minte' (1604, 33). Such resources enabled the invitation of continental mining experts to Godolphin and they contributed to substantial technological improvements in stamping (wet stamps) and smelting, at Godolphin mines, including Great Work, the 'inventions in tin matters' celebrated by Carew. These developments enabled the acceleration of capitalisation in tin mining at Godolphin and elsewhere in southwest Britain.

Godolphin continued to be a place of innovation for at least two more centuries, with Cornwall's earliest recorded use of blasting to expedite the breaking of lode-bearing rock, in 1689, taking place on Godolphin Mines, possibly at Wheal Vor, and in the second decade of the 18th century the earliest use of a steam or 'fire' engine (a Newcomen engine) to pump water from a Cornish mine, again possibly at Wheal Vor (Earl 1968, 38; Barton 1969, 16). By the time these last two breakthroughs in the development of Cornish mining had taken place the Godolphins themselves had largely left the exquisitely beautiful and remarkably architecturally advanced house, regarded in 1649 as a 'stately ancient palace' (Taylor 1649, 19). It was by some way the largest house in Stuart Cornwall, if the number of hearths (49) recorded for the Hearth Tax in 1664 is a guide to its scale (Stoate 1981).

The younger, more dynamic, Godolphin-born spawn of the last Sir Francis Godolphin to reside permanently at the family home, moved their affairs to London and by the turn of the 18th century, Sidney, the third child (b.1645), was one of the most powerful politicians of his day (Sundstrom 1992). He had been appointed First Lord of the Treasury in 1684 by Charles II, and again in 1690 and 1700 by William III. He was then given the highest political position in the country, Lord High Treasurer, by Queen Anne in 1702. He remained in post for eight years. Sidney proved effective at raising state funds and then utilising them to consolidate Protestantism in Britain and contain France within Europe. He was closely involved in overseeing the 1707 Acts of Union that created the Kingdom of Great Britain and in 1706 was made the 1st Earl Godolphin (*ibid*). 'Few ministers in English history have done so much to shape the future of their country' (Sundstrom 2014). Sidney's younger brother Henry later became Provost of Eton College (1695-1732) and the Dean of St Paul's cathedral (1707-26) (Sundstrom 1992).

It was tin (and later copper) that had produced the transformative wealth that took the Godolghans from being a modest farming family to the highest positions in state within four centuries. They changed their name to one, Godolphin, that was first easier for the English to say and second allowed them to use the dolphin, symbol of swiftness and love, as their device. Their home, now owned by the National Trust, retains on the sides of its main square court four clearly distinguishable phases, the earliest from

Figure 15 The 1630s north front of Godolphin House, for long the largest and most sophisticated house in Cornwall, and home to its most influential family, all built upon the wealth drawn from tinworking (Peter Herring).

Figure 16 Tinworking contributed to Cornwall's unusually diversified and commercialised medieval economy in which opportunities to thrive led to dismantlement of former communal ways of farming. At Boscastle Cornwall's last unenclosed strip field system, known as Forrabury Stitches (front right), lies within a more extensive pattern of former strip fields (e.g. beyond the town), enclosed piecemeal and then more systematically from the later medieval period onwards, turning a land of dispersed hamlets into one of dispersed and isolated farms (Peter Herring).

the 1470s, the last the 1630s, each of which was substantial, innovative and stylish, displaying status and taste, but also closeness to the pulse of British society (Herring 1997, 187-194; Fig. 15). The house partly overlies a large later medieval garden, one of the grandest to survive in Britain, and again a means of displaying status to influential visitors. Surrounding it was the large deer park whose creation was an appropriation of former common land (and thus an exercise in power) and involved the unabashed sterilisation and, perhaps, display to those who went hunting with the Godolphins, of two of the earliest tin lodes to be worked in Cornwall (above).

Other Cornish families benefitted from early tin wealth, some of them also ultimately derived from poor peasant households who took risks and received the rewards of success, though none quite so spectacularly as the Godolphins.

So tinworking affected the Cornish landscape by funding flowerings of ostentatious displays of the wealth gathered into the hands of tin lords, the grand houses, their deer parks and later their landscape parks, often, like Godolphin, and Tehidy immediately adjacent to the mines and the poorer homes of the miners. The Bassets' 14th-century deer park deliberately, even callously, enclosed its mining area's dominant hill, Carn Brea, taking the former common grazing into private use and replacing cattle and sheep with beautiful, sporty but, from a peasant's perspective, useless fallow deer (Herring 2003, 39).

We can also consider how tinworking contributed to revolutionary economic and then social changes at the lower, peasant levels of medieval Cornish society that in turn transformed the form, fabric and character of the two-thirds of Cornwall that make up its Anciently Enclosed Land. This transformation took place so long ago, half a millennium or more, that it is not closely documented in the records made for the state and the church, nor in the papers that survive from the manorial bureaucracies of estates, the sources that support most medieval histories of Cornwall. But the processes and their outcomes are still clearly visible in Cornwall's landscape and are recorded, analysed and interpreted by archaeologists.

In short, until the later 13th century, and from the Middle Bronze Age, Cornwall's rural settlements were hamlets, typically from two to half a dozen households, from round house groups through enclosed hamlets (the rounds) to the open hamlets that worked the small *tre*-estates in the early medieval period and the first centuries of the later medieval period. From the later 13th century these hamlets, and the communal and cooperative ways of organising land and work, sharing and minimising risk, and increasing and maintaining security, and the sociability and social pleasures that they supported (and upon which they depended) were increasingly replaced by single farmsteads (Herring 2006). Some of these were the result of amalgamation of holdings within a hamlet and then the shrinkage of the hamlet to a single household; the archaeological remains of such shrunken hamlets may be found across Cornwall, with the earthworks of many lost homesteads still visible in orchards, mowhays and yards. Other single farmsteads were new creations, established either within the reorganised open strip fields of the former hamlet or beyond them, as farmers colonised that other important part of the formerly more communal world, the common.

The shift from hamlets to single farmsteads began a considerable time before the climatic disasters and then plagues of the early and middle decades of the 14th century that are often turned to as determiners of much later medieval change. Other causes for those 13th-century changes identified in Cornwall must be sought and may be found in the consequences for communalism and cooperation of the rapid increase in commerce, driven in large part by tinworking.

The arrangements visible in many hamlets suggest there may have been a tension between their constituent households. Archaeological surveys indicate that each household had its own property and kept it close; cows were housed in the same building as the people, in the lower end of the longhouse, and the household's hay, corn, fuel etc. was ricked in the mowhay, usually placed on the far side of the longhouse when seen from the central communal townplace (Herring 2006). Each household had the potential to create more wealth, to have more cattle, and to grow, store and sell more goods. On the other hand, each household was also bound to the hamlet community. Each shared in the communal resources, whether land in the open fields and the common meadows and pastures, labour like herding, equipment like ploughs, infrastructure like wells, corn-dryers and bakehouses, and each shared in the risks. The consequence was that when a household was strong, its members healthy and capable, it may have felt held back by another that was less able to pull its weight.

Those working the land in later medieval Cornwall (and much of Devon) obtained it in ways that have been described as 'non-manorial' (Hatcher 1970a; 1970b). In contrast to middle England, land in Cornwall was largely held from its owner in return for money rather than labour. Farmers were therefore accustomed to taking their surpluses to the market

Figure 17 The cartouche of Thomas Martyn's map of Cornwall of 1748 displays Cornish mining scenes, including this very early image of a Newcomen steam engine pumping from a shaft. Note the external boiler and the balance bob. An earlier form of power, a waterwheel, is also shown (Harvard Map Collection, Harvard Library).

Figure 18 The Wheal Edward stamping engine house, was part of the Wheal Owles mine in St Just at the time of a terrible disaster in 1893 when 20 men drowned as miners broke through to flooded older workings (Peter Herring).

to obtain the coin with which they paid their rent. The introduction into this world of the fairly sudden ability to earn substantially more money, either through tinworking itself or through the victualling of its workforce, may have been the factor that caused the breakdown of cooperation and the rise of individualism in hamlet after hamlet. Those stronger households such as that of Alexander de Godolghan, could have and probably would have seen their earning power become even greater relative to the hamlet's weaker households and can be expected to have been encouraged by the examples seen in other neighbouring hamlets, leading to the numerous local decisions that eventually ended the long history of hamlets in Cornwall.

Tinworking would therefore have contributed to the shaping of much of Cornwall's post-medieval and modern landscape: the hedging in of formerly open fields, whether just one or two strips or groups of them and the creation of a settlement pattern of dispersed farmsteads rather than one of dispersed hamlets (Fig. 16). Much of Cornwall may therefore be seen to be, to varying degrees, the outcome of tin working, if not a tin-working landscape.

Miners were enabled by their Charters (from that of King John onwards), to dig where they would (with surprisingly few exceptions – graveyards and private gardens), and the remains of their endeavours are seen throughout Cornwall. The following of lodes has left lines of overgrown spoil heaps that cut across the patterns of earlier fields, as at Rosemergy in Morvah, Gwedna in Breage, or Halabezack in Wendron, amongst many other examples. Others run out onto wild promontories, like Zennor Head

(Johnson et al. 1995, *fig. 1*; Fig. 12), and up onto upland commons like Bosiliack and Ding Dong in Madron (Buckley 2009, 107; 110). Open shafts could therefore be encountered in much of the central spine of Cornwall, with hedges or fences installed to prevent valued grazing animals from falling in as much as to safeguard people. (*see* Sharpe 2008, *fig. 47* for an impression of what such early shafts may have looked like, and how hazardous they would have been.)

The introduction of steam engines in the 18th century (Fig. 17) enabled mines to be sunk substantially deeper, as shown graphically by Thomas Pryce's 1778 section drawing of part of the Dolcoath complex where two fire engines drew water from 90 fathoms (540 feet, or 165m) below surface to the mid-depths from which subterranean waterwheels pumped it up to the lowest drainage adit (Pryce 1778, plate IV). Wheal Vor had already, in the early part of the century, been pumped by its primitive Newcomen engine to around 60 fathoms (360 feet, 110m) deep through six lifts of ten fathoms each (Jenkin 1927, 99). James Watt's external steam condenser (introduced in 1765) improved engine efficiency and meant mines required less coal, making many more of them viable, so that by 1778 there were over 60 fire engines in Cornwall and Devon (mostly in Cornwall). Further improvements included those made in the first years of the 19th century by Camborne-born Richard Trevithick that enabled development of high pressure steam engines

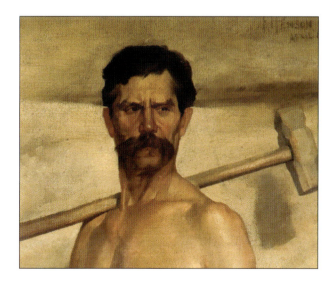

Figure 19 To be a successful miner involved considerable personal responsibility, strength and courage, all contributing to the heroic status of the miner, and all captured in this late Victorian painting, Cornish Miner, by Frederick Thomas Penson (1866-1951) (The Potteries Museum and Art Gallery).

The Tinworking Landscape of Dartmoor in a European Context: Prehistory to 20th Century

Figure 20 The Pridacoombe valley on Bodmin Moor is one of many marginal areas of Cornwall transformed in the early modern period by the creation of new farms stimulated by the market for foodstuffs swollen by the thousands of industrial workers. Some holdings, like these, created in the 1830s, were occupied by miners, streamers and labourers (Peter Herring).

at roughly the same time that plunger pumps finally replaced, in most but not all mines, the antiquated technology of rag-and-chain and bucket pumps (Barton 1969). Cornwall had often been several steps ahead of the 'industrial revolution', which swept much of the rest of Britain in the last quarter of the last millennium, but the technological improvements of the 18th and 19th centuries did enable even it to work its mines on different levels of production and depth so that by the later Victorian era nearly 3000 engine houses had been built in Cornwall. The main shaft at Dolcoath was then as deep as 550 fathoms, or 3300 feet, or one kilometre.

As noted, celebration of the profound effect of early modern Cornish mining technology on mining and society in Britain and around the world led to the inscription by ICOMOS in 2006 of the Cornwall and West Devon Mining Landscape World Heritage Site, a designation that has helped reinforce further the association of tin mining and Cornish (and West Devon) identity. Much effort has been taken since the 2006 inscription to draw out narratives of Cornish miners, emphasising how rewarding and dangerous their life was. Several horrific disasters have befallen Cornish miners below-ground (39 miners drowned in the East Wheal Rose lead mine in 1846, 20 more at Wheal Owles in 1893, and 31 fell to their deaths when the man-engine collapsed at Levant Mine in 1919), in addition to the much more numerous individual tragedies as men died by candlelight, falling down shafts, being crushed by rock falls and caught by blastings. Others succumbed to diseases caused or exacerbated through mining or had their lives reduced by the effects of grindingly hard work, bad air and poor food. Another calamity to which mines were susceptible was that caused by changes in economic circumstances, from the high costs of materials that made late medieval mining difficult, to the effects of fluctuations in global tin prices. Mines could be suddenly closed and communities thrown into turmoil as recently as the final decades of the 20th century (when Geevor (Fig. 1) and South Crofty mines were last closed). To work and survive underground required initiative, strength and skill; the risks (physical and economic) were so great that the tin miner was rightly transformed into a hero for the Cornish (Fig. 19).

Women and children also played vital roles in mining in Cornwall, and on Dartmoor, especially on the dressing floors. Their contributions, working conditions and lives are also being researched, enabling their history to be better understood, appreciated and celebrated. For example, Lynn Mayers (2008) has helped draw the 'bal maiden' from obscurity, bringing the lives of many child workers out of the darkness as she has done so.

The miner, the bal maiden and the boy or girl on the buddle or shaking table worked long days in poor conditions. When their shift was done most returned to simple homes, many of them in the villages that old farms and hamlets had swollen into, some like the churchtown of St Just having become small mining towns. New hamlets had also been created, like Minions, and rows or terraces of cottages housing miners' families were built in corners of fields and on commons convenient for the local mine (Sharpe 1992, 26-7). Not all miners, or those who worked in the numerous ancillary industries, were poor. The successful and the professional families built substantial houses, villas, on the edges of towns and in the country beyond them.

The post-medieval and early modern Cornish landscape was altered not just by the 3000 engine houses and the thousands of other related structures, the dressing floors and the dumps, pack-horse ways, tramways and railways, the terraces and villages and the noises and the smells of mining and the other associated industries, but also by another later wave of effects on farming landscape. This was largely in the form of extensions to field patterns, whether by the creation on rough grazing land of new farms and new smallholdings or by established farms extending their fields on to the rough ground in order to grow a little more for the ready market for foodstuffs required to feed the mining and manufacturing people. Lords benefitted again. As they received their toll or cut of the mines' profits, so they also drew still more in the form of rent from their farmland, as exemplified by the plans and the successes of the Rodds of Trebartha in creating the parish of Boldventure (later Bolventor) in the heart of Bodmin Moor. Here the new units were mainly farms of around 30 acres, taken on terms of three lives, and mainly by the families of tin streamers and clay workers. William Jory took on Middle Pridacoombe at a rent of £2 per annum and was required by the Rev Edward Rodd to take in fields from the 'wastrel' and within 12 months to build a dwelling-house and a chall (cowhouse). By 1841 he had done that and also enclosed and improved 26 acres (Herring and Giles 2008, 143-6; Fig. 20).

The labouring communities of Cornwall welcomed and nurtured Methodism and other forms of nonconformist Christianity. They had been poorly served in the 18th and early 19th centuries by the established Anglican church, both in terms of the inadequacy of the churches that could not accommodate their swollen populations and congregations on Sundays and in the service provided to them by clergy who were often absent or neglectful (Rowe 1993, 67.1-67.40). It should be noted that chapels and their congregations are found throughout Cornwall, not just in the mining areas (Lake et al. 2001). For example, the parish of North Petherwin, in the rural Culm Measures, had five chapels: two Wesleyan, two Bible Christian and one Free United Methodist. Most of the Cornish were affected by Methodism and the extent of their nonconformism reflects the connectedness of Cornwall's communities. Mining families were also often fishing, farming and quarrying families. Cornish people on meeting still enjoy establishing the various ways they may be related by blood, by friendship, by chapel, by work and by place. Much is and was shared, including ways of living and working that were hazardous and uncertain.

The emphasis in its teaching on taking personal responsibility and drawing reassurance from a shared faith in the face of danger and change, linked Methodism to a typically resourceful Dumnonian personal character that was reinforced by the unusual range of its uncertainties. In the end it may be this, coupled with the early commercialisation, or economic diversification of the Cornish, compared with much of the rest of Britain, that sets Cornwall and west Devon apart as a landscape that has been fundamentally affected by the ways people have responded to uncertainty and opportunity, including through industry. Methodism's importance now is its symbolisation of how the essence of being Cornish, and of being a tinworker, is and was living with and being open to uncertainty.

Acknowledgements

It was a pleasure to respond to Tom Greeves and Barry Gamble's request for a paper on the effects of tin mining on the Cornish landscape. Sandy Gerrard, Adam Sharpe and Nigel Thomas influenced how I surveyed and interpreted tin mining complexes and Nick Johnson and Pete Rose arranged the projects I worked on while with Cornwall County Council. Adam also kindly read and commented on a draft of this paper. Graham Fairclough helped me see landscape as people in place. Many thanks to Andrew and Ewa Thompson for their warm hospitality while in Tavistock, and to Deborah Boden and Ainsley Cocks of the Cornwall and West Devon Mining Landscape World Heritage Site team for their help there.

The Tinworking Landscape of Dartmoor in a European Context: Prehistory to 20th Century

Bibliography

Austin, D, Gerrard, G A M and Greeves, T A P 1989 'Tin and agriculture in the Middle Ages and beyond: landscape archaeology in St Neot Parish, Cornwall' *Cornish Archaeol* **28**, 7–251

Barton, D B 1969 *The Cornish beam engine*. Truro: D Bradford Barton

Brace, C 2006 'Landscapes and Senses of Place' in R J P Kain (ed) *England's Landscape: the South West*. London: Collins, 229-46

Brayshay, M 2006 'Landscapes of Industry' in R J P Kain (ed) *England's Landscape: the South West*. London: Collins, 131-54

Bristow, C M 2008 'Late 18th and early 19th Century forays into economic geology – some little known Franco-German papers describing Carclaze Old Tin Pit, near St. Austell, Cornwall' *Geoscience in South-West England* **12**, 1-8

Buckley, A 2009 *The Tudor Tin Industry, the tinners and tinworks of Penwith and Kerrier Stannary*. Camborne: Penhellick Publications

Buckley, J A (ed) 1994 *The Bailiff of Blackmoor, Thomas Beare. An examination of the history, laws and customs of medieval and sixteenth century tinners*. Camborne: Penhellick Publications

Carew, R 1602 *The Survey of Cornwall*.

Cornwall Council 2012 *Edge of Poverty? A local analysis of Experian's work on households on the edge of poverty*. Truro: Cornwall County Council

Cornwall Council 2013 *2011 Census; an overview of the headline figures for Cornwall*. Truro: Cornwall County Council

Council of Europe (CoE) 2000 *European Landscape Convention, European Treaty Series, no.176*. Florence: Council of Europe

Deacon, B 2014 'Cornwall, an inside-out industrial region' in Payton et al. (eds) 2014, 276-83

Earl, B 1968 *Cornish mining, the techniques of metal mining in the west of England, past and present*. Truro: Bradford Barton

Fairclough, G 2006 'Our Place in the Landscape? An Archaeologist's Ideology of Landscape Perception and Management' in T Meier (ed) *Landscape Ideologies, Archaeolingua*, **Series Minor 22**, 177-97

Fleming, A 1988 *The Dartmoor Reaves. Investigating Prehistoric Land Divisions*. Batsford: London.

Gerrard, G A M 1986 *The early Cornish tin industry: an archaeological and historical survey*. Unpub PhD thesis. St David's University College, Lampeter, University of Wales

Gerrard, G A M 1987 'Streamworking in medieval Cornwall' *J Trevithick Soc* **14**, 6-31

Gerrard, S 2000 *The Early British Tin Industry*. Stroud: The History Press Ltd

Gilbert, D 1838 *The Parochial History of Cornwall, four volumes*. London: J B Nichols

Greeves, T A P 1981 *The Devon Tin Industry, 1450-1750: an archaeological and historical survey*. Unpub PhD thesis, University of Exeter

Harvey, D 2006 'Landscape as Heritage and a Recreational Resource, in R J P Kain (ed) *England's Landscape: the South West*. London: Collins, 207-28

Hatcher, J 1969 'A Diversified Economy: Later Medieval Cornwall' *Econ Hist Rev* **22**, 208-27

Hatcher, J 1970a *Rural Economy and Society in the Duchy of Cornwall 1300-1500*. Cambridge:University Press

Hatcher, J 1970b 'Non-Manorialism in Medieval Cornwall' *Agr His Rev* **18**, 1-16

Herring, P 1997 *Godolphin, Breage, archaeological and historical assessment*. Truro: Cornwall County Council

Herring, P 1998 *Cornwall's historic landscape, presenting a method of historic landscape character assessment*. Truro: Cornwall County Council.

Herring, P 2001 'The deer park' in Cole, R, Herring, P, Johns, C and Reynolds, A (eds) *Godolphin, archaeological research and recording*. Truro: Cornwall County Council, 17-24

Herring, P 2003 'Cornish medieval deer parks' *in* R Wilson-North (ed) *The Lie of the Land, aspects of the archaeology and history of the designed landscape in the south west of England*. Exeter: The Mint Press, 34-50

Herring, P 2006 'Cornish Strip Fields' in S Turner (ed) *Medieval Devon and Cornwall*. Macclesfield: Windgather Press, 44-77

Herring, P 2008 'Commons, communities and fields in prehistoric Cornwall' *in* A M Chadwick (ed) *Recent approaches to the archaeology of land allotment*. Oxford: British Archaeological Reports, International Series **1875**, 70-95

Herring, P 2013 'Changing Cornish Commons' in I D Rotherham (ed) *Cultural Severance and the Environment, the ending of traditional and customary practice on commons*. London: Springer, 263-74

Herring, P and Giles, C 2008 'Agriculture' in Herring et al. 2008, 139-62

Herring, P, Sharpe, A, Smith, J and Giles, C 2008 *Bodmin Moor, an archaeological survey. Volume 2: the industrial and post- medieval landscape*. Swindon: English Heritage

Herring, P and Thomas, N 1990 *Kit Hill, archaeological survey*. Truro: Cornwall Archaeological Unit

Howard, P, Thompson, I and Waterton, E (eds) 2013 *The Routledge Companion to Landscape Studies*. London: Routledge

Jenkin, A K Hamilton 1927 *The Cornish Miner: an account of his life above underground from early times*. London: George Allen and Unwin

Johnson, N, Thomas, N, Herring, P and Sharpe, A 1995 'The survey and consolidation of industrial remains in Cornwall – a progress report' *Industrial Archaeology Review* **18.1**, 29-38

Lake, J, Cox, J and Berry, E 2001 *Diversity and Vitality: The Methodist and Nonconformist Chapels of Cornwall*. Truro: Cornwall County Council

Lewis, G R 1908 *The Stannaries, a study of the English tin miner.* Cambridge: Harvard University Press

Mayers, L 2008 *Bal Maidens*. Cinderford: Blaize Bailey Books

Norden, J 1604 *Speculi Britanniae Pars: a Topographical and historical description of Cornwall.* Published 1728, reprinted 1966, Newcastle-upon-Tyne: Frank Graham

Payton, P 2007 *Making Moonta, The Invention of Australia's Little Cornwall.* Exeter: University of Exeter Press

Payton, P, Kennerley, A and Doe, H (eds) 2014 *The Maritime History of Cornwall.* Exeter: University of Exeter Press

Pryce, W 1778 *Mineralogia Cornubiensis.* Truro: Bradford Barton (1972 reprint)

Rose, P and Herring, P 1990 *Bodmin Moor, Cornwall; an evaluation for the Monuments Protection Programme.* Truro: Cornwall County Council

Rowe, J 1993 *Cornwall in the Age of the Industrial Revolution.* St Austell: Cornish Hillside Publications (2nd edition)

Sharpe, A 1989 *Minions: an archaeological survey of the Caradon mining district.* Truro: Cornwall County Council

Sharpe, A 1992 *St Just: an archaeological survey of the Mining District.* Truro: Cornwall County Council

Sharpe, A 2008 'Mining' in P Herring et al. 2008, 29-82

Stoate, T L (ed) 1981 *Cornwall Hearth and Poll Taxes, 1660-1664.* Bristol: Stoate

Sundstrom, R A 1992 *Sidney Godolphin: Servant of the state.* Newark: University of Delaware Press

Sundstrom, R A 2004 'Godolphin, Sidney, first earl of Godolphin (1645–1712)' *Oxford Dictionary of National Biography*, Oxford University Press; online edn, May 2011

Taylor, J 1649 *Wandering to see the Wonders of the West.* Newcastle: Frank Graham (1967 reprint)

Turner, S 2007 *Ancient Country: the historic character of rural Devon.* Exeter: Devon Archaeological Society

World Heritage Site Bid Partnership 2005 *Nomination of the Cornwall and West Devon Mining Landscape for Inclusion on the World Heritage List.* Truro: Cornwall County Council

Tin Isotope Fingerprints of Ore Deposits and Ancient Bronze

Gerhard Brügmann[1], Daniel Berger[1], Carolin Frank[2], Janeta Marahrens[1], Bianka Nessel[2], Ernst Pernicka[1,2]

Abstract

The sources and origin of tin, and the dispersion of bronze technology in the 3rd and 2nd millennium BC, are the central research topics of our multi-disciplinary research project, funded by an Advanced Grant of the European Research Council (ERC). It has the general goal to establish the tin isotopic composition of tin ores and tin-bearing artefacts, and considers the influence of anthropogenic processes on the isotope ratios.

We discuss the tin isotopic composition of cassiterite from two major tin provinces in Europe: from Cornwall and Devon (Southern England), and from the Erzgebirge (Germany and Czech Republic). The samples from both tin provinces show a very large variation of isotopic compositions with $\delta^{124/120}$Sn-values ranging overall from -0.28 to 0.85‰. Although there is large overlap, on average, cassiterite from the Erzgebirge ($\delta^{124/120}$Sn = 0.09‰) is isotopically lighter than that of southwest England ($\delta^{124/120}$Sn = 0.18‰). This is due to a higher proportion of heavy isotope compositions in the samples from Cornwall and Devon.

In addition, we compare the ore data with preliminary tin isotopic systematics in Early Bronze Age metal artefacts from the Únětice Culture in Central Germany and from several ancient settlements in Mesopotamia belonging to the Early Dynastic III and the Akkadian Periods. Bronze artefacts of the Únětice Culture containing more than 3 wt.% tin have rather constant isotopic compositions ($\delta^{124/120}$Sn = 0.2 to 0.31 ‰), despite having highly variable trace element concentrations and tin contents. This suggests the intentional addition of an isotopically homogeneous tin raw material (metal or cassiterite) to the copper ore or melt. In contrast, the tin isotopic composition of artefacts from Mesopotamia (>3 wt. % Sn) show a much larger $\delta^{124/120}$Sn variation from -0.2 to +0.4‰. This is even observed in single settlements such as Ur. Since there is no sizeable tin mineralization in the vicinity, this implies that the tin demand of the ancient metallurgist was covered by trading tin from different ore sources.

1 Introduction

As early as the 19th century AD, researchers began to question the provenance of tin ores used for the production of the earliest bronzes of mankind. Scientists like Karl Ernst von Baer wondered why tin bronzes occurred exactly in those regions at first that are devoid of tin ores (von Baer 1876). During the late 4th and early 3rd millennium BC, first bronze artefacts were used in an area stretching from the Aegean region across Anatolia, the Levant, and Mesopotamia to the Arabian Sea (Fig. 1). Apart from small, and at most locally important mineralization, no tin sources that could have supplied metallurgists with tin are known in this region. It is therefore generally believed that tin and the technology of making bronze came from areas outside this territory, and Central Asia seems to be the most plausible at present. Besides written documents claiming that tin was delivered from the east (Dercksen 1999), large tin deposits are known from Afghanistan, Uzbekistan and Tadzhikistan whose exploitation could be traced back into the 2nd millennium BC (Thomalsky et al. 2013; Garner 2015). Earlier evidence, however, is lacking, and it is no surprise that the provenance of the earliest tin source is still an unsolved issue in archaeological and archaeometallurgical research.

Moreover, neither the spread of bronze technology can be reliably pursued, nor is it known whether

---

[1]Curt-Engelhorn-Zentrum Archäometrie gGmbH, D6,3, 68159 Mannheim, Germany. *www.cez-archaeometrie.de*

[2]Institut für Geowissenschaften, Universität Heidelberg, Im Neuenheimer Feld 234–236, 69120 Heidelberg, Germany

The Tinworking Landscape of Dartmoor in a European Context: Prehistory to 20th Century

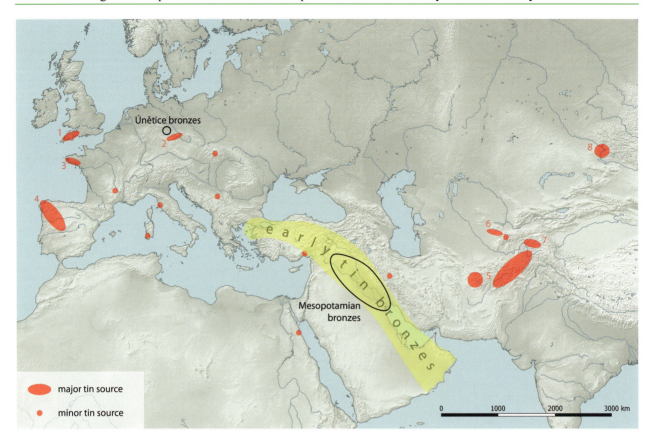

Figure 1 Map showing major and minor tin resources in Eurasia, the region of the earliest tin bronzes and the areas of the objects analysed by our research group.
1 – Cornwall/Devon; 2 – German/Bohemian Erzgebirge; 3 – Bretagne; 4 – Iberian Peninsula; 5 – Western and Eastern Afghanistan; 6 – Uzbekistan; 7 – Tadzhikistan; 8 – Kazakhstan.

bronze invention occurred at a single centre or multiple locations. The scarcity of archaeological evidence of prehistoric mining activities is a major reason for that, but the subject is also complicated by the lack of analytical fingerprinting tools that help associate artefacts to ore deposits. Lead isotopy and trace elements are rarely useful for linking tin metal and tin bronzes to their parental tin ores, because most elements in tin ores do not partition into the tin metal during smelting. Lead contents in tin ores (mainly cassiterite) are very low, making lead isotope analysis only meaningful in special cases, like for pure tin metal. Lead contained in tin bronze is dominated by the contribution of the copper ore and it is therefore not a tracer of the tin source.

Chemical and physical processes, such as ore formation or smelting, can modify an element's isotope abundance pattern, producing what is commonly referred to as mass fractionation of the isotopes. With modern high-resolution multi-collector mass spectrometers (those with inductively coupled plasma ionisation (MC-ICP-MS) for example) the induced fractionation effects can be resolved even in heavier elements, such as tin. The interdisciplinary ERC research project, Bronze Age Tin, aims to use the variation of stable tin isotope ratios as a novel diagnostic element in the study of tin provenance. Meanwhile, the isotopic compositions of tin ores and artefacts are routinely analysed by our research group. In addition, laboratory and field experiments are carried out with ores and metals in order to unveil possible mass fractionation effects during pyrometallurgical processes (smelting, casting, recycling).

This paper discusses methodological issues in measuring tin isotope ratios in tin ores and metal objects. Also, some preliminary data are presented on tin ores from southern England and Germany as well as Early Bronze Age (EBA) artefacts from the Únětice culture in Germany, Early Dynastic III and Akkadian periods in Mesopotamia (Fig. 1). The results expand and substantiate published tin isotope compositions and are combined with archaeological context information, providing an improved understanding of raw material distribution and the production processes of tin bronze in prehistory.

2 Determination of the isotopic composition of tin in cassiterite, tin metal and bronze artefacts

The tin isotopic composition in artefacts made of tin bronze (Cu-Sn alloy), and in tin metal obtained from the experimental reduction of tin ores (cassiterite) at high temperatures, will be presented. The procedure of reducing cassiterite is described in detail in the following chapter. The reduction yields tin beads, which were hand-picked and, like the bronze alloys, dissolved in a mixture of HCl and H_2O_2. The solution of the tin metal can be directly measured after appropriate dilution with H_2O and HNO_3. However, the solutions from bronze artefacts, containing high concentrations of copper and other metals (Pb, Sb, As, Ag, etc.) have to be purified chromatographically in order to minimize matrix effects and to avoid isobaric interferences during isotope measurements (Brügmann et al. 2017).

The tin isotopic analyses (TIA) were performed with a Thermo Scientific Neptune Plus MC-ICP-MS, equipped with nine Faraday Cups. Tin has ten isotopes covering a mass range of 12amu between masses 112 and 124. The measurement of the seven high mass Sn isotopes (^{116}Sn, ^{117}Sn, ^{118}Sn, ^{119}Sn, ^{120}Sn, ^{122}Sn, ^{124}Sn) was preferred, because they have the highest abundances, which helps to attain data with the highest analytical precision. This mass range also fits more closely to that of Sb (121–123) which was used for mass bias correction. Samples were run in a blank-standard-blank-sample-blank-standard bracketing setup. The calculation of the isotope ratios, the mass bias correction using the exponential law (Russell et al. 1978; Baxter et al. 2006) and δ-value calculations, were done off-line with Excel spreadsheets. The data will be given with the conventional delta notation where

$$\delta^{124/120}Sn = \left(\left[\frac{^{124}Sn}{^{120}Sn}\right]_{sample} \Big/ \left[\frac{^{124}Sn}{^{120}Sn}\right]_{Standard} - 1 \right) *1000$$

Although isotope ratios such as $^{124/116}Sn$ would yield larger values because of the larger mass fractionation, the $\delta^{124/120}Sn$ values presented in this study are more precise and accurate, because of minimal systematic errors during mass fractionation correction.

The combined uncertainty (reproducibility) of the measurements is given by 2 standard deviations (2 SD) and includes the analytical uncertainties introduced during the measurement and by sample processing (*e.g.* dissolution, wet chemistry, anion exchange chromatography). (Brügmann et al. 2017) investigated in detail the analytical uncertainty of reference materials made of bronze. Separate dissolutions of BAM 211 (G-SnBz10, Bundesanstalt für Materialprüfung, Berlin, Germany) were processed giving a combined uncertainty between 0.01 and 0.06 ‰ depending on the isotope ratio to be considered. For example, $\delta^{124/120}Sn$ varies by ±0.025 ‰.

3 Tin ore preparation for isotope analysis

One of the main challenges of the project was the preparation and reliable dissolution of the tin ores. Cassiterite as the main tin ore for prehistoric craftsmen and the main subject of our studies is highly resistant to most chemicals. The oxide cannot be readily dissolved in acids and bases that are commonly used in isotopic research. The task was to find a method which completely breaks down cassiterite without any loss of tin. Several methods of decomposition have been reported in the literature:

1. Dissolution with hydroiodic acid (Caley 1932; Yamazaki et al. 2013)
2. Chemical reduction with metallic zinc and hydrochloric acid (Hosking 1974)
3. Chemical reduction with various salts (Hall 1980)
4. Thermal reduction with carbon/carbon monoxide (McNaughton and Rosman, 1991; Clayton et al. 2002)
5. Thermal reduction with potassium cyanide (Haustein et al. 2010).

The first two methods only partially decomposed the cassiterite and were not followed up. The latter three methods were re-evaluated (*cf.* Berger et al. submitted) in order to investigate in detail the potential tin loss and its impact on the isotopic composition. Evaporation of tin during the reduction as a result of the formation of volatile stannous oxide (SnO) is a well-known problem in tin pyrometallurgy that can lead to significant tin loss (Wright 1982; Smith 1996; Zhang et al. 2015). Moreover, tin is easily slagged by silicates (always present in tin ores), which can also result in considerable tin loss. Both processes are of great importance for the fingerprinting of cassiterite, since any loss of tin during the decomposition of cassiterite, or during the metallurgical process, can induce isotope fractionation. In this case, the measured tin isotopic composition would not be representative of the cassiterite ore.

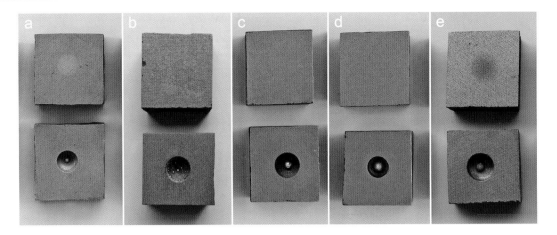

Figure 2 Results of experimental reduction of stannic oxide in the laboratory: Reduction with (a) carbon monoxide, (b) potassium cyanide, (c) sodium carbonate, (d) copper and (e) cupric oxide.

Several laboratory experiments with synthetic and natural cassiterite were designed that tested the different methods of thermal reduction. Besides reduction experiments with carbon/carbon monoxide (C/CO) and potassium cyanide (KCN), tests were carried out using sodium carbonate (Na_2CO_3) as a flux. In addition, two methods have been incorporated that involved the reduction of cassiterite either in the presence of metallic copper or cupric oxide (CuO). Both experiments, so-called co-smelting (co-reduction of tin and copper ores) and cementation (reduction of cassiterite with copper), are techniques likely to have been used to produce bronze in antiquity.

Most of the experiments were done in polished graphite plates. Sample material (ca. 10 mg synthetic or natural SnO_2) was loaded into drilled pits with or without additives (Cu, CuO, KCN, Na_2CO_3). The graphite plates were put into corundum crucibles and embedded in active carbon. Depending on the reduction method, the whole assemblage was heated to 950 °C and up to 1100 °C for several hours (heating up + dwell time at temperature maximum) in a muffle furnace. The samples were documented and weighted thoroughly after reduction.

Figure 2 shows photographs of the experiments with synthetic and natural cassiterite; these examples show representative results for the whole range of our investigations. Besides silvery or reddish metal beads within the drill holes, tarnishes can be seen at the lids of some experiments (Fig. 2a and e). In cases where the reduction was done without additives (C/CO), a white tarnish consisting of tiny tin beads precipitated at the lid (Fig. 2). It formed by condensation and reduction of the tin oxide vapour, confirming previous studies reporting that cassiterite cannot be reduced thermally without the loss of tin. In our experiments the tin loss amounted to 2–15 %. Tin loss was also observed during the co-smelting of SnO_2 and CuO. Apart from large bronze beads and some unalloyed tin in the drill holes (Fig. 2e), little bronze beads occurred at the lids of the trials suggesting the simultaneous evaporation of tin and copper. Yet the loss of tin was less than 5 %. In contrast, no fuming and hence no loss of tin was observed when cassiterite was reduced in the presence of KCN, Na_2CO_3 or Cu (*cf.* Fig. 2b–d). These reduction methods would thus be preferred for the characterization of tin ores provided that the isotopic composition can be measured precisely. After analysis of a large number of samples, reduction with KCN turned out as the most reliable method, although special care is required due to the toxicity of the cyanide. No fractionation as a consequence of the reduction was detected (Fig. 3). The reduction of synthetic and natural cassiterite in the presence of Na_2CO_3 and copper, induced small but significant variations of the tin isotopic compositions. In addition, this procedure would necessitate a further chromatographic clean up step before the isotope measurements. Even higher deviations of tin isotope ratios ($\delta^{124/120}Sn \approx 0.1$ ‰) were found for the samples that have been reduced with C/CO and in presence of CuO (Fig. 3). Evaporation of tin oxide thus affects the tin isotopic composition in such a way that the light isotopes preferentially escape, *i.e.* the vapour is isotopically lighter than the residual tin metal. Moreover, incomplete alloying of tin and copper, as observed for the co-smelting of SnO_2 with CuO, also effects the isotopic composition decreasing the precision and accuracy of the data. Both reduction

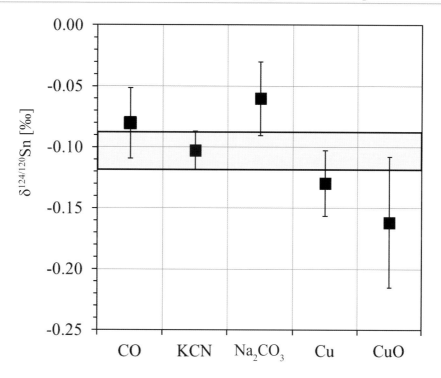

Figure 3a Average isotopic composition ($\delta^{124/120}Sn$) of the tin metal and bronze obtained by reduction of synthetic cassiterite with five reduction methods applied in the laboratory (grey area defines the true isotopic composition of the sample).

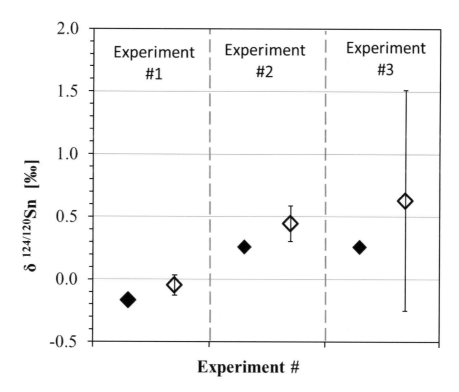

Figure 3b Average isotopic composition ($\delta^{124/120}Sn$) of the tin metal and bronze obtained by smelting in the field with cassiterite from two different ore deposits on the Iberian Peninsula. Experiment #1 and #2 were done in crucibles, whereas experiment #3 was carried out without one. Incomplete reduction during experiment #3 caused large isotopic variation. Open symbols represent the composition of tin metal; filled symbols are the isotopic composition of the cassiterite reduced in the laboratory with the KCN reduction method. Error bars represent 2 standard deviations of the mean.

methods are hence not suitable for fingerprinting the tin ores.

4 Pyrometallurgical experiments in the field

The laboratory experiments described above were designed to minimize evaporation and loss of tin during the reduction of cassiterite. However, they are not well suited to understanding the tin isotopic systematics on the scale of a field experiment where the prehistoric metallurgical process can be simulated more realistically. To investigate this aspect, experiments were conducted, in cooperation with Portuguese and Spanish colleagues (Berger et al. 2016; Figueiredo et al. 2016), which tested different smelting techniques of cassiterite (direct reduction, cementation, co-smelting), but also other pyrometallurgical processes that could have an impact on the isotopic composition of tin. Amongst these are the casting and re-melting (recycling) of bronze and tin.

Smelting experiments with cassiterite took place in the field using a primitive, open furnace structure (cf. Figueiredo et al. 2016). As already observed in earlier investigations (Earl 1966; Timberlake 1994), tin recovery was also rather low in these experiments. A maximum of 30 % of the theoretically possible value was recovered as tin metal. The remaining tin was lost either as vapour, tied up in slag or survived as unreacted SnO_2. Surprisingly, the extreme tin loss affected the isotopic composition of the tin metal to a much lower degree than anticipated by theoretical considerations (Budd et al. 1995). The difference was just about 0.1–0.15 ‰ ($\delta^{124/120}Sn$), which is in the same order we observed in our C/CO laboratory experiments, where markedly better recoveries had been possible (Fig. 3). The variation of the tin isotopic composition in tin ores is significantly larger (>1 ‰ in terms of $\delta^{124/120}Sn$, see below). Thus, the relatively small isotopic variation induced during the smelting of cassiterite appears not to be significant and provenance studies of tin should provide consistent and sensible results. However, if cassiterite is smelted incompletely – i.e. there is still unreacted cassiterite (cf. Earl 1986 and our own experiments) – the isotope ratios of the tin metal do not reflect those of the parental ores (cf. Fig. 3b, Exp. 3; Berger et al. submitted; Berger et al. forthcoming).

The influence of other pyrometallurgical processes turned out to be distinctly less critical. For instance, only small isotopic variations were observed after repeated melting of bronze in a reducing atmosphere, or after open-mould casting. These typical steps in the processing of tin and bronze do not seem to hamper the investigations on tin provenance. The details of the experiments will be described in forthcoming publications.

5 Tin isotopic variation in tin ores: Southern England and Erzgebirge

One major subject of the ERC project is the investigation of the distribution of the tin isotopic composition in the most important tin provinces of the Old World, comprising the European tin deposits in Southern England, the Iberian Peninsula and the Erzgebirge of Germany/Czech Republic, as well as the Central Asian deposits in Afghanistan, Uzbekistan, Kazakhstan and Tadzhikistan (cf. Fig.1).

Prehistoric mining activities dating to the European Bronze Age, have only been found in southern England (Tylecote et al. 1989) and the Iberian Peninsula (Merideth 1998; Rodríguez Díaz et al. 2013). In Cornwall and Devon, tin mining is documented over the past 3500 years from Late Bronze Age until the 20th century AD. But prehistoric evidence is limited to a few slag finds containing tin, and prehistoric remains in tin placers (Penhallurick 1986; Tylecote et al. 1989). The oldest of the slags, excavated in a burial in Caerloggas Downs near St. Austell, is dated from the 16th to 14th century BC (Miles 1975). Near the tin and copper deposits in the Erzgebirge, a number of Bronze Age settlements and other traces of occupation have been found (Bouzek et al. 1989). Perhaps in Bohemia and Saxony some local sources of copper and tin might have been exploited, the latter metal by panning from the river and creek beds (Bartelheim and Niederschlag 1998).

A common feature of the European tin ore provinces is their association with late Variscan granites. The primary mineralization occurs in granitic pegmatites and in hydrothermal greisen, quartz and polymetallic veins. The principal tin mineral exploited is cassiterite (SnO_2), although locally stannite (Cu_2FeSnS_4) might also be of some importance. Cassiterite is a hard, dense, weathering-resistant mineral, and during the erosion of the granite and the mineralization the mineral is deposited in fluvial placer deposits in economically important concentrations.

The granitic rare metal pegmatites are late, high temperature (>600 °C) crystallisation products of mainly per- to metaluminous granites and contain a complex ore mineralogy with Nb-Ta-Ti oxides and cassiterite. The mineralization in the veins precipitated from hydrothermal fluids probably at temperatures of less than 400 °C. The ore mineralogy of the quartz veins is relatively simple, containing mainly cassiterite or wolframite and only small amounts of stannite and other sulphide minerals. Current research supports an internal derivation and enrichment of the metals from the granitic melts continuing into the hydrothermal regime (Cerny et al. 2005). The wide-ranging compositions of the mineralisation reflect variable composition of the source material of the granitic melt, different degrees of anataxis, fractional crystallisation and eventually aqueous fluid-melt processes. Leaching of metals from the country rocks by hydrothermal interaction appears to be of inferior significance (Cerny et al. 2005).

The tin mineralisation in southwest England is associated with a series of granite plutons, which intruded during the Upper Carboniferous-Lower Permian *ca.* 270–290 million years ago (Chen et al. 1993; Chesley et al. 1993). We determined the tin isotopic composition of ore samples (cassiterite) from pegmatitic and hydrothermal mineralization associated with the major granite plutons of southern England (Land's End, Carnmenellis, St. Austell, Bodmin Moor and Dartmoor). The Central European tin province belongs to the Saxothuringian zone of the Bohemian Massif which represents the easternmost part of the European-Variscan belt. The late-orogenic to post-orogenic extensive silicic plutonic and volcanic activity at 330–290 million years was the foundation of the wealth of mineral deposits in this area, including tin. We analysed ore samples from deposits in Germany and the Czech Republic (Fichtelgebirge, the Saxon-Bohemian Erzgebirge, Vogtland, Kaiserwald). Haustein et al. (2010) had already studied the tin isotopic composition of cassiterite from both tin provinces. We re-analysed several samples from the previous study because modern equipment now available at our institute provides more precise data. In addition, we extended the data set by analysing new samples.

The samples from both tin provinces show a very large range of isotopic compositions, and the $\delta^{124/120}$Sn-value ranges overall from -0.28 to 0.85 ‰ (Fig. 4). Although Haustein et al. (2010) did not measure this isotope ratio, their $\delta^{122/116}$Sn-values show a similar variation. The average and median $\delta^{124/120}$Sn-values for Cornwall (0.18 ‰ and 0.15 ‰, respectively) and the Erzgebirge agree well (0.09 ‰ and 0.10 ‰, respectively) indicating a normal distribution of the tin isotopic composition in the tin ores of both provinces. The isotopic composition of cassiterite from the Erzgebirge is, on average, isotopically lighter than that of southern England, which reflects the higher proportion of very low $\delta^{124/120}$Sn-values (Fig. 4) in samples from the Erzgebirge, and the high proportion of heavy isotope composition in Cornwall. The isotopic composition of cassiterite from pegmatites and hydrothermal veins overlaps and it is not possible to differentiate among different ore types. Even in individual ore districts, large isotope variations occur, which in detail, however, display subtle differences. For example, several districts display skewed frequency distributions, but it is not clear as yet, whether this reflects the presence of different types of tin ores in these districts.

In order to distinguish different ore types and their petrogenesis in detail, one has to answer the basic question: what causes the isotope fractionation? Unfortunately, the behaviour of tin and its isotopes during the complex process of tin ore formation, from partial melting deep in the source area, fractional crystallization of the granitic melt to precipitation in a cooling hydrothermal aqueous fluid, is not even qualitatively understood and needs more research in the near future.

6 Tin isotopic composition in Early Bronze Age artefacts

The archaeological Metal Ages are traditionally considered to begin with the Bronze Age shortly before the beginning of the third millennium BC in the Mediterranean and at the end of that century in Central Europe. We present some preliminary isotope data on Early Bronze Age artefacts from both areas (Fig. 1):
  a. Artefacts from the Únětice culture, the main EBA culture in Central Europe
  b. Artefacts from Mesopotamia belonging to the Early Dynastic Period III and the Akkadian Empire (2600 to 2200/2100 BC).

a. Isotopic composition of bronze artefacts from the Únětice culture in Central Germany

The Únětice culture is dated between 2300 and 1500 BC and is generally divided into an early (A1, 2300–1900 BC) and a younger or classical phase (A2, 1900–1500 BC) (Zich 1996). Typical materials are found between northern Lower Austria, the western part of Slovakia, Moravia and Bohemia, the greater

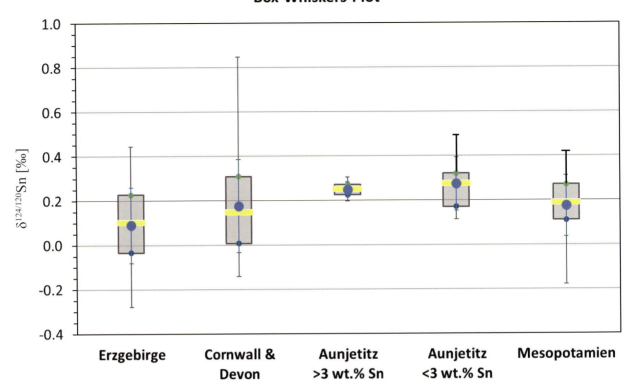

Figure 4 Box-Whiskers diagram showing the variation of the δ[124/120]Sn ratio in tin ore deposits from the Saxon-Bohemian Erzgebirge and from Cornwall and Devon in southern England as well as in EBA bronze objects belonging to the Únětice culture in Central Germany and to the Early Dynastic III and the Akkadian Periods of Mesopotamia. Yellow lines represent the median values, blue dots the averages of the isotope distributions. Data of tin ore deposits from Marahrens (unpublished); Data of Mesopotamian objects from Frank (unpublished).

region of Middle Germany, Silesia and greater Poland. Tin bronze is found in graves and numerous hoards The latter sometimes contain several hundred items like tools, jewellery, weapons and ingots. In the area of the Únětice culture several potential ore sources are known; however, specific mineral deposits, which can be directly related to Early Bronze Age metal artefacts, have not been identified. Nevertheless, import of raw metal from the copper mines in the eastern Alps is highly likely (Lutz and Pernicka, 2009). Whether tin was also imported or whether the people of the Únětice culture mined it in the Erzgebirge or the Slovakian Ore Mountains is currently under discussion.

We focus the discussion on artefacts belonging to the Central German or Saxon-Thuringian subgroup near the city of Halle (Fig. 1). The samples are from different hoards laid down in a rather short period of about 200 years (1950 to 1750 BC). Lutz and Pernicka (2009), who systematically studied the composition of these metal finds, estimated that about 90 % of the bronze artefacts were made of copper smelted from the mineral fahlore. Such copper is characterized by high concentrations of arsenic and antimony (>1 wt.%) and about 1 wt.%. silver. To this group belong the bronze artefacts from the hoards of Dieskau II and III, Kanena II and III and Schkopau. In contrast, the objects from the hoards of Gröbers-Bennewitz and Burgstaden have systematically lower antimony and silver contents (<1 wt.%). These differences indicate that the ancient smelters have used a different copper ore type as well, probably one which was rich in chalcopyrite, when producing the bronze of the two hoards. The tin contents of the bronze objects are highly variable; in the analysed objects they vary from 0.11 to 14.4 wt.%.

The $\delta^{124/120}$Sn ratios in the Únětice objects vary from =0.12–0.51 ‰ (Fig. 4). No significant differences can be observed among the objects from the different hoards. Thus, the isotopic composition does not depend on the type of copper ore (fahlore or chalcopyrite) used to alloy with tin. In addition, the isotopic composition cannot discriminate between objects with different functions (jewellery, weapons, tools, and ingots). Interestingly, this large range of the isotopic compositions is observed in bronze objects with low tin contents, less than 3 wt.% (Fig. 4). The isotopic composition in tin bronzes having more than 3 wt.% tin is on average similar to the tin-poor ones, however, the variation of $\delta^{124/120}$Sn is significantly smaller, ranging from just 0.2 to 0.31 ‰ (Fig. 4). The addition of less than 3 wt.% of tin to the copper would not distinctively change mechanical, optical and metallurgical characteristics of the copper metal. Thus, there is no apparent point in adding such a small amount of tin during the smelting process. It implies that the tin had not been added intentionally to the copper ore or copper metal. More likely, tin represents a natural impurity of the ore. However, adding more than 3 wt. % tin improves the casting characteristics of the melt and produces a harder, but malleable alloy with a golden colour. This suggest that the tin of the high-tin objects has been intentionally added to the copper.

Furthermore, the uniform isotopic composition of these bronze artefacts implies that the tin added to the copper was rather homogenous. This could signify that tin was derived from a single ore source or a single mineralization. However, there are alternative scenarios. If cassiterite had been added to the copper metal then the tin ore was most likely derived from a placer-type deposit. Such a deposit consists of cassiterite collected from a large area and is likely to include different types of tin ore, and therefore, contains cassiterite whose individual grains have very different isotopic composition. However, panning of a large number of grains would homogenize the metal content and should produce a concentrate with a rather uniform isotopic composition. Alternatively, isotopically homogeneous tin metal could have been added to the copper melt, which has been previously produced by smelting of stocks of cassiterite. Considering the large number of bronze artefacts deposited in this period in the area of the Únětice culture, the latter two scenarios would suggest that there was a well-organized trade system already during the EBA supplying the tin to the metallurgist.

Even if one assumes a European source of tin for the high-tin objects of the Únětice culture, its origin cannot explicitly be defined. This is due to the large overlap of the isotopic compositions of the tin ores from southern England and Germany as discussed above. On average the $\delta^{124/120}$Sn ratios in the Únětice objects are higher than those of the two ore provinces (Fig. 4). The high-tin objects have higher ratios than about 70% of the ores from the Erzgebirge. This would imply that this province is not a very likely source of the Únětice tin. However, if additional concrete evidence, for example the archaeological context, could suggest a relationship to the Erzgebirge, then the special, heavy, isotopic composition of the tin in the objects would considerably reduce the number of potential ore districts providing the tin ore. However, such evidence has not been found, despite intensive search (Bartelheim and Niederschlag 1998).

b. Isotopic composition of bronze artefacts from Mesopotamia

The studied artefacts from Mesopotamia belong to the Early Dynastic III and the Akkadian Periods (2600 to 2200/2100 BC); the allocation is based on their find context or typological markers. The objects are predominantly from the settlements of Ur, Tell es-Suleimeh, Tell Asmar and Khafajah (Fig. 1) and encompass weapons (mostly shaft-hole axes, spear heads and daggers), jewellery (mostly needles), as well as metal vessels (bowls).

The Mesopotamian objects contain 3.5 to 17.2 wt.% of tin and low concentrations of silver (<0.24 wt.%), arsenic (<3 wt.%) and antimony (<1 wt.%). It is therefore believed that the tin was intentionally alloyed with copper by the ancient metallurgist, and that the copper source, possibly Oman, did not contain a large proportion of fahlore, if at all. The variation of the tin isotopic composition in the bronze artefacts is significantly larger than that of the Únětice culture. The $\delta^{124/120}$Sn ratios extend in particular to lighter isotopic composition (-0.18 ‰) and ranges up to 0.44 ‰ (Fig. 4). This large range is even characteristic for individual finds; on average however, the heavier isotopic composition dominates as suggested by median and average $\delta^{124/120}$Sn ratios of 0.19 ‰ and 0.17 ‰, respectively.

Currently, it is not possible to define the tin provenance for the Mesopotamian objects. The main reason is the lack of isotope data for potential tin ore sources in Central Asia. However, the large variation of the $\delta^{124/120}$Sn ratios overall and in single graves would suggest that several tin deposits supplied tin either as cassiterite concentrates or as already semi-finished products (ingots) of tin metal. The large isotope variation within settlements could even suggest the presence of several metallurgist, each one having his own special tin supply. There is no sizeable tin mineralization in the vicinity; this implies that the tin demand of the ancient metallurgists was covered by trading tin from different sources and far-ranging tin trade is likely.

7 Summary

Great progress has been made with regard to the provenance of copper by comparing in particular lead isotopic compositions and trace element contents of bronze objects and copper ores. Unfortunately, the origin of tin remains as one of the knottiest problems in the archaeology of metal sources, specifically with regard to the 3rd and 2nd millennium BC. It looks like tin bronze was first produced and used in regions of Anatolia or Mesopotamia where no significant tin deposits are known. In addition, early objects of tin bronze are found in regions that are separated by long distances from each other. Thus, the provenance of Bronze Age tin and the origin of the bronze technology are the central research topics of our multi-disciplinary research project 'BronzeAgeTin'.

The project uses state of the art instrumental equipment (MC-ICP-MS) and develops chemical and experimental techniques to determine the tin isotopic compositions of ore deposits and archaeological objects. The tin isotopic composition can define a specific isotopic fingerprint of an ore and an artefact, because chemical-physical processes fractionate isotopes according to their mass differences. For example, the tin isotopic composition of a tin ore deposit will depend on its specific magmatic-hydrothermal evolution: the inherited isotopic composition of the source, mass fractionation during partial melting forming the granite magma, and eventually during the precipitation and concentration of the ore minerals from the magma and the hydrothermal fluid. Pyrometallurgical processes (smelting, casting, recycling) for making archaeological metal objects potentially change the isotopic composition as well and could therefore overprint the original provenance signal.

Evaporation of tin oxide during smelting of cassiterite, for instance, affects the tin isotopic composition in such a way that the light isotopes preferentially escape, *i.e.* the vapour is isotopically lighter than the residual tin metal. However, our experiments suggest that the pyrometallurgical process does not hamper the investigation of tin provenance. Even low tin recoveries of 30 % caused only small isotopic differences of 0.1–0.15 ‰ ($\delta^{124/120}$Sn) between ores and smelted tin which is not significant regarding the large variation in tin ores. However, large isotopic variations can be caused by incomplete reduction of cassiterite or alloying of tin and copper during co-smelting of tin and copper ores as observed in some experiments. In these cases the isotope ratios of tin do not reflect those of the parental tin ores.

Tin deposits in Southern England and in the Saxon-Bohemian Erzgebirge are potentially important tin sources for Bronze Age objects in Central Europe. Overall the isotopic composition in cassiterite varies by more than 1 ‰ in terms of the $\delta^{124/120}$Sn ratio. However, the isotopic composition from both provinces overlap to a large degree, although on average the $\delta^{124/120}$Sn ratios in deposits from Cornwall (0.18 ‰) tend to be higher than those from the Erzgebirge (0.09 ‰). This observation makes distinct assignments of bronze artefacts to one of the two provinces very difficult. Exceptions are bronze objects having extreme heavy or light isotopic compositions; in these cases even an assignment to a specific ore district or deposit might be possible as exemplified by artefacts of the Únětice culture. Tin bronzes (>3 wt. % Sn) from several large hoards of the Únětice culture show a fairly small isotopic variation ($\delta^{124/120}$Sn = 0.25±0.03 ‰). Less than 25 % of the isotope data from the Erzgebirge have such heavy isotope compositions making it fairly unlikely that the tin was supplied from this area. However, if ore deposits with such heavy isotope compositions exist in the Erzgebirge, these would be excellent prospects. The homogeneous isotopic composition of the bronze objects implies a tin supply with a similar homogenous composition over a time span of about 200 years. Although this could indicate the exploitation of a single ore deposit, the large amount of EBA bronze artefacts laid down in the area of the Únětice culture favours a pooling of cassiterite before being alloyed with copper.

Near Eastern bronzes from the 3rd and 2nd millennium BC, which were found in graves and hoards of Ur, Tell Asmar, Tell es-Suleimeh and Khafajah display overall and in individual graves rather large isotopic variation as $\delta^{124/120}$Sn varies from -0.2 to +0.4 ‰. This suggests that tin has been supplied by several ore sources. Because no significant tin deposits are known in the immediate neighbourhood the presence of a network of a far-ranging tin trade must be assumed. We are currently investigating whether Central Asian tin ores have been involved in this network. Additional evidence provided by the archaeological context and by multi-proxy approaches would be necessary in order to provenance specific tin deposits.

Acknowledgements

This study is part of the research project *'Bronze Age Tin-Tin isotopes and the sources of Bronze Age tin in the Old World'* which is financially supported through the Advanced Grant no. 323861 of the European Research Council awarded to E. Pernicka. We would like to thank the conference organizers for the kind invitation to the *Celebration of the tinworking landscape of Dartmoor in its European context: Prehistory to 20th Century* in Tavistock. We owe special thanks to Dr Tom Greeves, Dr Barry Gamble and the colleagues of the Dartmoor Tinworking Research Group for their unlimited support in Tavistock and further cooperation. We are also most grateful to Dr Newman for editing the publication.

References

Bartelheim, M and Niederschlag, E 1998 'Untersuchungen zur Buntmetallurgie, insbesondere des Kupfers und des Zinns, im sächsisch-böhmischen Erzgebirge und dessen Umland' *Arbeits- und Forschungsberichte zur Sächsischen Bodendenkmalpflege* **40**, 8-87

Baxter, D C, Rodushkin, I, Engstrom, E, Malinovsky, D 2006 'Revised exponential model for mass bias correction using an internal standard for isotope abundance ratio measurements by multi-collector inductively coupled plasma mass spectrometry' *Journal of Analytical Atomic Spectrometry* **21**, 427-30

Berger, D, Brügmann, G, Pernicka, E (submitted) 'Laboratory reduction experiments of stannic oxide for evaluation the suitability for tin isotope analysis in archaeological research' *Archaeological and Anthropological Science*

Berger, D, Figueiredo, E, Brügmann, G, Pernicka, E (forthcoming) Tin isotope fractionation during experimental cassiterite smelting and its implication for tracing the tin sources of the Bronze Age.

Bouzek, J, Koutecky, D, Simon, J 1989 'Tin and prehistoric mining in the Erzgebirge (Ore Mountains): some new evidence' *Oxford Journal of Archaeology* **8**, 203–12

Brügmann, G, Berger, D, Pernicka, E 2017 'Determination of the Tin Stable Isotopic Composition in Tin-bearing Metals and Minerals by MC-ICP-MS' *Geostandards and Geoanalytical Research.*

Budd, P, Haggerty, R Pollard, A M, Scaife, B and Thomas, R G 1995 'New heavy isotopes studies in archaeology' *Israel Journal of Chemistry* **35.2**, 125–30

Caley, E R 1932 'The action of hydriodic acid on stannic oxide' *Journal of the American Chemical Society* **54**, 3240–3

Cerny, P, Blevin, P L, Cuney, M, London, D 2005 'Granite-related ore deposits' *Society of Economic Geologists 2005 100th Anniversary* 337-70

Chen, Y Clark A H, Farrar, E, Wasteneys, H A H P, Hodgson, M J and Bromley, A V 1993 'Diachronous and independent histories of plutonism and mineralisation in the Comubian Batholith Southwest England' *Journal of the Geological Society, London* **150**,1183-91

Chesley, J T, Halliday, A N, Snee, L W, Mezger, K, Shepherd, T J and Scrivener, R C 1993 'Thermochronology of the Cornubian Batholith in southwest England: implications for pluton emplacement and protracted hydrothermal mineralisation' *Geochimica et Cosmochimica Acta* **57**, 1817-35

Clayton, R, Andersson, P, Gale, N H, Gillis, C and Whitehouse, M 2002 'Precise determination of the isotopic composition of Sn using MC-ICP-MS' *Journal of Analytical Atomic Spectrometry* **17**, 1248–56

Earl, B 1986 'Melting tin in the West of England: Part 2' *Journal of the Historical Metallurgy Society* **20.1**, 17–32

Dercksen, J-G (ed) 1999 *Trade and Finance in Ancient Mesopotamia* MOS Studies 1 Leiden

Figueiredo, E, Lackinger, A, Comendador Rey, B, Silva, R J C, Veiga, J P, Mirão, J 2016 'An experimental approach for smelting tin ores from Northwestern Iberia' *Materials and Manufacturing Processes* **32.7–8**, 765–74

Garner, J, 2015 'Bronze Age tin mines in central Asia, in: Archaeometallurgy in Europe III' in A Hauptmann, D Modarressi-Tehrani(eds) Der Anschnitt Beiheft *Proceedings of the 3rd International Conference, Deutsches Bergbau-Museum Bochum, June 29 – July 1 2011* **26**, 135–43

Hall, A 1980 'The determination of total tin content of some geological materials by atomic absorption spectrophotometry' *Chemical Geology* **30.1–2**, 135–42

Haustein, M, Gillis, C and Pernicka, E, 2010 'Tin isotopy – a new method for solving old questions' *Archaeometry* **52.5**, 816–32

Hosking, K F G, 1974 'Practical aspects of the identification of cassiterite (SnO_2) by the "tinning test"' *Bulletin of the Geological Society of Malaysia* **7.6**, 17–26

Lutz, J, Pernicka, E 2009 'Spurenelementchemische und bleiisotopische Untersuchungen an frühbronzezeitlichen Metallfunden aus Mitteldeutschland' in G Borg, H Pöllmann, and K Friese (eds) *Hallesches Jahrbuch für Geowissenschaften* DMG-Tagung 2009 13-16 September in Halle 149

Lutz J, Pernicka E, 2013 'Prehistoric copper from the Eastern Alps' in R H Tykot (ed) Proceedings of the 38th International Symposium on Archaeometry – May 10th-14th 2010, Tampa, Florida *Open Journal of Archaeometry* 122-7

McNaughton, N J and Rosman, K J R, 1991 'Tin isotope fractionation in terrestrial cassiterites' *Geochimica et Cosmochimica Acta* **55.2**, 499–504

Merideth, C 1998 *An archaeological survey for ancient tin mines and smelting sites in Spain and Portugal Mid-central western Iberian geographical region 1990–1995* British Archaeological Reports International Series **714**. Oxford

Miles, H 1975 Barrows on the St Austell granite *Cornish Archaeology* **14**, 5–81

Penhallurick, R D 1986 *Tin in antiquity.* London:The Institute of Metals

Rodríguez Díaz, A, Pavón Soldevila, I, Duque Espino, D, Ponce de León Iglesias, M, Hunt Ortiz, M A, Merideth, C 2013 'La explotación tartésica de la casiterita entre los ríos Tajo y Guadiana: San Cristóbal de Logrosán (Cáceres)' *Trabajos de Prehistoria* **70/1**, London 95–113

Russell, W A, Papanastassiou, D A and Tombrello, T A 1978 'Ca isotope fractionation on the Earth and other solarsystem materials' *Geochim Cosmochim Acta* **42**, 1075–90

Smith, R 1996 'An analysis of the processes for tin smelting' *The Bulletin of the Peak District Mines Historical Society* **13.2**, 91–9

Timberlake, S, 1994 'An experimental tin smelt at Flag Fen' *Journal of the Historical Metallurgy Society* **28.2**, 121–8

Thomalsky, J, Bräutigam, B, Karaucak, M and Kraus, S 2013 'Early mining and metal production in Afghanistan: The first year of investigations' *Archäologische Mitteilungen aus Iran und Turan* **45**, 199–230

Tylecote, R F, Photos, E, Earl, B 1989 'The composition of tin slags from the south-west of England' *World Archaeology* **20**, 434–45

von Baer, K E 1876 'Von wo das Zinn zu der ganz alten Bronze gekommen sein mag?' *Archiv für Anthropologie* **9**

Wright, P A 1982 *Extractive metallurgy of tin.* Amsterdam: Elsevier

Yamazaki, E, Nakai, S, Yokoyama, T, Ishihara, S and Tang, H 2013 'Tin isotope analysis of cassiterites from Southeastern and Eastern Asia' *Geochemical Journal* **47.1**, 21–35

Zhang, Y, Liu, B, Su, Z, Chen, J, Li, G and Jiang, T 2015 'Volatilization behaviour of SnO_2 reduced under different CO–CO_2 atmospheres at 975 °C–1100 °C' *International Journal of Mineral Processing* **144**, 33–9

Zich, B. 1996 'Studien zur regionalen und chronischen Gliederung der nördlichen Aunjetitzer Kultur' *Vorgeschichtliche Forschungen* **20**. de Gruyter: Berlin

Leats and tin streamworks of the 16th century in the Krušné Hory/Erzgebirge, Czech Republic

*Petr Rojík**

Abstract
This paper contributes to knowledge of surface mining for cassiterite from the 16th to the 19th centuries in the western Krušné Hory/Erzgebirge region of the Bohemian Massif, Czech Republic. Although the area studied is one of the key tinworking regions of Europe, conditions for the preservation of mining heritage are difficult because of historical, demographic, linguistic, cultural and environmental damage since 1939. The primary greisen deposits are accompanied by extensive 'wet' streamworks and 'dry' placers in a hilly landscape. To extract and process the ore, a network of leats was in operation from the middle of the 16th century. The author has revealed a leat, 13km in length, near Rudné/Trinksaifen. Besides the results of archival, literary and field research he presents new GPS and LiDAR measurements and granulometrical and chemical analyses of the leat fill. The data allows interpretation of the age and use of the leat.

Introduction

The paper focuses on the Czech part of the Krušné Hory (Erzgebirge) in the Bohemian Massif, close to the border between the Czech Republic and Germany.

The German word 'Erzgebirge' and the former Czech name 'Rudohoří' originally meant 'Ore District' and now in modern language 'Ore Mountains'. The recent Czech name Krušné Hory is derived from 'krušit', which means to crush ore, and 'krušec', which means crushed ore.

The tin deposits of the Krušné Hory (Erzgebirge) originated in a Hercynian collisional mountain ridge. Long-term erosion and levelling revealed large parts of the granite plutons with associated tin deposits. During the Oligocene and Miocene, the flat relief of NW Czechia was compressed by the Alpine orogenesis, uplifted and subsequently broken down along the axis of uplifting. The resulting Ohře/Eger graben was filled with volcanic ejecta and sediments. The lignite seams represent the main energy source of the country. Opencast mining for lignite and processing of coal in power and heat stations caused considerable environmental damage. At the base of the graben buried kaolins are being extracted near Karlovy Vary spa. The kaolins, derived from Hercynian tin-bearing granites, belong to the best chinaclays in the word. The tectonic jointing of the lithosphere formed channels for the recent ascent of heat, gas (CO_2) and mineral springs (Karlovy Vary spa, Františkovy Lázně, Mariánské Lázně, Jáchymov).

Figure 1a & b The miners' village Chaloupky/Neuhaus: comparison of the 1920s (left photo by Rupert Fuchs) and now.

---

*Email: *rojik@suas.cz*

The Tinworking Landscape of Dartmoor in a European Context: Prehistory to 20th Century

The region of Krušné Hory/Erzgebirge along the Czech/German border has been densely settled by people who came from the territory of Germany and possibly also from the Netherlands and Cornwall/Devon in several colonisation waves during the 12th to 17th centuries. After WW2, in 1945-1946, more than 3 million German inhabitants were forced to leave their homes and were transferred to Germany. As a consequence, the mountain regions with hundreds of towns and villages, have remained abandoned (Fig. 1). Knowledge about mines and miners disappeared for decades and, in some cases, forever. The rest, comprising scattered local German manuscripts and literature, reports and memories, remained almost inaccessible to most of the 'rootless' inhabitants who came later from the central Czech region, Slovakia and other eastern countries. Some Czech researchers deal with the 're-revealing' of old, previously known and sometimes published material. To understand the geography and history of the region it is necessary to use both the new Czech names and the original German terms (e. g. the village Rudné/Trinksaifen).

The upland of the Czech Erzgebirge is covered with dense spruce forests, with wet meadows spread in the places of abandoned villages and with peat bogs where traces of tin streamworks, mines, mills and smelting houses disappeared. Many miners' villages were destroyed by the Czechoslovak army in the 1950s (Fig. 1). Some houses were rebuilt in the 1960s and 1970s as holiday family dwellings.

Today, in the Czech Krušné Hory/Erzgebirge there are two key activities:

- establishing natural protection zones also on previous mining sites, for their biodiversity
- tourist use, including building of facilities for accommodation, gastronomy, sports and adventure, sometimes in previous mining areas.

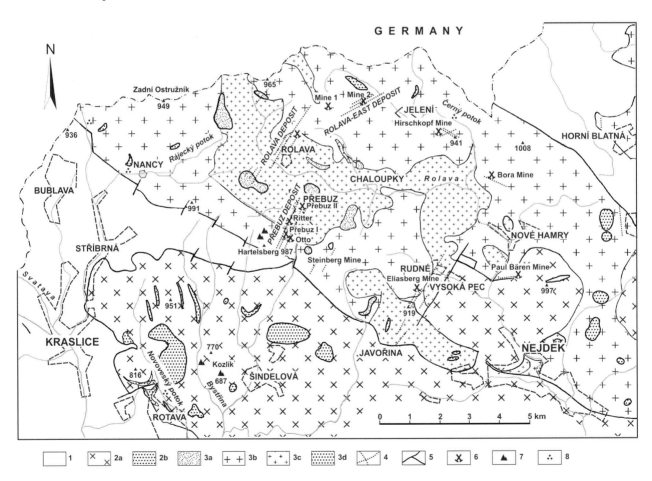

Figure 2 Geological map of the area studied with the deposits forming the 'tin circle'.
Key: 1 Crystalline schists; 2 Older intrusive complex: 2a Porphyritic 'medium-grained' biotite granites; 2b Fine-grained muscovite-biotite granites; 3 Younger intrusive complex: 3a Porphyritic fine-grained biotite granites with bimodal groundmass; 3b Porphyritic and porphyroblastic 'coarse-grained' biotite granites often with bimodal groundmass; 3c Porphyritic 'medium-grained' muscovite-biotite granites, in places with bimodal groundmass; 3d Fine-grained muscovite-biotite granites; 4 Greisens; 5 Faults; 6 Abandoned mines; 7 Outcrops (related to the text); 8 Alluvial blocks.

The Czech and German governments and EU policy encourage future mining. Although the European countries belong to the main consumers of tin, Europe (Portugal) shares only 0.02 % of world tin ore output (Reichl et al. 2016, 149). The Czech Republic has three industrial tin deposits (Cínovec, Horní Slavkov – Krásno, and Krásno) with total reserves of 163,809 tonnes of metallic tin, besides associated lithium, tungsten, copper etc.

Geological setting

The granite plutons in the Krušné Hory/Erzgebirge exhibit two main groups of rocks: the older complex, which is rather barren, c.332 - 323 Ma in age, and the younger tin-bearing complex, c.325 - 290 Ma in age. The younger granites, rhyolites, ignimbrites and eroded subvolcanic pipes contain increased concentrations of the lithophile elements F Li Rb Cs B Ga Ge Nb Ta TR P Sn U. This fact is reflected in the assemblage of the accessory minerals: topaz, monazite, apatite, tourmaline, cassiterite, and mica with increased contents of F Li Rb Cs Sn. Some granites exhibit specific textures (a granulometric bimodality of the groundmass and a rhythmical stratification) which indicate shallow, subvolcanic conditions for their origin.

The tin deposits in the area studied belong to the pluton of Karlovy Vary – Eibenstock (Western Krušné Hory/Erzgebirge). In the present erosion level the younger granites build an oval trace which is parallel to the NW-SE elongation of the pluton. The tin deposits are concentrated in an oval 'tin ring' in the youngest fractionated granites. The ring is marked by the historical tin deposits (clockwise): Přebuz, Rolava, Rolava – East, Jelení - Hirschkopf, Jelení - Bora, Nové Hamry (Paul-Bären Mine), Rudné/Javořina (Eliasberg mines), and Přebuz - Steinberg (Fig. 2).

The tin deposits are composed of packets of almost parallel greisen bands, which follow subvertical, short, vicarized joints penetrating all granitic rocks. (The terms greisen, granite and gneiss came from the German Erzgebirge. The etymology of greisen expresses its similarity to both granite and gneiss.) The greisens in the area studied are grouped into joint sets, up to 5km long and up to 300m broad, segmented into parallel packed zones. The greisens tend to converge at depth. The tin content decreases with depth. Workable ores reach to the depth of 120m (Přebuz and Rolava – East deposits). Laterally, toward the centre of the 'tin ring', the tin content in greisens decreases and the depth of the workable greisens gets gradually shallow. In the centre of the ring, in the vicinity of the former village Chaloupky/Neuhaus (Fig. 2), mining trials mark the occurrence of poor quartz greisens. There, the greisens may be more deeply eroded and/or the ore forming fluids escaped by the unsealed roof of the granite body, which is indicated by the abundance of the xenoliths of phyllites, skarns and tin-bearing garnets in the streamworks.

Figure 3 Greisen with intercalated vein of cassiterite and topaz, Přebuz mine.

Some greisens are sandwiched by veinlets of coarse-grained cassiterite, löllingite, topaz, hematite, microcline, and quartz (Fig. 3). The dykes continue to the minimum depth of 385m (drilling works in the Rolava – East deposit, Janečka et al. 1973, 36). Both greisens and dykes have been repeatedly tectonized and mineralized. These facts support a concept of tectonic predisposition of ore mineralization and of a deep source of tin related to a deep and late intrusion of the fractionated granite.

The area is densely jointed with young Cenozoic fractured zones filled with quartz and lenses of iron and manganese ores which became the basis for local glass works and ore mining trials.

Summary tin mining history

The area studied is intersected by several primary greisen deposits associated by streamworks and leats (from NW to SE).

The primary Rolava deposit runs in the direction SW-NE. Its shallow, extractable part was 3km long, while the greisen structure marked by stone debris, trials and streamworks reaches 5 km. The seasonal streamworks for cassiterite were first noticed in 1494. Several miners' dwellings adjoined the village

The Tinworking Landscape of Dartmoor in a European Context: Prehistory to 20th Century

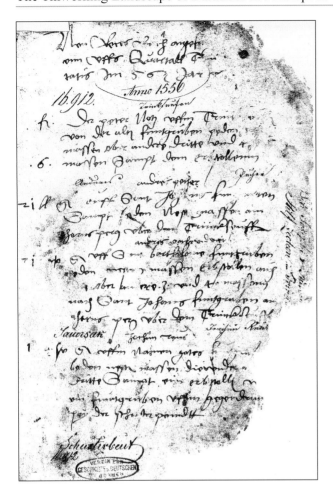

Figure 4 The title sheet of the Neudek Miners's Book from 1556 (State Central Archive in Prague).

of Sauersack in the Nejdek/Neudek county between 1602 and 1654. The historical peak of streamworking along the Rolava creek developed in the middle of the 16th century when the county was owned by the Schlick family (Fig. 4). The huge St. Antonie adit, 1470m long, completed in 1859, could not have been used then. The tin miners' village Rolava/Sauersack, which was inhabited by 1,060 people before WW2, has been abandoned since the 1950s. The most important mining sites of the Rolava deposit are: the streamworks in the Rolava valley (16th to 18th centuries), shafts and rows of pits (Kronesberg, 16th to 19th centuries), the openwork Grosse Rappenpinge, Kassel adit (16th century to 1793), St. Antonie adit (1811 – 1859) with associated heaps and with one removed mortarstone. The Rolava and neighbouring Rothenmuth deposits are intersected by the 6 km-long leat of Přebuz/Frühbuss.

The most important Přebuz tin deposit runs in the direction SW-NE. The whole ore structure is almost 5km long but its workable part is 2.5km in length, 300m broad and up to 120m deep. Hundreds of greisen bands, with an average concentration of 0.43 % Sn, contain crystals of cassiterite mostly 0.01 to 0.03 mm in size. The area of the Přebuz deposit was part of the former Jindřichovice/Heinrichsgrün county. The start of streamworking along the Rolava creek predates 1340. The first miners' settlement of Přebuz/Frühbuss (originally Friebes) is documented in 1543. Count Schlick gave the town rights to the settlement (1553) and established a mining office board (1556). After the Thirty Years War (1618 – 1648) Count Nostitz gave new rights to Přebuz/Frühbuss (1670, 1683, and 1698) and established a mining office board (1677). The mines were closed by 1815. Underground tin mining regenerated in 1933 and reached its historical maximum during WW2 up until 1945. Drilling and mining exploration in 1953 – 1958 did not lead to the reopening of mines. Now Přebuz (71 inhabitants) includes important mining features – church, frame houses, termination of the Přebuz leat (16th century) with the associated Karl graben, reservoir, stamping mill (site of), one removed mortarstone, large streamworks along the river Rolava/Rohlau (Figs 5a,b) and its tributaries (16th century to c.1727), adits (16th to 20th centuries), openworks and rows of pits (Hartelsberg, Schmidtenberg, Kronesberg, Steinberg, Rothenmuth, 16th to 20th centuries), the framework of the Main Shaft (1942 – 1958) and of the dressing plant for tin and arsenic ores (1942 - 1945).

The primary Přebuz – Steinberg deposit runs in the direction SW-NE. Its shallow workable part, known till now, was only 1km long and 300m broad. But the author has mapped the ore structure for a further 3km to the NE, to the former village Chaloupky/Neuhaus where it is marked by underground trials and by extensive 'dry' and 'wet' streamworks. The streamwork deposits are connected with the 13km long Rudné/Trinksaifen leat and several shorter branches of the leat that convey water to shafts, mills and infrastructure. The streamworks in the valleys of Rolava and tributaries (Kellerbach and Tanelbach) are among the most important mining remains, but are threatened by a planned water reservoir. Some streamworks have been known since 1560 in the Schlick period, in the Jindřichovice/Heinrichsgrün and Nejdek/Neudek areas, but may have existed already by 1340 in the previous Plick period. Streamworks are accompanied by many short leats, trial shafts and adits. Other openworks and lines of trenches and pits are known on the Steinberg hill near Přebuz, where a tin mill and smelting house are documented but not visible. The remnants of miners'

Figure 5a and 5b The main streamwork from the 16th century along the river of Rolava/Rohlau, NW of Neuhaus/Chaloupky, photos (top) and LiDAR map (below).

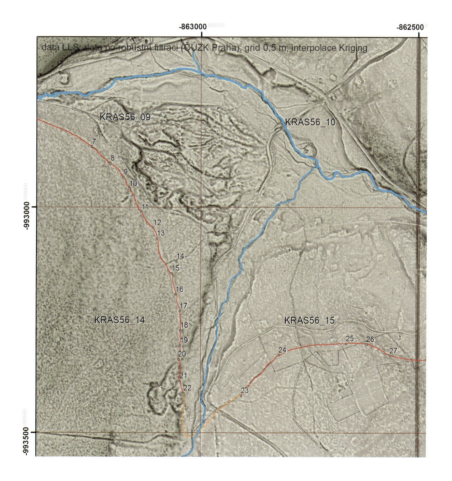

and blacksmiths' dwellings from c.1654 – 1950 are visible in the landscape of former Chaloupky/Neuhaus.

The primary Rudné deposit runs from SW to NE. It is 5km long, c.300m broad and reaches from the former Ahornswald/Javořina village over Rudné/Trinksaifen to the NW vicinity of Nové Hamry/Neuhammer. Historical documentation about tinworking in the vicinity of Trinksaifen (Saifen = streamworks), in the Neudek county owned by the Schlick family, dates from 1556 (Anon 1556 – 1651, Fig. 4). Many surface and shallow underground mines on the hills Eliasberg, Ahornsberg, Zechengrund and Rabesberg, which have been working from the 16th century to 1813, follow outcrops of the greisen zones. The Rudné deposit is twice intersected by the 13km-long Rudné/Trinksaifen leat. Prominent tinworking evidence includes the Rudné/Trinksaifen leat, the rows of pits, adits, sunken areas and short leats along the whole ore structure.

Figure 6a and 6b The Rudné / Trinksaifen leat.

The leats and streamworks of Rudné/Trinksaifen

In the area described, scores of leats were created across the cassiterite-bearing areas in order to bring water energy to the primary and secondary (residual, deluvial and alluvial) deposits. The most important and longest leat was in the vicinity of the Rudné/Trinksaifen miners' village (ruda = ore, Saifen = streamwork). The leat was fed from the river Rolava/ Rohlau, NE of Přebuz/Frühbuss, 842m above sea-level (Fig. 6). The leat meets the large alluvial streamworks and deluvial placers in the Rolava/Rohlau and Kellerbach valleys (Fig. 5a,b). The leat continues through the former Chaloupky/Neuhaus village and a large forested area around the hills Chaloupecký vrch/Neuhauser Berg) and Vysoký vrch/Hochberg). It supplied tin streamworks along the Kellerbach creek (tributary of Rolava/Rohlau) and also the 'dry' works on the slopes of the Chaloupecký vrch/Neuhauser Berg (top 900 m), Vysoký vrch/Hochberg (883 m), Havran/Rabesberg (841 m) and Bedřichův vrch/Pritzenberg or Fritzenberg (828 m) hills. Then the leat makes a huge arc around Rudné/Trinksaifen and terminates in the SW part of the village, on the outcrop of the Rudné tin deposit. At the miners' settlement called Pochlowitz (pochen, which means to stamp ore) or Zechengrund (Zeche, which means a mine), a stamping mill near the houses Nr. 169 and 214 may have been working (Dittrich 1928, 32-33), but no mortarstones, sand or other traces of dressing have been found around the rebuilt houses. The leat may also have supplied 'dry' works and mine waterwheels. Water ran from mining operations to the little Rudenský/Trinksaifen creek, where it supported extensive tin streamworks (Anon c. 1830), and finally to the Rolava/Rohlau river north of the town Nejdek.

On the east slope of the Vysoký vrch/Hochberg, the leat branches into two channels (Fig. 6), which are interrupted by agricultural and forestry activities. Possibly, the lower branch may have supplied water to the streamworks on the Bedřichův vrch/Pritzenberg greisen outcrops. Similarly, a short parallel ditch conveyed water to the deluvial part of the main streamworks near Chaloupky/Neuhaus (Fig. 5, close to the GPS point 11).

The presence of tin streamworks high above the river and creeks would not be explicable without the existence of the leat. The tinworks on the hills in Rudné/Trinksaifen, Havran/Rabesberg and Bedřichův vrch/Pritzenberg were first mentioned in

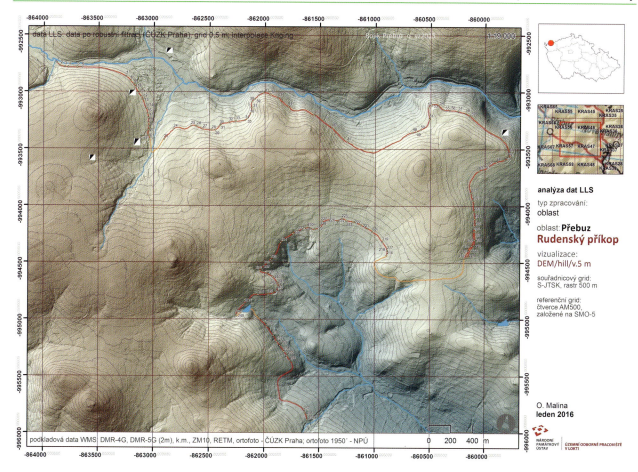

*Figure 7 Combination of the GPS and LiDAR maps, route of the Rudné / Trinksaifen leat.
Red line = measured intervals, orange line = interpolated intervals.*

a miners' book (Anon 1556 – 1651). Later, the leat was drawn on a schematic map (Anon c.1830). The watercourse, as shown, roughly corresponds to the newly measured course of the leat. Surprisingly, the dominant Rolava/Rohlau creek is not shown on the map in the gap below the start of the leat. Probably all the water was used for the leat. Although mining activity in Rudné/Trinksaifen finished by 1813, the leat was used until the end of the 19th century as a water source for dwellings, corn mills and agriculture in Rudné/Trinksaifen (Dittrich 1928, 32-33). Since then the leat has remained dry, but disturbed many times by forestry and agricultural activities during recent decades.

In spite of some general knowledge of the existence of the leat, even the former German inhabitants of the 19th and 20th centuries knew nothing of its age and original use (Dittrich 1928, 32-33). A settler from Chaloupky/Neuhaus village ended his recollections with a suggestive question: 'Who could have created this ditch, and why?' (Ullmann 1970, 3).

The course of the leat was revealed and its purpose explained recently (Rojík 2000, 122-124).

The leat was measured with precision GPS by Mr. Martin Procházka in 2014. The area was processed from LiDAR measurements by Mr. Ondřej Malina (Czech National Heritage Survey in Loket) in 2016. For the compilation of both measurements see Fig. 7.

The sediments of the leat underwent X-ray diffraction analyses (Mr. Michal Řehoř, VÚHU Institute, Most), granulometric analyses (Mr. Pavel Jedlička, KMK Krásno – see Fig. 8) and chemical analyses for tin and iron (Ms. Michaela Nováková, SU Sokolov). The latter confirm increased content of tin and iron in the relatively well-sorted sands.

On the other hand, searching for dendrological samples, and remnants of stamping, milling and smelting, were not successful. In the vicinity of the leat, iron slags from the 19th century and copper slags from the 18th century were found and analysed for their chemistry and isotopic (C14) age, in the laboratories of SU in Sokolov, in the Czech Academy of Sciences in Prague and in the isotopic laboratory in Debrecen (Hungary). The results will be evaluated for other interesting connections. All the analyses, measurements, mapping and archive researches

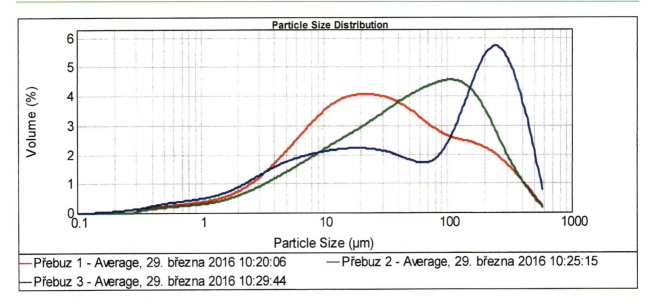

Figure 8 Granulometry of loams in different parts of the leat fill.

Locality	Tin content (method AAS, per cent)	Iron content (method AAS, unit per cent)
Start of the leat, NE of Přebuz / Frühbuss, red sandy loam	0.13	2.35
Leat fill at Chaloupky / Neuhaus, fine sand	0.24	1.86
Leat fill NE of Rudné / Trinksaifen, sandy loam	0.004	1.11
Greisen, Přebuz – Otto mine	1.41	2.60
Rich dyke, Přebuz – Otto mine	21.70	2.95

Table 1 Chemical analyses of the leat fill and of the primary ores.

were obtained as a result of the private activity of the author.

The total length of the Rudné/Trinksaifen leat amounts to c.13,080 m. Of this, the preserved and measured parts comprise 11,400m and the interpolated parts c.1,680 m. The difference in altitude between the start and supposed termination of the leat is 70 m.

The Rudné/Trinksaifen leat was probable built in the mid-16th century. This extremely long leat essentially changed the hydrological regime in the landscape by transferring water from one drainage area to another. The leat has influenced the water supply of streamworks, mines and works along the river of Rolava/Rohlau for centuries. The leat intersects two former administrative areas – that of Jindřichovice/Heinrichsgrün in the NW and that of Nejdek/Neudek in the southeast. This fact presumes good cooperation between both counties instead of conflict. The only time when both areas were owned by a single family (Schlick) was in the period between 1446 and 1602. The Schlick family greatly encouraged mining everywhere in the areas owned by them. Other well dated leats in the broad region originated in the 1540s and 1550s. The first evidence of tin streamworks on the Rabesberg and Pritzenberg hills above Rudné/ Trinksaifen is dated to the intensive mining phase that began in 1556 (Anon 1556 - 1651). The idea of cooperation between both areas is supported by the common register of claims in Neudek/Nejdek in 1557 – 1558 (Rojík 2000, 53).

The Rudné/Trinksaifen leat was operating at least from 1556 - 1580 in order to supply 'wet' tin streamworks, 'dry' eluvial and deluvial works, besides stamping mills along the whole course of the leat, especially along the creeks Rolava/Rohlau, Kellerbach and Rudenský potok/Trinksaifener Bach, on the slopes of the hills Vysoký vrch/Hohenberg, Havran/Rabesberg and Bedřichův vrch/Pritzenberg and in the Rudné/Trinksaifen tin deposit, where surface and underground mining and ore mills exist. Later, the existence of a running leat was noticed in the 19th century in the post-mining period. By then the leat was supplying corn mills, various works and agriculture.

Results

The paper supplements knowledge about surface mining for cassiterite in the Czech part of the Krušné Hory/Erzgebirge. To extract and process the primary deposits, and especially the secondary alluvial ('wet' streamworks) and eluvial and deluvial deposits ('dry' placers), a network of leats was operated.

A very long leat (13 km) near the municipality Rudné/Trinksaifen was recently revealed by the author. The archive and literature searches indicate that the leat was constructed in the middle of the 16th century (in 1556 or earlier). The purpose and use of the leat was to supply water energy to the primary and secondary 'wet' and 'dry' tin deposits in the water-deficient hilly area. Surface mining in the 16th century revealed that the tin deposits Rudné, Přebuz and Přebuz-Steinberg intersected by the leat had a larger extent than supposed. The leat was recorded in the field using precision GPS and LiDAR measurements. Its fill was characterized through granulometrical and chemical analyses.

Acknowledgements

I am very thankful to Dr Tom Greeves and DTRG members who encouraged me to undertake this work and who refined the text. I thank very much Ing. Martin Procházka for the GPS measurement, to Dr Ondřej Malina for the processing of the LiDAR maps, to Ing. Michaela Nováková and Ing. Pavel Jedlička for the laboratory analyses.

Bibliography

Anon 1556 – 1651 *A New Miner's Book etc.* – Manuscript, State Central Archive Prague, section Upper Miner's Authority Jáchymov, Miner's Authority Nejdek, sign. 600a (in German)

Anon *c.*1830 *Map of the surroundings of the miner's town Fribus etc.* - Map 1:38210, manuscript, Archive Czech Geol. Survey Prague, sign. P114 (in German)

Dittrich, J 1928 *Municipality's Chronicle of Trinksaifen.* – Manuscript, State Regional Archive in Karlovy Vary, section Collection of Municipalities's Chronicles, Archive of the Municipality Rudné (in German)

Janečka J et al. 1973 *Final report on the geological exploration of Sn-W deposits of the Bohemian Massif.* – Czech Geol. Survey Prague, sign. P 116.1973 (in Czech)

Reichl, C, Schatz, M and Zsak, G 2016 *World Mining Data 2016.* – Fed. Ministry of Sci., Research and Economy, Vienna, 248

Rojík, P 2000 *History of the tin mining in western Krušné Hory.* – Sokolov, 232 pp. (in Czech)

Rojík, P 2005 'Tin deposits Přebuz and Rolava in the Krušné hory/Erzgebirge Mts. (Czech Republic): classic localities, new challenges, *Journ. Czech Geol. Soc.* **50**, 3-4, 157-165, Prague

Ullmann, E 1970 'Neuhaus – origin and destruction of a village' *Neudeker Heimatbrief* **22.1**, 2–3. Hersbruck (in German)

National Cultural Monument Jeronym (Hieronymus) Mine, near Rovna, Czech Republic

Michael Rund*

Abstract

The Jeronym (German Hieronymus, English Jerome) Tin Mine provides unique evidence of the mining culture and skills of our ancestors. The mine is located to the southwest of the former town of Čistá/Lauterbach (Czech Republic) and was already registered by the mining authority in 1548. In 1551, King Ferdinand I granted mining rights to Čistá and the privileges of a royal town, which were acknowledged and expanded by subsequent rulers. The town had its own tin scale, tin smeltery and unlimited logging rights in the royal forests. At the start of the 17th century, the mines were not profitable in spite of the rapid development of mining, and were sustained for the sole purpose of retaining the mining town status of Čistá. During the course of its history, the Jeronym Mine produced approximately 500– 700 tonnes of tin. Although the mine was never as rich and renowned as other workings in the area, much of it has survived in its original form. Imposing underground chambers from the 16th century are located in the central part of the mine. In many places, the walls and ceilings are blackened by soot, which accumulated from fires associated with fire setting, and the walls are grooved by the hammers and picks of past miners. In 2008, the Jeronym mine was declared a national cultural monument. From autumn 2013 part of the mine (SDD1-OMW 1[1]) was opened to the public, followed in 2014-15 by the construction of an entrance and car park.

Description

The mine complex consists of several parts, but before 1982 the only known section was referred to as ODD[2]. In this section, corridors and two chambers of the 16th century, as well as later periods, are located. The last drivings were completed in this location during World War 11.

In 1982 Mr. František Baroch discovered a hitherto unknown part of the Jeronym Mine, to be later referred to as SDD1 (Fig. 1). This part of the mine was abandoned in the 1700s century and there are no traces of subsequent mining activity within it. In the deepest part of SDD1, called Chamber S, a date inscription for the year 1624 was found carved in the rock, which corresponds to the likely beginnings of mining in this part of the mine, approximately 100-150 years earlier.

In May 2014, a new and very interesting underground space complex, which was previously inaccessible, was discovered (SDD2-OMW2) (Fig. 1). It comprises large-scale chambers, connected by manually driven corridors with a small-profile, where for hundreds of years no one has entered . They may date from the 16th to the 17th century.

The newly discovered spaces are dominated by two chambers, oriented with their longer proportions along the slope of its ore position (about 35 °). The average height of these chambers is between 3-4m with a width of 5-9m. The length of the larger chamber reaches 45m along the bow of the deposit (37m horizontally). The elevation between the highest and the lowest discovered place is about 30m. The area is relatively well preserved; roughly half of the area is clear, the other half is filled with the rubble from rockfalls and sediments emanating from the space above, or completely embedded spaces. In several places some water is retained. The total length of the tunnels in this newly discovered area is nearly 350m. It is likely that further, similar discoveries will be made as exploration continues.

This space is interesting in several respects. Compared with other parts of the mine, evidence of mining 'along the vein' is more perceivable. In one of the chambers a small stone dam survives, built by 'old men', probably in the 16th century, and it is still partly functional. Well-preserved traces of pockets

---

* Sokolov Museum, Czech Republic. Email: *sokorund@gmail.com*

The Tinworking Landscape of Dartmoor in a European Context: Prehistory to 20th Century

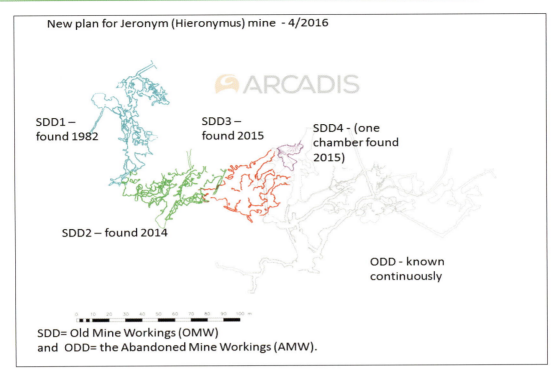

Figure 1 New plan of Jeronym Mine –April 2016, showing newly discovered (2014 -15) chambers (Sokolov Museum Archive).

Figure 2a (top left) Montan Archaeologist Ondrej Malina completing a field sheet underground (M. Rund); b (top right) Chamber K1 in ODD area (I. Klatečka); c (bottom left) penultimate Chamber in SDD2 area (I. Klatečka); d (bottom right) cut sockets for mine timbers in SDD2 area (Sokolov Museum Archive).

used to store various pieces of wood and miners' lamps are amply represented in these spaces (Fig. 2d). The remains of old timbering, a few fragments of mining picks and timber pipes for pumping water were also discovered. Although an attempt was made to determine the age of wood from the surviving pieces using dendrochronology, unfortunately this was unsuccessful, so an accurate date for these artefacts is not yet available.

The 'new' areas are also very interesting in terms of their colour. They are dominated by red (probably trivalent iron compounds released by oxidation during the heating and cooling process). Multiple yellow traces are also present.

When a well known geologist, Mr Václav Cílek, visited the mine, we were able to have a closer look at evidence for the work of the 'old men' who had worked the mine. Mr Cílek was able to identify traces made with hammers and picks left in one of the chambers by at least three generations of miners. Part of SDD2 was measured and a detailed map was created by Martin Šefrna and Petr Olišar from the Arcadis Company. A 3D laser scan of the largest chamber was also carried out, and archaeological and historical research were conducted. Among the participants of the archaeological surveys were Ondřej Malina, Filip Prekop, and Jakub Chaloupka from the NPU (National Heritage Board), Loket. The survey method is, at least in the Czech context, completely new and is still being improved. Here we present the method outline. Its aim is to create an inventory of important spaces, surfaces, artefacts and details.

The two objectives of the mapping are:
1) to assess the monumental and historical values of all the parts of the mine.
2) To contribute to the technological and chronological interpretation of the mine.

The method is based on a book of maps, of which:
- the field sheets are printed in monochrome, with a pre-defined grid system, overlaps, and a navigation window
- the grid on each sheet represents a square of 10m, based on the values of a S-JTSK coordinate system[3], established from geo-referenced auxiliary survey points. The grid covers the whole of the known area of SDD and ODD and includes surface artefacts
- the definition and annotation of the evaluated area is then performed in the field, when the walls are outlined, with emphasis on every sheet of the levels (height). Two sets of map sheets are therefore necessary
- four colours are used to signify different elements of each chamber's working methods
- the legend is applied with thematic variation (e. g. right and left hatching, etc.) and some details are drawn onto thematic layers. Generally, the denser the hatch and the thicker the lines are, the more significant a surface or wall is
- the basis of the mapping is to define the evaluated area (sub-chambers), this layer is then used as a basis when exporting all thematic layers
- the spaces are divided according to interpretive (height) levels

Survey is undertaken using four thematic layers, which are mapped separately: walls, ceiling, footwall, other details (including constructions). The data is evaluated later during the interpretation (synthesis) phase by combining the findings in the various thematic layers.

In conjunction with the programme of work partly financed by the Karlovy Vary Region, Georgius Agricola Foundation, the Slavkov Forest Region, and the Ministry of Industry and Trade of the Czech Republic, it was possible to open and access the secured part of the mine to the public in the autumn of 2013. This section of the mine dates at least from the 16th century.

In 2014 and 2015 the mine was open from May to mid-October. Also, in 2014-15 the construction of the operations building (so-called 'background') of the Jeronym Mine took place. The construction was financed from the Regional Operational Programme of the Northwest region and was supported by the European Regional Development Fund. Co-financing was ensured by the Karlovy Vary Region. The construction cost 13.8 million CZK in total, and was completed in April 2015.

Also in 2015, new discoveries of additional space - space SDD3 (OMW3) - old mine workings and the three separate chambers SDD4 (OMW4) were made. Their location is marked on the attached plan. The area is currently (May 2016) being surveyed and plans will be prepared; archaeological research is also being undertaken. The spaces are unique with a well-preserved floor and shards found here have been dated to the 15th and 16th centuries. Thanks to the discovery of the 'new' areas, which have increased the space preserved in its original 15th-17th century

The Tinworking Landscape of Dartmoor in a European Context: Prehistory to 20th Century

Figure 3 Card from year 2010 (Arcadis Company -Sokolov Museum Archive).

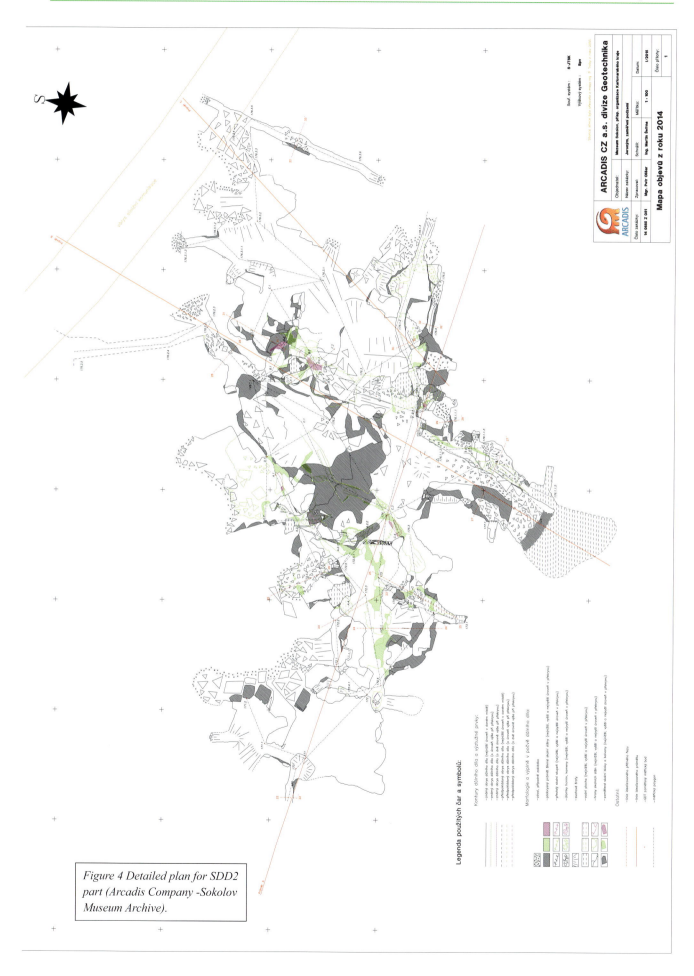

Figure 4 Detailed plan for SDD2 part (Arcadis Company -Sokolov Museum Archive).

The Tinworking Landscape of Dartmoor in a European Context: Prehistory to 20th Century

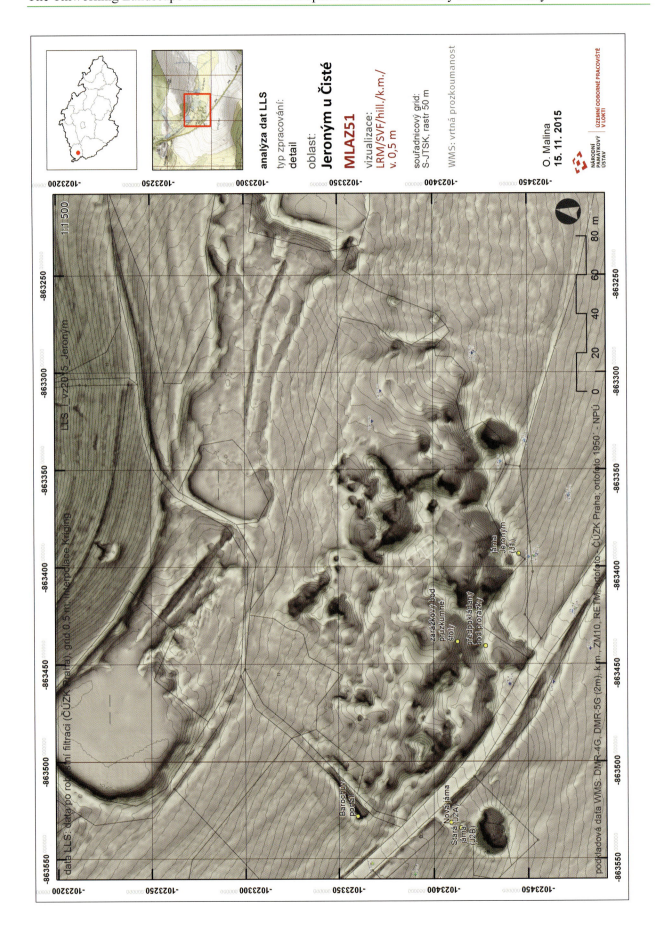

Figure 6 An iron pick found in the mine (Sokolov Museum Archive).

Figure 7 Wooden pipe found in Chamber R – SDD1 area (Sokolov Museum Archive).

form threefold, the Sokolov Museum can circulate information about these discoveries to experts on an international level, and the future goal would be eventually to enlist the mine to the UNESCO World Heritage List.

The museum also wishes to cooperate with CHKO Slavkovský les (nature conservation area), to promote endangered bats through regular events called Bat Nights. The Jerome Mine area is not only an important wintering area for the bats but also a so-called bats swarming area. In co-operation with the National Heritage Board, a branch of Loket, a company called Terra Incognita and the Georgius Agricola Foundation, as well as the Slavkov Forest Region, the museum wants to undertake further research. This will include mapping and salvage operations of the relics found in a former town called Čistá, which was destroyed in the late 1940s during several military exercises. The entire area surrounding the Jeronym Mine including the placer-mining sites, mining ponds and other remains, is also being mapped using modern survey methods, such as (LiDAR).

Notes

1. OMW – Old Mine Workings.
2. ODD - a Czech abbreviation for abandoned mine workings.
3. S-JTSK is the national mapping coordinate system used in the Czech Republic, equivalent to the Ordnance Survey National Grid in the UK.

Figure 5 (opposite) Example of LiDAR image showing surface evidence of mineral extraction (NPU Loket – O. Malina).

Further reading

Agricola, G 1556 *De re metallica libri XII*. - Basilae

Beran, P, Jangl, L, Majer, J, Suček, P, Otfried, W 1995 *1000 let hornictví cínu ve Slavkovském lese*. Okresní muzeum Sokolov.

Beran, P 1999 *Nerosty cíno-wolframových ložisek Slavkovského lesa.* - (*Minerals in the tin-tungsten deposits of the Slavkovský les area.*) Okresní muzeum a knihovna Sokolov

Beran, P 2000 *Cín roku 2000 v regionu střední Evropy (Tin in the year 2000 in the Central European Region)*. (minulost, současnost, budoucnost) : sborník příspěvků mezinárodní konference, Sokolov 4-8. Září. Okresní muzeum a knihovna Sokolov

Beran, P. 2001 *Královské horní město Horní Slavkov (Horní Slavkov and its history of Royal Mining Town)*. Město Horní Slavkov ve spolupráci s Okresním muzeem Sokolov.

Cílek, V, Korba, M and Majer, M 2015 *Podzemní Čechy*.

Kuna, M, Danielisová, A 2015 *Archeologický atlas Čech*.

Prokop,V and Smola, L 2014 *Sokolovsko,Umění, památky a umělci do roku 194*.

Journal, newsletter and magazine articles

Beran, P and Sejkora, J 2006 'The Krásno Sn-W ore district near Horní Slavkov: Mining history, geological and mineralogical characteristics' *Journal of the Czech Geological Society* **51**, 3-42.

Janečka, J, Just, J, Kušnír, I 1966 Zpráva o výzkumu a výpočet zásob Sn-rud na ložisku Jeroným v Čisté ve Slavkovském lese (stav ke dni 1.7.1966). Loket: MS, Ústřední ústav geologický Praha, 86pp.

Malina, O 2016 Jeronym Mine SDD2 Pasport. Unpublished

Tomíček, R 2010 Důl Jeroným – Čistá. (Hieronymus Zeche - Lauterbach.) Unpublished, 59pp, 150 figs.

Žůrek, P, Kořínek, R, Kaláb, Z, Hrubešová, E, Knejzlík, J, Daněk, T, Kukutsch, R, Michalčík, P, Lednická, M a Rambouský, Z 2008 *Historický Důl Jeroným v Čisté*. Monografie, VŠB – Technická univerzita Ostrava a Ústav geoniky AVČR, v.v.i. Ostrava, ISBN 978-80-248-1757-6, 82 stran

Internet References

Arnika 2/2014 New Finds in Jeroným Mine
http://www.casopis-arnika.cz/cisla/arnika_14_2/index.html [accessed 15-Jun-2016]

Sokolovsko 2/2015 New Finds in Jeroným mine
http://mas-sokolovsko.eu/wp-content/uploads/2016/01/Sokolovsko-2015-2/#1 [accessed 15-Jun-2016]

Tunel 2012
http://www.ita-aites.cz/files/tunel/2012/1/tunel_1_12-10.pdf [accessed 15-Jun-2016]

Archeologický atlas Čech (Archeological Atlas of Bohemia)
http://www.archeologickyatlas.cz/en/lokace/cista_so_dul_jeronym [accessed 15-Jun-2016]

Jeroným Mine, Czech Republic — Contribution to the Geomechanical Stability Assessment
http://agp2.igf.edu.pl/agp/files/M-29/Kalab_et_al.pdf [accessed 15-Jun-2016]

Initial Recording of the Radon Activity Concentration in Jeroným Mine
http://www.caag.cz/egrse/2013-1/04_kalab.pdf [accessed 15-Jun-2016]

Jeronym Mine, hydrogeology
http://slon.diamo.cz/hpvt/2012/Sekce%20V/V%2016.pdf [accessed 15-Jun-2016]

The Jeroným Mine in Čistá: Past, Present and the Future
http://www.uur.cz/images/5-publikacni-cinnost-a-knihovna/casopis/2010/2010-02/16_dul.pdf [accessed 15-Jun-2016]

Opening of the medieval Jeroným Mine in the Czech Republic to the public
http://actamont.tuke.sk/pdf/2003/n2-3/9zurek.pdf [accessed 15-Jun-2016]

Introduction of Jeroným Mine in geophysical journal named EGRSE
http://docplayer.cz/8533023-Prof-rndr-zdenek-kalab-csc-ing-marketa-lednicka-ph-d-t-11-predstaveni-dolu-jeronym-v-geofyzikalnim-casopise-egrse.html [accessed 15-Jun-2016]

Pinge in Jeronym area
http://media.archeologicky-atlas.cz.s3.amazonaws.com/production/source/documents/%C4%8Cist%C3%A1%20u%20Rovn%C3%A9/Kukutsch_Stolarik_2008.pdf [accessed 15-Jun-2016]

History of Jeronym mine
http://docplayer.cz/15026207-Ing-tomicek-rudolf-t-10-nastin-historickeho-vyvoje-dul-jeronym-v-ciste.html [accessed 15-Jun-2016]

Archaeology in Town Lauterbach near Jeronym Mine
https://www.academia.edu/23086280/Archeologick%C3%A9_vyhodnocen%C3%AD_elikt%C5%AF_intravil%C3%A1nu_st%C5%99edov%C4%9Bk%C3%A9ho_hornick%C3%A9ho_m%C4%9Bsta_Lauterbach_%C4%8Cist%C3%A1[accessed 15-Jun-2016]

Northwestern Iberian Tin Mining from Bronze Age to Modern Times: an overview

Beatriz Comendador Rey[1]*, Emmanuelle Meunier[2], Elin Figueiredo[3], Aaron Lackinger[1], João Fonte[4], Cristina Fernández Fernández[1], Alexandre Lima[5], José Mirão[6], Rui J.C. Silva[3]

Abstract

The northwestern Iberian Peninsula has been well known for its mineral wealth since classical times, including for gold and for tin. In fact, the Iberian tin belt is the largest in western Europe (covering an area of c.200,000 km²), containing tin deposits that were accessible from ancient times. Nevertheless, few archaeological studies have been dedicated to ancient tin mining in the region, unlike gold mining, for which major mining complexes are known from Roman times (e.g. Las Médulas, N Spain, and Três Minas, N Portugal). In this paper, evidence for tin mining in different periods, from the Bronze Age to modern times, is discussed, based on selected case-studies, using various approaches developed for the study of ancient and modern tin mining, by members of the present Iberian Tin Research Group. An introduction to the geographical and geological contexts of Iberian tin, and the history of investigation on Iberian tin mining, is included.

1 Introduction

In his chapter dedicated to Iberia, Roger Penhallurick (1986, 95-103) stated that the Iberian tin belt is large and three times the length of the Cornish-Devonian field. In fact, the Iberian tin belt is not just much larger than the Cornish-Devonian field, it is the largest extension with tin ores available in Western Europe. Nevertheless, its importance has not been widely debated in archaeological historiography, resulting in some periods of strong affirmation, and others of almost total invisibility, depending on historical context at particular times, or on specific interests of individual researchers.

Unlike the intensive and detailed studies on Roman gold mining and Pre-Roman copper mining that have taken place, tin mining has not received a similar level of research commitment, particularly in Iberia. This runs counter to the role that tin is known to have played in ancient times: knowing that tin ores are not evenly distributed in the European territory, tin must have had far-reaching exchange routes needed for bronze fabrication, particularly to Eastern Mediterranean areas where tin sources lack.

Reasons often given for the lack of research in ancient tin mining are that early tinworks supposedly exploited mainly alluvial deposits. This was a system of mining that is believed to have left very few remains, if any, whereby more recent mining works (as for wolfram and tin in the 20th century) destroyed earlier evidence, particularly in the case of mining in primary deposits. An additional reason for the low profile of tin mining in archaeological literature might be that field evidence of many secondary placer mining works have, traditionally, been attributed to gold, but could have also been for tin. In fact, since tin and gold are present in the very same districts, and gold mining has been far more appealing to researchers, few proposals as to the possibility of tin

---

[1] Grupo de Estudos de Arqueoloxía, Antigüidade e Territorio (GEAAT), Universidade de Vigo, Spain

[2] Laboratoire TRACES (CNRS), University of Toulouse Jean Jaurès, France

[3] Centro de Investigação em Materiais (CENIMAT/I3N), Faculdade de Ciências e Tecnologia, Universidade NOVA de Lisboa, Portugal

[4] Institute of Heritage Sciences (Incipit), Spanish National Research Council (CSIC), Santiago de Compostela, Spain

[5] Instituto de Ciências da Terra (ICT, Pólo da UP), Departamento de Geociências, Ambiente e Ordenamento do Território, Faculdade de Ciências, Universidade do Porto, Portugal

[6] Laboratório HERCULES, Universidade de Évora, Portugal

*Corresponding author. Email address: *beacomendador@uvigo.es*

The Tinworking Landscape of Dartmoor in a European Context: Prehistory to 20th Century

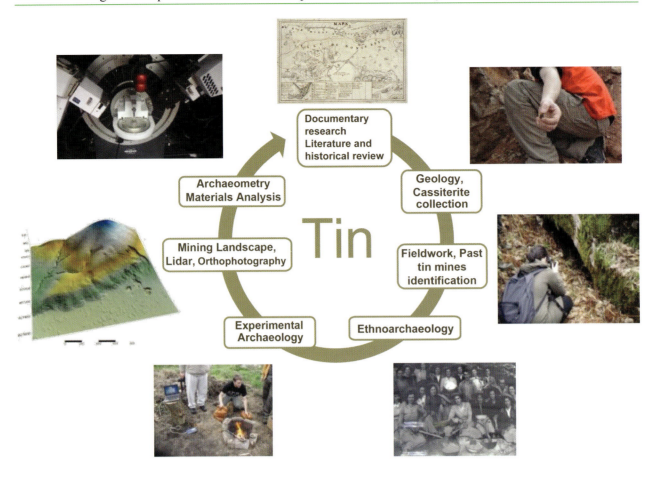

Figure 1 Multidisciplinary approaches to ancient tin research.

mining are presented in archaeological discussions.

Thus, the supposedly small impact of ancient tin mining on the landscape might be due to a lack of detailed/focused investigations, or a poor understanding as to the nature of the Iberian tin resources itself. In truth, tin ores are distributed throughout a large area of Iberia; they are easily available at surface and lower depths, and can be mined by very simple techniques. Based on numerous descriptions by previous visitors to the tin works in Iberia, Penhallurick (1986, 97, 100) stated that 'enough has been said to indicate that alluvial tin and outcropping lodes are abundant … it is clear that the tin is common at or very close to the surface … differing from the alluvials of Cornwall'. This particular morphology of Iberian tin deposits could have generated rather superficial exploitation, easily erased in the landscape. Clearly, a combination of factors can contribute to the present scarce knowledge of the extent, intensity, and chronology of tin mining in Iberia.

Despite the lack of focused studies, there are some positive factors showing the potential for ancient Iberian tin mining. The Iberian tin belt, along its large extent, has a high density of mineralization available, following criteria suited for exploitation in the prehistoric and Roman periods, which are, according to O'Brien (2015, 13-15) outcropping deposits (which can include placers, as they are visible from the surface) with a grade high enough to enable ore recovery with manual or simple mechanical processes. Also, the existence of numerous settlements with significant evidence of metallurgical activity during the Bronze Age and Iron Age, in areas rich in tin, suggests that deposits in those areas were exploited since these early periods. Examples are the *Baiões/Santa Luzia* cultural group (Late Bronze Age, Central Portugal), where bronze metallurgical remains have been recorded (Senna Martínez 2011, 2013) some of which are presented in more detail below. Also, the Iron Age hillforts (called *castros*) in Northern Portugal and Galicia (NW Spain), from which the case-study of Carvalhelhos will also be detailed below. In addition, some classical sources (amongst others: Pliny the Elder *Naturalis Historia* XXXIV) mention the *Lusitania* and *Gallaecia* regions as the origin of tin for the Mediterranean areas, and both regions correspond to the Iberian tin belt area.

However, the richness of Iberia in tin seems to have been totally forgotten, at least among the rest of Europe, during the medieval period. In fact, Iberian tin-rich mining provinces only become 'known' again in international circles by the end of the 17th and 18th century, mostly with the tin mines in the mining province of *Monterrei* (Ourense, Spain) (Meijide Pardo 1963). Later, from the beginning until the mid-20th century, numerous mines were opened for wolfram and/or tin along the extension of the Iberian tin belt, resulting today in numerous abandoned mining complexes. From these latest mining works, the rush for tungsten during the two world wars has been the most attractive and investigated aspect, leaving the tin mining almost invisible in the more recent historiography.

Aware of the great lack of archaeographic records on ancient tin mining, The Early Tin Iberian Group was formed in 2010 as a synergy between researchers from several institutions in Spain, Portugal and France, sharing an interest for tin in antiquity. Being an interdisciplinary group it aims to broaden the study of ancient tin in North West Iberia in a variety of directions (Fig. 1), such as documentary research, archaeometallurgical analysis and field survey to recognise ancient mining works and sample cassiterite, relying on the expertise of each researcher and institution. The group also integrates ethnological data to generate interpretative models and perform experiments with the aim of producing tin and bronze from Iberian ores. Besides the present authors, other researchers also contribute to focused studies; some of them have already been published, while others are in different stages of development.

In this paper, will be presented an introduction to the geographic and geological contexts of tin in the Iberian Peninsula, as well as a review of past archaeological investigation on tin mining since the 18th century. Some selected case-studies related to Iberian tin mining will be presented and a discussion of some investigation approaches. Some of the case-studies are extracted from past published works by other authors, while others are part of on-going works by the present authors.

2 Geographical and geological contexts

The Iberian Peninsula is a large territory with almost 600,000 km², administratively divided between two countries, Spain and Portugal. The peninsula has a long coastline, bordered on the southeast and east by the Mediterranean Sea, and on the north, west and southwest by the Atlantic Ocean. The peninsula is separated from the rest of continental Europe by the Pyrenees Mountains, to the northeast.

The Iberian territory is predominantly formed by plateaus at the centre and in southwestern areas, with major mountain systems in the northwestern, northern and southeastern areas. The southern extremity is separated from the African coast by less than 20 km at the Strait of Gibraltar, known in antiquity as 'Pillars of Hercules'. This strait also separates the Mediterranean Sea from the Atlantic Ocean.

Environmentally, the Peninsula can be divided into two regions, one at the north and northwest with Atlantic climate influences and an Arctic flora, and another at the south and southeast with Mediterranean climate influence and a Mediterranean flora (Sánchez Goñi et al. 2002).

The Iberian coast has been inundated over time, since the Last Glacial Maximum (LGM) to *c*.3,500 years BP when the present sea level was reached. Prehistoric and historical sea level variations are little known, but it appears that coastline shaping was controlled mostly by a climatically biased balance between erosion and supply of terrigenous sediments to the shore, as well as by deforestation and increasing agricultural land use in more recent times, resulting in a series of minor transgressions and regressions (Dias et al. 2000).

The Iberian tin belt is located in the northwest region, covering an area of *c*.200,000 km², in an extension of *c*. 600 km northwest to southeast (Fig. 2). It is the largest area with tin available in Western Europe. All major rivers that flow through the Iberian tin rich areas follow a path westwards (e.g. Tejo, Mondego, Douro, Minho) with their lower course in the Portuguese territory, reaching the Atlantic coast and not the Mediterranean.

Studies of fluvial navigation have shown that until as recently as the mid-19th century, most of the major rivers were navigable several kilometres inland, in some cases up to 200 km, as the case of the Douro and Tejo rivers (Blot 2003). The strategic importance of the fluvial routs in past times was significant, and it would make interior tin sources very accessible to long distance maritime trading (Fig. 2). Several Phoenician settlements are known along the Iberian Atlantic coast, most situated at the head of past marine embayments or on estuary margins with easy access to the sea. This type of settlement exhibit a topographical criterion familiar from Phoenician trading-stations and merchant outposts in the

The Tinworking Landscape of Dartmoor in a European Context: Prehistory to 20th Century

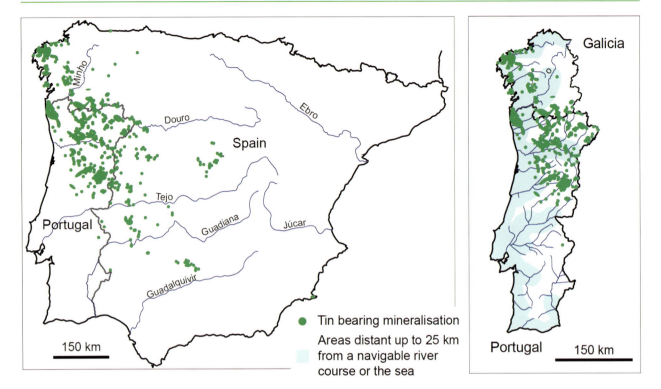

Figure 2 Left: Tin bearing mineralisation in Iberian Peninsula (Sources: SIORMINP, IGME). Right: Limits of navigability until the mid-19th century in Portugal (adapted from Blot 2003).

Mediterranean (Wachsmann et al. 2009).

The relationship between the tin-tungsten ore deposits and magmatism, is widely recognized in the general context of the European Variscan Belt metallogenic provinces. In western Iberia, the primary Sn-(W) ore deposits, possibly exploited in ancient times, are located almost only in the Central Iberian Zone (CIZ) and Galicia-Trás-os-Montes Zone (GTMZ). Embedded in the Hercynian cratonic block these two paleographic units are differentiated by Precambrian, predominantly mafic-ultramafic rocks, and Silurian-Devonian metasedimentes (GTMZ), or neoproterozoic to carbonic metasedimentary and metavolcanic rocks (CIZ) (Fig. 3)[1].

In the two zones, the primary Sn-W ore deposits are spatially associated to granitoids emplaced mainly during and following the ductile deformation phase D3 of Namurian–Westphalian age after the collision between Gondwana and Laurentia. These granites can be split in two: mica syntectonic granites associated with migmatites, and the biotite post-tectonic granites type. The Sn deposits are related to the first type of granitic rocks that are slightly enriched in Sn. The hydrothermal characteristic of the ores is clear and the role of magmatic fractional crystallization is demonstrated by the granite–aplite/pegmatite sequence. Besides some contributions of meteoric or metamorphic fluids, the ore results mainly from the interaction of residual Sn-rich fluids, separated from the crystallizing magma, with some parts of the cooling granite or metasedimentary wall rocks.

The mineralogy of the aplite–pegmatite veins and sills are compatible with a granitic rock. The accessory minerals comprise beryl, tourmaline, wolframite, uranium and rare earth elements phosphates, Nb-Ta oxides and Li minerals. The only important Sn mineral is cassiterite.

3 THE HISTORY OF INVESTIGATION

3.1 From the 18th to mid-20th century: between classical texts and geological prospection

The northwestern Iberian Peninsula has been well known since classical times for its mineral wealth, which includes gold and tin. Authors such as Diodorus Siculus (*Bibliotheca historica*), Strabo (*Geographica*, III) or Pliny the Elder (*Naturalis Historia*, IV & XXXIV) all described and wrote about it. They all agreed that the origin of tin for Mediterranean countries was in the extreme Occident, but they kept their descriptions at a regional level, referring to western Iberia (*Lusitania* and *Gallaecia*), southern Great Britain and the Cassiterides Islands[2] (Fig. 4) but do not refer to any specific mine. The Cassiteride Islands, somewhere in the Atlantic Ocean, have so far proved impossible to locate, but

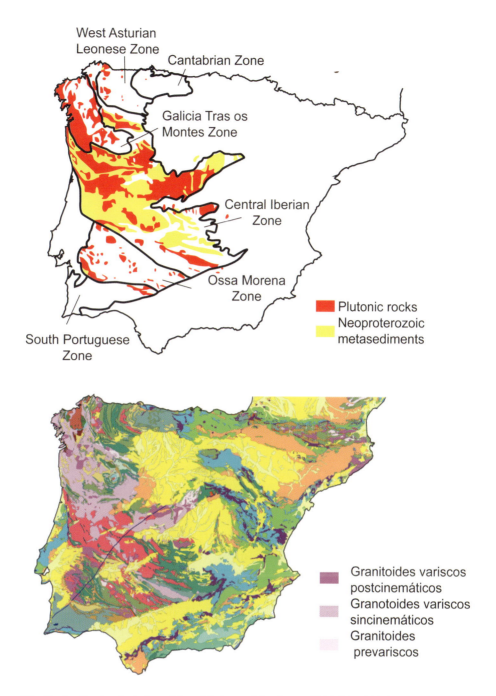

Figure 3 Geological map of the Iberian Peninsula (adapted from Ribeiro and Sanderson 1996; Vera 2004).

this mystery was also the triggering factor for the beginning of investigation on early tin mining. Since the 18th century, both Iberian and British writers wanted to prove that the Cassiterides were near their coast. The islands off the Galician coast were first identified as being the Cassiterides by Sarmiento in the second half of the 18th century (Sarmiento, 1758-1769). A few years later, Cornide Saavedra proposed a similar interpretation, contrary to the claims of the British writer, William Camden who identified the Cassiterides with the Isles of Scilly. Given the absence of tin mines in the Isles of Scilly, Cornide Saavedra provides the name of three places with tin mines in Galicia and northern Portugal, including one island: Ons Island, Monterrei and Lafoes (Cornide Saavedra 1790).

During the 19th century, this question had new developments with the growth of the mining industry. The search for minerals was an opportunity to re-discover some ancient mines, and the mining engineers published notes and some extended papers about early tin mining based on what they could observe in the landscape (Pérez Domingo 1831; Borlase 1897). In Portugal, the encyclopaedic

The Tinworking Landscape of Dartmoor in a European Context: Prehistory to 20th Century

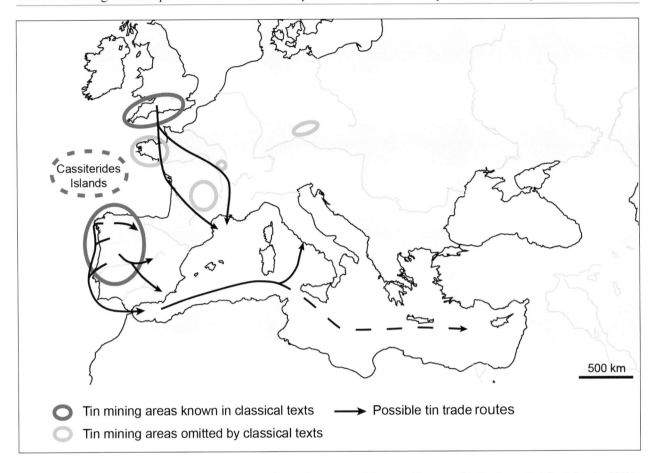

Figure 4 Tin producing areas in Europe according to classical sources and the possible routes for the tin trade (after Meunier 2011).

description of the district of Bragança by Alves (also known as Abade de Baçal) made use of this information in his book about mineral resources (Alves 1913). Later in the 20th century, the technical side of the mining research became stronger but some evidences of ancient works were still being recorded in the mining engineers' reports.

As a result, the combined historical, technical and geological reports open a first window to the part played by Iberian tin in a large scale trade from the Bronze Age to Roman period, which the following phases of investigation will hopefully confirm with archaeological data.

3.2 Since the 20th century: a slow encounter between archaeology and mining

After the mining engineers, archaeologists started to focus their interest on the question of tin supply. They started with the classical texts, but soon considered bronze objects in their discussion. One of the most emblematic type of artefact considered were the single or double-looped palstaves from the Bronze Age which had a strong local character and were found in large quantities as isolated item or in hoards in northwest Iberia. The finding of moulds that served to produce them were recurrent, and these facts were considered to be strong arguments for local tin mining. Additionally, the distribution of this type of artefact, with a distinguished local shape, across the Iberian Peninsula (including areas with absence of tin sources) and along the Atlantic and Mediterranean coasts (with many examples found in modern Italy) was considered as a result of the tin trade (Joleaud 1929, Serpa Pinto 1933, Monteagudo 1954). Iberian geological data and mining developments were also being taken into account in these syntheses. All of this continued feeding the discussion about the location of the Cassiterides, moreover knowing that in some of the small islands in the Galician coasts, as in the Ons Island, ancient and modern tinworking existed (Obermaier 1944-1945, Monteagudo 1953, Madroñero 1994). The discussion and texts devoted to the location of the Cassiterides eventually subsided, while more recently it has been proposed that the Cassiterides were only the generic name for the occidental tin producing areas, and not a specific location within the Iberian Peninsula or the British Isles (Balboa 1997).

The emergence and subsequent development of mining archaeology since the 1970s has placed an increasing importance on fieldwork and multidisciplinary approaches. However, very few investigations were carried out to examine tin from the point of view of mining archaeology, so that knowledge on this theme has not evolved until recently. From Muhly's book in 1973 to Domergue's synthesis about mines in Antiquity in 2008, we find nearly the same scenario: after reviewing the classical texts, the geological data is used to identify where tin deposits are situated, and the same few sites quoted are attributed to Roman works.

This situation can be explained partly by the reasons given above: part of the cassiterite must have come from tin bearing alluvium from the numerous rivers crossing the Galician or Portuguese territory and the exploitation of secondary placers left very few traces. Also, archaeologists often overlook tin mining traces, in part due to inadequate training and in part to considering it, *a priori*, as an impossible task. As a consequence, the lack of objective data about ancient mines prevents any reliable estimation of the amount of metal produced in ancient times. These intrinsic difficulties are known in literature as 'the problem of tin' (Mohen 1992, 101; Giumlia-Mair and Schiavo 2003; Rovira 2007: 22-24; Chakrabarti 1979). But even in this peculiar investigation context, tin resources are frequently used to explain some phenomena observed in northwestern Iberian societies since the Bronze Age. The possible tin trade routes are reconstructed from indirect sources of evidence such as the distribution of bronze objects, the distribution of menhir statues and warrior stelae (attributed to Bronze Age and showing frequently metallic objects), but also the spread of materials from areas in need of tin, such as Phoenician or Mediterranean affiliated objects, as found along the Atlantic Iberian coast and in inland central and northern Portugal (Ruiz-Gálvez Priego 1986; Martins 1996; Senna Martínez 2011, 2013).

In the last 20 years, only two academic works have examined the ancient exploitation of Iberian tin in detail. The first was by C. Merideth (1998a), who focused on the central area of Portugal and Spain and relied on data from a field survey of 42 sites. From these sites, he was only able to provide connections to ancient exploitation of tin at two archaeological locations: Cerro de San Cristóbal (Logrosán, Cáceres) and Torre Romana de Centum Cellas (Belmonte, Portugal); details for these two sites are presented below. More recently, focusing in northern Portugal and Galicia (NW Spain), E. Meunier (2011) undertook a documentary and bibliographical review of nearly 300 references and was able to highlight the potential for ancient tin mines in this region (*see* details below).

Relating to more recent tin exploitation, some academic works have been produced, including ethnoarchaeological studies. These include: the works of Fernández in the south of the Ourense province (Fernández 2011; Fernández et al. 2014); Ayán Vila et al. (2007) in the coastal area of southern Galicia; Alves (1999) on the mines of Panasqueira (Portugal); Fernandes (2008) on the Ervedosa mines (North Portugal).

4 Case studies

The cases presented here illustrate different aspects of recent tin mining research or investigations on archaeological remains carried out in Iberia by different researchers, including the present team. Case-studies are presented following their geographic location, from south to the north of the Iberian territory (Fig. 5).

4.1 Cerro de San Cristóbal (Logrosán, Cáceres, central Spain)

The Cerro de San Cristóbal has been subjected to archaeological work from 1998 to 2002 (coordinated by C. Merideth until 2005) during which, tin mining and metallurgical remains were identified (Merideth 1998b, 1988c; Rodríguez Díaz et al. 2001, 2013). Despite disturbance by modern mining works, prehistoric layers have been recorded and attributed to the Late Bronze Age/Orientalizing period, between the 9th-8th/7th-6th centuries BC. More recently, a new programme of archaeological work and mining prospection in the Caceres region has begun, by the initiative of the Logrosán City Council, which included new archaeological excavations on the site during the summer of 2013 (Rodriguez Díaz et al. 2014). The following is an overview of the site, based on this previous archaeological work.

One of the interesting facts is that this site is located at the very same place where cassiterite was mined, and metallurgical activity is documented too. The cassiterite is present in quartz veins, with associated arsenopirite and stannite, accompanied by smaller amounts of chalcopyrite, pyrite and sphalerite (Merideth, 1988c). During excavations at the mines, stone mining tools were found in undisturbed layers,

The Tinworking Landscape of Dartmoor in a European Context: Prehistory to 20th Century

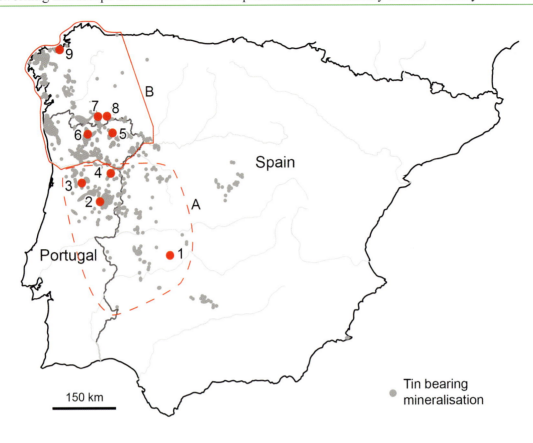

Figure 5 Location of the case studies presented in this paper. 1: Cerro de San Cristobal, Logrosán. 2: Centum Cellas, Belmonte. 3: Castro de Nossa Senhora, Baiões. 4: Vale do Mouro, Coriscada. 5: Tuela Tin Mine, Ervedosa. 6: Castro de Carvalhelhos, Boticas. 7: Laza. 8: A Gudiña. 9: Punta Muros. A: Field survey Merideth 1998a. B: Bibliographic inventory Meunier 2011.

and attributed to the Bronze Age. The site has circular or elongated huts, and materials related to metallurgy include crucible and mould fragments. Others related to ore dressing comprise heaps of gangue (mainly quartz), some crushing or grinding stones and mills.

A particularity of the site is that many of the protohistoric habitat structures have been constructed over the mining vestiges, which stratigraphically relates the beginning of tinworking to the Bronze Age.

Also in the area, local miners in the 1950s documented quartz veins with malachite, as well as the occasional appearance of gold nuggets, during the mining and concentration of cassiterite.

Analysis of a slaggy surface on one crucible fragment has suggested that very fine ground cassiterite was added directly to copper (or copper ores) to produce bronze. The most recent excavations have uncovered tuyeres and metallic prills. Analyses have shown that prills are of bronze or copper with some arsenic.

The role of the cassiterite mined in Cerro de San Cristobal among ancient trade networks is not known; nevertheless, in the case of cassiterite or metal exportation, the most natural way out would have been the southern valley of Guadiana river, which in turn would have provided an easy connection with Phoenician coastal contexts (Rodriguez Diaz et al. 2014).

4.2 Torre Romana de Centum Cellas (Belmonte, central Portugal)

Centum Cellas is a monument of central Portugal classified of national interest (*Monumento Nacional*), which comprises ruins of a Roman tower and other buildings. It is located near the confluence of two streams, whose placers are known to have been mined since ancient times. Archaeological excavations that took place from 1993 to 1998 (coordinated by IPPAR and directed by H. Frade), suggested that Centum Cellas would have been a *villa* or *vicus*, constructed at the mid-1st century AD. The *villa* belonged to a roman citizen named Lucius Caecilius, who was probably a tin trader (Frade, 2002; Alarcão, 2012).

During the archaeological work, iron slags and tin slags of dark-blackish colour and of relatively large

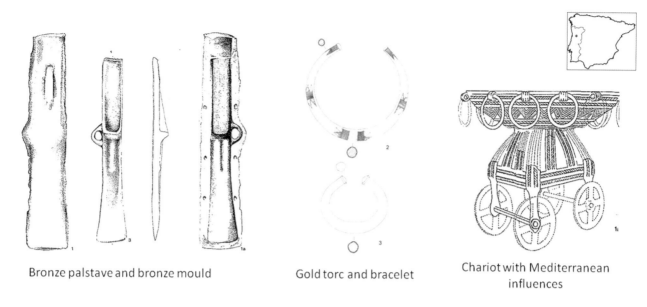

Bronze palstave and bronze mould   Gold torc and bracelet   Chariot with Mediterranean influences

Figure 6 Diversity of materials from the Late Bronze Age site of Baiões: bronze artefacts, artefacts with Mediterranean affiliations and gold artefacts (adapted from Silva 1986 and Kalb 1986). Other materials such as an iron knife and numerous metallurgical remains, including smelting slags and a small fragment with metallic tin were also found.

size were found. Merideth (1998a) analysed some of these tin slags and some others that were at the surface of the site. SEM-EDS analysis showed that all tin slag fragments had tin contents that varied considerably (from 2.2% to 20% Sn), and that most areas measured also contained varying but high percentages of the elements niobium, titanium and tantalum.

The presence of these tin slags at the site shows that the *villa* or *vicus* probably developed around tin mining in the region, with tin smelting occurring on the site. The production of metallic tin would most likely have had commercial purposes.

4.3 Castro de Nossa Senhora da Guia, Baiões (Viseu, central Portugal)

The Castro de Baiões is one of the most emblematic Late Bronze Age archaeological sites in central Portugal. It received the attention of archaeologists when two torques and a bracelet made of massive gold were found in 1947 (Kalb 1990-92). Later, in 1971, another chance find provided several bronze palstaves, with a local northwestern Iberian typical shape from Bronze Age. Later, in the 1970s and 80s, some archaeological excavations took place, from which many more artefacts were retrieved, including various metallic objects attributed to the Late Bronze Age (e.g. socketed spearheads, bifacial double looped palstaves, unifacial single looped palstaves, daggers, rings, *tranchet*, chisels, etc.), as well as numerous metallurgical remains (Fig. 6). The metallurgical remains include fragments of moulds (as for palstaves), artefacts newly produced (still with the casting seams), and numerous fragments of diverse artefacts, among other metallurgical debris of difficult classification. Since then, other Late Bronze Age sites in the immediate vicinity (lying in a cluster within about 1-2 km of each other) have also been investigated and evidence of local metallurgical production has also been recorded. This group of sites has since been labelled the Baiões/Santa Luzia cultural group, and is located in most of the inland basins of the Mondego, Vouga and southern Douro rivers (Senna-Martinez 2000). Most artefacts found in this group are related to the 'Atlantic Bronze Age' traditions, but many artefacts are also clearly related to Mediterranean models (e.g. bowls with *omphalos* bottom; articulated roasting spit fragments; old types of fibulae fragments and early iron daggers from 12-10th century BC contexts). Radiocarbon dates show that these sites were occupied between 1250 and 550 BC (Senna-Martinez and Pedro, 2000; Vilaça, 2007).

In the last decade, elemental and microstructural analyses of metallurgical debris from Baiões have identified bronze metallurgy. In one particular study (Figueiredo et al. 2010), a slag fragment had copper and tin species present in different microconstituents, and a bronze prill with one side covered with metallic tin, which showed an interdiffusion process between the metallic tin and bronze, were also described. These two findings show that the site did not simply perform bronze recycling, but that metallic tin, or

The Tinworking Landscape of Dartmoor in a European Context: Prehistory to 20th Century

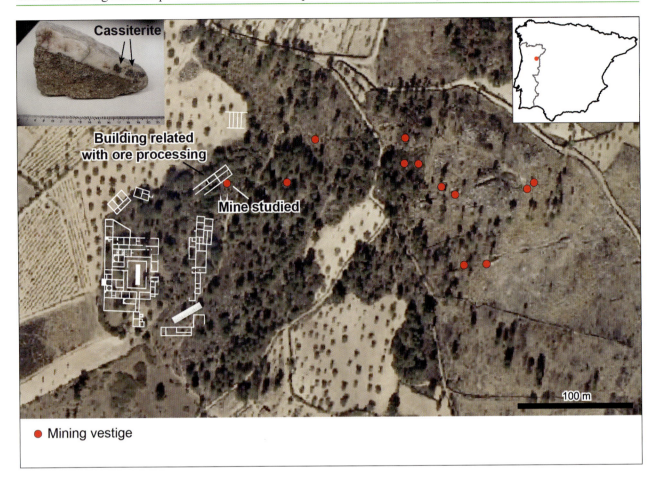

Figure 7 The Roman villa of Vale do Mouro and the mining vestiges, with an example of a tin bearing quartz vein. Orthophoto: WMS service of igeo.pt.

cassiterite, was known and circulated among the local metallurgists. Given the location of Baiões in a rich tin area, it is likely that during the Late Bronze Age, the local communities were exploiting their tin resources. In fact, at São Martinho de Orgens, just 15 km SE of the Baiões site and within the Baiões/Santa Luzia cultural group area, during the re-opening of a tin mine in 1941, the miners found a bronze dagger of the 'Porto de Mós' type (from the Bronze Age) which indicates that previous tin mining works could have been performed in that place (Vilaça et al. 2014)[3].

The piece of metallic tin found in Baiões is, until now, the only Bronze Age tin fragment found or recognized in Iberia[4]. Other tin objects, such as bars or ingots, have been described in archaeological literature; however no scientific analysis has been made to confirm if they are of tin or other material. However, taking into account the numerous metallurgical remains from hundreds of Bronze Age sites in Iberia that have never been analytically studied, it would be no surprise if more tin samples are found during future investigations.

4.4 Vale do Mouro – Coriscada (Mêda, central Portugal)

The archaeological site of Vale do Mouro (Coriscada, Mêda, N Portugal) is a Roman *villa* excavated by T. Silvino and A. Sá Coixão, between 2003 and 2009. This *villa*, one of the largest ever studied in Portugal, had its main period of activity by the end of the 3rd century AD. The production of olive oil and wine is well documented and was an important source of wealth for the owners of this establishment (Sá Coixão and Silvino 2010; Silvino and Sá Coixão 2010). Very close to this *villa*, a few metres eastward, more than ten opencast mines are still visible (Fig. 7). These opencast mines were known among the local town inhabitants who, during the 20th century, were mining for tungsten and tin in the region.

However, during 2014 a new excavation campaign uncovered a Roman building with important remains of waste material, made of blocks of quartz. This kind of remains is of a type known for sorting the ore before starting the metallurgical process, and provided evidence of mining activity linked to the *villa*.

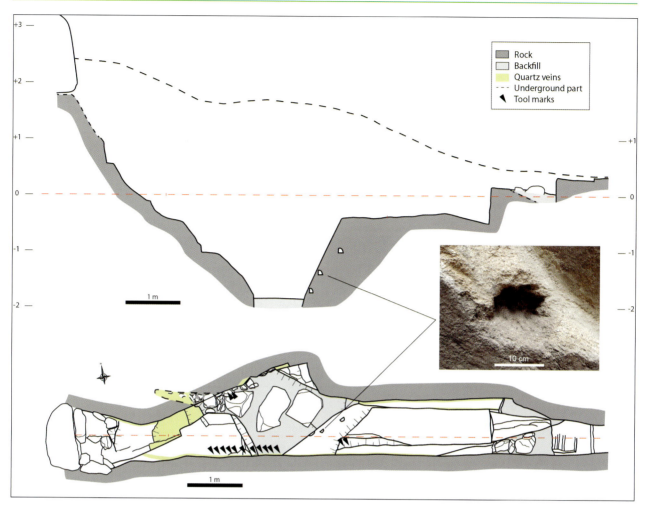

Figure 8 Section and plan of the opencast trench closest to the villa buildings.

A first survey of one of the mines was carried out in 2015 by E. Meunier and E. Figueiredo. The mine chosen was the closest to the Roman buildings (less than 50m). It proved to be an opencast trench, oriented east to west, of 27m length and between 0.5 and 1.6m width, and with a depth from a few cm to several metres, following some quartz veins in a granitic context. During this first survey it was possible to clean it along 9m and to a depth of 4.25m, though this was not the bottom of the mine (Fig. 8). The characteristics of the working are consistent with ancient mining.

The width of the trench is delimited by two veins, still visible in some points of the southern and northern walls where the miners left them, because they were too thin or barren in that level (we did not find any mineralization in the samples from the remaining quartz veins). The two veins are crossing themselves in the western end of the trench. In the lower part, the miners followed this larger vein with an underground excavation.

In the southern wall, tool marks made by picks are visible and well preserved. The use of picks is not specific to any particular period but neither discordant with an exploitation in Roman times, as known from many other sites (Domergue 2008). This type of mark is also visible in three notches in the eastern wall. These notches could be used to support a wooden structure to help to climb out of the mine. Their size and shape is similar to the lamp niches known in some Roman mines, but at this depth within an opencast trench, there would have been no need to illuminate the works.

A survey was also made of a large amount of rock found in the Roman building, and some samples of quartz vein were found with cassiterite. Preliminary SEM-EDS analysis to the cassiterite showed it to be composed by zones of very pure cassiterite as well as zones with impurities (e.g. Fe).

Despite not reaching the archaeological levels in the mine, which could have confirmed the Roman exploitation, during this first survey, the relation between some buildings of the *villa* and the ore sorting wastes leaves no doubt about a Roman phase of

Figure 9 At left a photograph from the Ervedosa Sn mining works, from the personal archive of Carlos Lindley (1930s), adapted from Fernandes (2008). At right images of crushing and grinding stone tools found during the modern mining works, believed to have served in the processing of cassiterite at protohistoric/Bronze Age period (adapted from Veiga Ferreira and Castro 1949; Fernandes 2008; and photographs from the authors).

mining. These works could have been contemporary with the main phase of the *villa* (3rd century AD) but could also have begun as early as the 1st century AD, to which some archaeological materials recovered in the site belong to. Other phases of exploitation are of course also possible, and future works will try to reveal further data on the mining periods.

4.5 Tuela Tin Mines (Ervedosa, North Portugal)

The Ervedosa mines (Vinhais, North Portugal) began to be explored from the beginning of the 20th century, and until 1927 were worked by three concessions; the Borralheira, Pereiro, and Alto do Vale da Veiga. The mines were all in the southern margin of the Tuela river, having the washing and enrichment processing on both sides of the river. In 1938, they were merged as the 'Couto Mineiro de Ervedosa', and were explored by a company, Tuella Tin Mines Limited, which worked until 1969 (Fernandes 2008). The mine reached production of 150 up to 300 tons of cassiterite concentrate (at 65-67% Sn) per year, which was almost exclusively exported to England.

The extraction took place along a principal vein, of large thickness, with a direction N 40°W and inclination 70-80°NE. This vein was little mineralized, but secondary veins with irregular shapes and with only a few centimetres in thickness were rich (stockwork type). Thus, the mining works resulted in an important network of galleries and shafts. The mineralized areas were formed by 0.6-1.3% cassiterite, 2-4% arsenical pyrites, chalcopyrite, some iron and vestiges of zinc and gold (Gomes 1996).

During the hydraulic working at one of the mines, crushing and grinding stone tools were found that were believed to have served in the processing of cassiterite, attributed to the protohistoric/Bronze Age period (Veiga Ferreira and Castro 1949; Fernandes 2008) (Fig. 9).

Roman and pre-Roman occupation sites are known in the region. Specifically, in a hill over the Tuela river, near the mining works, there is a Bronze Age(?)/Iron Age hillfort called Muradal, which however, has never been archaeologically excavated.

4.6 Carvalhelhos hillfort (Boticas, North Portugal)

The Carvalhelhos hillfort (Boticas, North Portugal) was excavated through several campaigns directed by J. R. dos Santos Júnior from the 1950s to the 1980s. It is a fortified *castro*, and its occupation is attributed to the Iron Age/Roman transition, between the 2nd century BC and the 1st century AD (Fonte 2015).

The site is located in a region very rich in tin resources. The area of Barroso is known for aplite

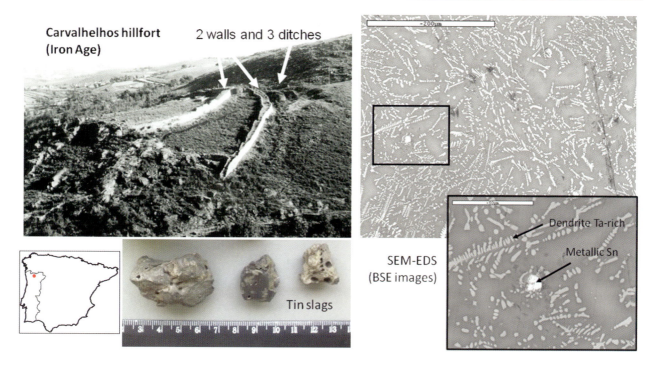

Figure 10 Iron Age Carvalhelhos hillfort at top left and samples of tin slags found in the hillfort at bottom left. At right, SEM-EDS (BSE) images of a typical microstructure of the tin slags.

bodies associated with tin mineralisation (Ferreira & Noronha 1987). Most of these aplites with tin mineralisation were described as countless, thin (metre-size, on average), mainly aplitic dykes and veins, commonly converted to kaolinite which contain low-grade (<3 kg/t) cassiterite mineralisation (Charoy et al. 1992). Frequent occurrence of cassiterite in the greisens surrounding the pegmatites have been reported in this area, and were exploited for tin on a small scale after the Second World War (Martins & Lima 2011).

During the archaeological excavations, several kilograms of slags, pottery, and some metal artefacts such as fibulae, rings and pins, as well as a few Roman coins dated to the 26-25 BC and 41-54 AD, were recovered (Fonte 2015). Also near the site, a 200 kg cassiterite deposit was found, which was interpreted as a 'hiding place made by the inhabitants in the imminence of an attack, possibly by the Romans' (Santos Júnior 1984).

An early study of a slag sample, by Maia e Costa (1966), suggested that this particular slag was a result of tin smelting activity. However, the very high iron (Fe) content and rather low tin (Sn) content within the sample, created some uncertainties about this interpretation (Tylecote et al. 1989). More recently, in an attempt to better understand the metallurgical activities at this site, more slag samples have been analysed, and the results show effectively that tin, as well as iron, extractive metallurgy was performed there. This study is still being developed; nevertheless, the presence of tin slags has now been confirmed. The results even show some similarities with the Centum Cellas examples (*see* above; Merideth 1996): the tin content varies considerably although is frequently upwards of ~30%, and the significant percentages of the elements niobium, titanium and tantalum are also present (Fig. 10), which are common occurrences in cassiterite from the Iberian tin belt.

After years of excavations, Santos Júnior (1984) concluded that 'the inhabitants of Carvalhelhos were skilled miners who exploited the cassiterite tin ore … which was exploited in some pits dug on the periphery of the village'. These pits and other remains are difficult to identify today, in part due to mid-20th century mining works that destroyed evidence of previous episodes, and due to the intensive afforestation that the region underwent in the second half of the 20th century.

Currently, the Carvalhelhos is the only Iron Age hillfort from which tin slags have been identified and analysed. Nevertheless, as previously mentioned for the Bronze Age sites, future analytical studies examining metallurgical remains of the thousands of *castros* in northwestern Iberia could provide more evidence for tin extractive metallurgy in pre-Roman times.

The Tinworking Landscape of Dartmoor in a European Context: Prehistory to 20th Century

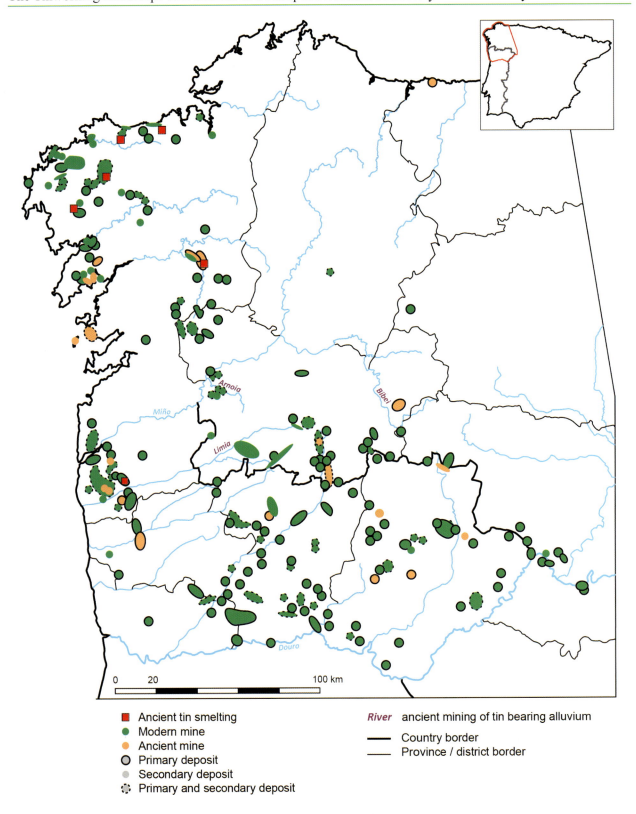

Figure 11 Tin exploitation sites in the north-western Peninsula (Meunier 2011).

4.7 Punta Muros (Arteixo, Northwest Spain)

Due to the recent construction of a harbour in Punta Langosteira (A Coruña), a small fortified settlement located in the top of a cliff which was going to be destroyed was subjected to archaeological excavations. This site, called Punta Muros (Arteixo, A Coruna, Spain), is of the Late Bronze Age, with some features that make it unique and exceptional in the far northwest of the Iberian Peninsula. Large, elongated and aligned houses have been uncovered, all with outside fireplaces and basins carved into the rock for metallurgical uses. It has been interpreted as a fortified factory dedicated to the production of bronze in its two forms: binary (copper-tin alloy) and ternary (copper-tin-lead alloy) (Cano 2011; Cano & Gómez, 2010). Of particular importance was the find of a lead ingot. The researchers of the site propose that crushed cassiterite was introduced directly during the metallurgical processes. They also claim that the origin of galena or cassiterite was close to the site. Galena could have been found between the pegmatitic rocks.

5 INVESTIGATION APPROACHES

Beyond more traditional archaeological investigations, other approaches have been applied to specific questions relating to tin exploitation. Three examples, carried out by members of the present team are here presented.

5.1 Documentary survey: mapping modern and ancient tin mining in NW Iberia

Documentary synthesis, carried out by E. Meunier for the area to the north of the Douro River, resulted in the mapping of tinworks, whose chronology runs from the Bronze Age to the 20th century (Meunier 2011, 2014). The documentary sources used to produce this database are very diverse. Archaeological publications were used, but the main source was geological databases and mining engineers' reports. The objective was to compile a list of places where mining activity took place, during different chronological periods.

This investigation served to provide the first detailed database of past tin mining evidence in northern Portugal and Galicia (northwest Spain). Nevertheless, documentary sources are limited. For example, the locations of tin mines are known only where previous archaeological or geological surveys have been completed, resulting in written documents; archaeological surveys are very few in number, but there are many geological surveys available, produced at the behest of the mining industry. Thus, the map resulting from this process shows information concentrated into locations/areas where modern mining interests prevail, so many tin resources and ancient mining activities are overlooked. Inevitably, therefore, the list is incomplete, and future field surveys still have to be undertaken.

The second constraint that hampers the work is the different forms of available documentation depending on its country of origin. For Spain, most of the reports from the IGME[5] are available in an online database, providing many details on each mining site. For Portugal, only a database with mineral occurrences is online[6]. In this case, the information is mainly geological and mineralogical; the mining works are never described. Another problematic issue is the chronology of the mines. If, in some cases, mining engineers recorded the presence of 'old' works, there is seldom any indication of how old they were. In a few cases, they recorded the presence of archaeological remains (Roman coins, ceramics) or highlighted the ancient morphology of the works (nearly always considered of the Roman period), but mostly, there are no detailed descriptions. Archaeological documentation allows completion of the information in only a few cases.

The resulting list was used to prepare a map (Fig. 11), which presents the recorded mining sites, distinguishing the ancient ones from the modern or undated ones.[7] The wide, spatial spread of tin mining works is notable, despite the empty zones that result from the limitations of geological surveys. Another point of interest is the known location of ancient works in many areas, despite the very few archaeological investigations carried out in order to characterise them.[8] Primary and secondary deposits are also indicated. It can be shown that old works were recorded in both primary and secondary geological contexts.

Despite its limitations, this documentary work has presented an encouraging body of new data revealing great potential for future fieldwork directed towards early tin mining.

5.2 Ethnoarchaeology: the example of modern mining in Laza and A Gudiña (Ourense, Northwest Spain)

The southeastern area of Galicia (Ourense province), which includes the municipalities of Laza and A Gudiña, is characterised by an undeniable landscape value, but also by its industrial and mining heritage. During two research projects, the 'Archaeological Intervention project in the Monte Urdiñeira environment (A Gudiña and Riós municipalities)' and the 'Upper Támega Project', both directed by the University of Vigo,[9] research was carried on the exploitation of tin resources in recent times.

The main aim was to obtain information about the usage and benefits of tin mining in a wide, cross-border region. The methodology followed an interdisciplinary approach, integrating the mining documentary collection from the Arquivo Histórico Provincial in Ourense (AHPOu), field surveys, and the involvement of the local community, as well as interviews with older miners.

Tin mining works in the region have been recorded from the second half of the 19th century onwards, based on accounting ledgers, files and payment of taxes, namely in sites such as Trabisquedo and Valgrande (A Gudiña) (Fernández 2011), or Arcucelos (Laza) (Fernández et al. 2014). Field surveys confirmed a substantial level of tin exploitation, locating many examples of drift mining with multiple passageways, and evidence of industrial infrastructure. In addition, two open-pit mines (located in Vilameá, Laza and O Tameirón, A Gudiña) were detected, which could be related to the exploitation of gold.

The local community offered a social perspective as a first-hand resource, since many inhabitants had close associations with the recent mining works. The information they provided, clarified different aspects of the exploitation of tin ore, including the extraction technique, ore quality, and the gender-based segregation in the work environment. Moreover, many details regarding tin smuggling were documented, since this was a frequent activity, due to the cross-border nature of the area.

Two main conclusions can be highlighted from this investigation. First of all, the chronology of the contemporary tin exploitation is well documented between 1856 and 1964 in the AHPOu files. These documents also reveal the existence of remains of 'ancient works', which would need to be further investigated by archaeological prospection, to provide further details about possible mining activities during prehistory or antiquity. On the other hand, the two open-pit mines discovered would require further detailed investigation. The possibility to combine research into gold and tin mining in that area would be of great interest in the study of ancient patterns of metal exploitation.

5.3 Experimental archaeology: extractive metallurgy and tin or bronze production

In the context of the 'problem of tin', particularly the difficulty caused by the lack of a comprehensive archaeological data on extractive metallurgy, ethnoarchaeology and experimental archaeology are two tools of great potential. They represent an empirical way of better understanding bronze and tin production specificities, bringing some answers to a topic that is short on information.

Recently, during the ethnoarchaeological interviews with the local population in the region of Laza and A Gudiña (see details above) an opportunity to document a traditional way of producing a tin ingot with local ores occurred. One inhabitant who had been a tin miner in the mid-20th century and a former blacksmith, told about the way he and others used to produce tin for local consumption (as for tinning spoons and other utilitarian objects). He was very keen to put his old blacksmith workshop to work, to demonstrate tin production, which was duly documented.

This was an exceptional ethnological opportunity, during which it was possible to observe different stages of the metallurgical process: cassiterite reduction in open fire with absence of fluxes or container; fabrication of a mould using a turnip (a potato could also have been used, depending on the season); separation of metallic tin prills from slags and charcoal, and melting together in an iron frying pan; casting of tin in the turnip mould. The process was done in a traditional forge, with charcoal as fuel and manual bellows to fan the fire, and took less than half an hour. The ores used were of local origin (Lackinger et al. in press).

The information obtained from this ethnological experience, together with some archaeological data about ancient smelting procedures, were used to design some smelting experiments that were performed by the team using Iberian ores. With these experiments, it was aimed to get a clearer understanding of the degree of difficulty/facility in metal production; to have some estimates on the efficiency using different ores or smelting techniques; and it was aimed to obtain materials that could be analytically studied and compared to archaeological samples. Additionally, the experiments were an opportunity to bring prehistoric metallurgy to a wide-ranging audience, from university students to professional archaeologists, including the general public, by performing public events.

Such metallurgical experiments have been performed since 2011 until the present, and involved the cementation process, co-smelting processes (simultaneously reducing copper ores and cassiterite for direct bronze production), and cassiterite reduction, for the production of tin. All the experiments were conducted in small-scale open fire structures, as a small pit dug into the ground. Fluxes were never added, and in some cases clay crucibles

Figure 12 (left) Experimental tin smelting operation performed in an open pit recreating prehistoric technologies; (right) tin prills recovered from the smelting experiment.

were used, while in others the reduction was made directly at the bottom of the pit. Two bellows were always used, with the tuyeres directed to the centre of the pit (Fig. 12). Variations in the bellows design, size and depth of the pit were included in some of the experiments.

Some of the experiments were more successful than others in producing metal. In respect to tin production, it has been generally perceived that the larger the cassiterite grains the higher recovery rates are attained (and with larger prills), and that the use of small open fire smelting structures can result in large amounts of tin loss due to the volatilization of Sn species (namely SnO) (Figueiredo et al. 2016).

In Table 1, the characteristics of the experiments performed and a summary of the results obtained are presented.

6 SOME FINAL NOTES

Tin resources in the Iberian Peninsula were available over a wide territory. Despite the absence of well dated ancient mines, there is indirect evidence for mining activities from the Bronze Age, Iron Age and Roman times.

With respect to modern times, mining activities have been documented since the 17th century only in a few places, but in the 20th century tin mining was performed in all provinces where tin resources occur.

So far, there are no elements to estimate the amount of tin produced in ancient times, but the regular presence of metallurgical vestiges in archaeological sites makes one presume that the exploitation of the local tin sources could have been performed on a regular basis from Bronze Age to Roman times, and in the various provinces of the Iberian tin belt.

Difficulties in recognising ancient mining evidence in the field, and the lack of metallic tin in archaeological excavations, constrain the research on ancient tin in Iberia. However, this is not unique to the Iberian territory.

Recently, there has been new interest in re-opening some mining complexes, namely for Critical Raw Materials (as Ta and Nb). This could represent a new threat for any ancient remains not studied or recorded yet. This, combined with a general lack of interest in mining heritage preservation and the scarcity of funded projects in Portugal and Spain to perform such studies, seriously threatens the development of tin mining and metallurgy archaeological investigation in the Iberian Peninsula.

The building up of a multidisciplinary team, from different institutions and countries, has been a first step to try to overcome some of these problems. The possibility to apply for international projects, and to tackle different case studies with the most appropriate methodology, is now an opportunity. Also, recent progresses in the archaeometric field, such as the possibility of using tin isotopes to determine the provenance of tin in antiquity, may contribute to the development of wider interest in tin studies in the Iberian territory among the research community.

Experiment	Material involved	Type of furnace; duration of the reaction	Production; archaeometrical results	Ref.
Cementation: bronze production with cassiterite added to melted copper in a crucible				
MazCe2011 Mazonovo (Asturias) 06/07/2011	- Cassiterite [1]: 37 g + Melted copper: 150 g - Charcoal made with heather roots	- Simple circular and open pit furnace, covered with clay (diam: 50 cm; depth: 20 cm) with a ceramic bowl (diam:- 12 cm). Volume max: 75 l. - 2 bellows of pig skin. - 2 ceramic tuyeres. L: 65 cm; ext. diam: 6 cm; int. diam. 2 cm. - 150 min.	- 169 g of bronze - Without archeaometrical records nor temperature measurements	Lackinger 2012
Co-reduction of copper and tin ores				
TarCo2012 Taramundi (Asturias) 12/05/2012	- Cassiterite [1]: 30 g + Malachite [2]: 120 g included in 3 loads - Charcoal made with heather roots	- Simple circular and open pit furnace (diam: 40 cm; depth: 30 cm) with a ceramic bowl (diam: 16 cm). Volume max: 75 l. - 2 bellows of pig skin. - 2 ceramic tuyeres. L: 65 cm; ext. diam: 6 cm; int. diam. 2 cm. - 50 min.	- Several scattered slag fragments containing some binary bronze droplets. It was not possible to quantify the global amount of metal produced.	Lackinger et al 2013
CaLam2016 PAAR Campo Lameiro (Pontevedra), 23/04/2016	- Cassiterite [1]: 68 g + Malachite [2]: 328 g 3 simultaneous loads - Charcoal made with heather roots	- Simple circular and open pit furnace without clay cover surrounded by stones. Diam: 35 cm; depth: 10cm. Volume max: 19 l. - 2 bellows of horse skin. - 2 ceramic tuyeres. L: 65 cm; ext. diam: 6 cm; int. diam. 2 cm. - 57 min.	- Slag dough containing metallic droplets. - Temperatures around 1000°C or between 1200-1340°C depending on who activates the bellows.	
Reduction of tin ore				
PenEtno2013/1 PenEtno2013/2 Pentes, A Gudiña (Ourense) 05/05/2013	Local cassiterite [3] 1º trial: 5 handfuls 2º: 1 handful	- Traditional forge with manual bellow; ethnographical observation - 1º: 3 min. - 2º: 9 min.	- 1º: only slags - 2º: metallic tin ingot of 37 g.	Lackinger et al. in press
OuSn2015/1 Campus de Ourense de la Universidad de Vigo, 27/02/2014	- Cassiterite [1]: 304 g included in 3 loads - Charcoal made with heather roots	- Simple circular and open pit furnace, covered with clay, surrounded by granitic blocks (diam: 38 cm; depth: 40 cm) with ceramic bowl (diam: 13 cm). Volume max: 19 l. - 2 bellows of horse skin. - 2 ceramic tuyeres. L: 65 cm; ext. diam: 6 cm; int. diam. 2 cm. - 37 min.	- The ceramic bowl was completely destroyed during the process. - Many vitreous slags. - 65.2 g of metallic tin. - Temperature: Max: 1360°C; average: 1100-1200°C; Max. according to slag analyse: 1500°C.	Figueiredo et al. in press
OuSn2015/2 Campus de Ourense de la Universidad de Vigo, 28/02/2014	- Cassiterite [4]: 40 g - Charcoal made with heather roots	- Simple circular and open pit furnace, covered with clay, surrounded by granitic blocks (diam: 38 cm; depth: 40 cm) with ceramic bowl (diam: 9 cm). Volume max: 19 l. - 2 bellows of horse skin. - 2 ceramic tuyeres. L: 65 cm; ext. diam: 6 cm; int. diam. 2 cm. - 18 min.	- Vitreous slag. - 2.3 g of metallic tin - Temperatures: between 1132 and 1292°C	Figueiredo et al. in press
OuSn2015/3 Campus de Ourense de la Universidad de Vigo, 28/02/2014	- Cassiterite [4]: 40 g - Charcoal made with heather roots	- Simple circular and open pit furnace, covered with clay, surrounded by granitic blocks (diam: 38 cm; depth: 30 cm), with a granitic block in the bottom of the pit. - 2 bellows of horse skin. Volume max: 19 l. - 2 ceramic tuyeres. L: 65 cm; ext. diam: 6 cm; int. diam. 2 cm. - 7 min.	- Slag dough where no metallic tin was recorded.	Figueiredo et al. in press

Table 1 Synthesis of the archaeological experimentation. [1]: from Penouta Mine, Viana do Bolo, Ourense, Spain. [2]: from O Seixo Mine, Petín, Ourense, Spain. [3]: from Trabisquedo Mines, A Gudiña, Ourense, Spain. [4]: from Gondiães Mine, Cabeceiras de Basto, Braga, Portugal.

Acknowledgments

Part of the research presented in this paper was financed by the Portuguese Science Foundation (FCT-MCTES) through the grants SFRH/BPD/97360/2013 and SFRH/BD/65143/2009 to EF and JF, and through the Projects UID/CTM/500025/2013 to CENIMAT/I3N, UID/Multi/04449/2013 to Hercules Lab and PEst-OE/CTE/UI0039/2014 to ICT.

The Projects 'Archaeological Intervention in the Urdiñeira Mountain and its surroundings' (REF 2009-INOU-04) and 'Upper Támega: Actions in Heritage Landscape' (INOU13-02 CITI131H 647) were supported by the Campus of Ourense Vice-Rectory, University of Vigo.

Footnotes

1: Besides the Iberian tin belt which is associated with Hercynian magmatism, in Sierra de Cartagena district (SE Spain) are the only Tertiary tin deposits in Europe. These deposits were discovered at the turn of the 19th to the 20th century. Up to present no vestiges of old mining works have been identified or were documented during the 20th century exploitations. The ore appears in veins related to volcanic and subvolcanic rocks and also in stratiform deposits in carbonate levels which it impregnates. The mineral paragenesis of the former is cassiterite-pyrite-galena-sphalerite-iron oxides, and the latter cassiterite-stibnite, and possible carbonates of Pb, Zn and Fe. Gravimetric concentration of these ores is difficult due to their fine grain size (Marina, 1987: 84).

2: For a more detailed revision of classical texts about tin in NW Iberia, see Meunier 2011.

3: Some 80 km East of Baiões site, in Cabeço da Quinta das Flores (Guarda) a bronze axe from Late Bronze Age was also found during extractive tinworking at a depth of 2 metres (Vilaça et al. 2014).

4: A few objects of tin have been found in Orientalizing or Iron Age contexts. These are a tin sheet with perforations found in an assemblage of materials of Phoenician and autochthonous affiliation dating to 900-770 BC in the city of Huelva (S Spain); six tin ingots (of various shapes) found in a Phoenician wreck at Bajo de la Campana (Murcia, SE Spain) dated to the 7th-6th century BC; a tin ingot and fragments found in a Greek wreck at the Cala Sant Vicenç, in the Mallorca isle, dated to the 6th century BC. Additionally, a few Iron Age tinned artefacts (from the second half of the first millennium BC) are also known from the Iberian Peninsula (Rovira et al. 1996).

5: Spanish Institute of Geology and Mining (http://info.igme.es/catalogo/?tab=2).

6: Database SIORMINP (http://geoportal.lneg.pt/geoportal/egeo/bds/siorminp/), from the National Laboratory of Energy and Geology of Portugal.

7: The chronological data for ancient works are presented in Meunier 2014, fig. 3. It is to be noted that further ancient works are very probable to be discovered when archaeological field survey is to be carried out.

8: C. Domergue's survey of Roman mines in the Iberian Peninsula is one of the few examples of this kind of investigation (Domergue 1990)

9: Proyecto de intervención arqueolóxica no Monte Urdiñeira e o seu contorno (Concellos de Riós- A Gudiña, Ourense). 2009 REF 2009-INOU-04, 102A 209/417; Proyecto Alto Támega: Acciones en el Paisaje Patrimonial 2013 CITI 131H647.

Bibliography

Alarcão, J 2012 'Notas de arqueologia, epigrafia e toponímia – V' *Revista Portuguesa de Arqueologia* **15**, 113-37

Alves, F M 1913 *Memorias arqueológico-históricasdo Distrito de Bragança*, **II** Guedes

Alves, H 1999 'Minas da Panasqueira: uma introduçao à arqueologia da paisagem mineira: da superficie ao trabalho subterráneo' (Oliveira, V. coord.). *3º Congresso de Arqueología Peninsular. Vila Real,* Vila Real: UTAD: 421-38

Ayán Vila, X, Modelo, X, González, L, González de Agüero, E 2007 'Etnoarqueoloxía e paleometalurxia de Os Castros de Neixón (Boiro, A Coruña)'. (López, M L & Alvarez-Campana, J M coord.) *Introducción á minería do Barbanza,* Cámara Oficial Mineira de Galicia, 83-120

Balboa, A 1997 'Mito e realidade na imaxe clásica das costas galaicas' (Alonso-Troncoso, V coord.) *Ferroltera Galaico-Romana*. Concello de Ferrol, Facultade de Humanidades, Ferrol, 155-66

Blot, M L P 2003 'Os portos na origem dos centros urbanos' *Trabalhos de Arqueologia* **28**

Borlase, W 1897 'Tin mining in Spain, past and present' *Ancient Science Tracts* **429**

Chakrabarti, D K 1979 'The problem of tin in early India' *Man and Environment* **3**, 61-74

Charoy, B, Lothie, F, Dusausoy, Y & Noronha, F 1992 'The Crystal Chemistry of Spodumene in some Granitic Aplite-Pegmatite from Northern Portugal' *The Canadian Mineralogist* **30**, 639-51

Cano, J (coord) 2011 *Punta Muros: un poblado fortificado de finales de la Edad del Bronce*. A Coruña: Arqueoloxía do NW S.L.U

Cano, J, Gómez Filgueiras, F 2010 El yacimiento de Punta de Muros: un poblado de producción metalúrgica en el NO de la Península Ibérica. *Anuario Brigantino* **33**, 27-56

Cornide Saavedra, J A 1790 *Las Casiterides o islas del estaño, restituidas a los mares de Galicia*. Madrid: Imprenta de Don Benito Cano

Dias, J M A, Boski, T, Rodrigues, A, Magalhães, F 2000 'Coast line evolution in Portugal since the Last Glacial Maximum until present – a synthesis' *Marine Geology* **170**, 177-86

Domergue, C 1990 *Les mines de la péninsule Ibérique dans l'Antiquité romaine*. Coll. Ecole Française de Rome, Rome

Domergue, C 2008 *Les mines antiques*. Paris

Fernandes, C M B 2008 *As minas de Ervedosa (1906-1969) Efígie de memória e narrativa*. Master thesis, Universidade Autónoma de Lisboa

Fernández, C I 2011 'Una aproximación etnoarqueológica al trabajo del estaño en el Valle del Río Ribeira y la zona del Tameirón (A Gudiña, Ourense, NW Peninsular)'. (Martins, C, Bettencourt, A M S , Martins, J P , Carvalho, J coords.) *Povoamento e exploração dos recursos mineiros na Europa Atlântica Ocidental*. Braga: CITCEM/APEQ, 261-277

Fernández, C I, Comendador, B, Amado, N 2014 'Heritage landscape of metal mining in the Upper Támega Valley (Ourense, Spain): Arcucelos mines' (Fontes, L and Marins, C dir) *Simpósio Internacional Paisagens Mineiras Antigas na Europa Occidental. PAVT-Parque Arqueológico do Vale do Terva* (Município de Boticas e Unidade de Arqueologia da Universidade do Minho)

Ferreira, N M R & Noronha, F 1987 'Pospecção de estanho em áreas envolventes dos maciços das serras do Gerês, Barroso e Cabreira. (Exploration of tin in surroundings of Gerês, Barroso and Cabreira granitic massives)'. *IX Reunião do Oeste Peninsular (Porto 1985), Univ. do Porto, Faculdade de Ciências, Museu e Laboratório Mineralógico e Geológico, Memórias* **1**, 433-49

Figueiredo, E, Lackinger, A, Comendador Rey, B, Silva, R J C, Veiga, J P, Mirão, J 2016 'An experimental approach for smelting tin ores from Northwestern Iberia' *Materials and Manufacturing Processes,* DOI 10.1080/10426914.2016.1244837

Figueiredo, E, Silva, R J C, Senna-Martinez, J C, Araújo, M F, Fernandes, F M B, Inês Vaz, J L (2010) 'Smelting and recycling evidences from the Late Bronze Age habitat site of Baiões (Viseu, Portugal)' *Journal of Archaeological Science* **37**, 1623-34

Fonte, J 2015 *Paisagens em mudança na transição entre a Idade do Ferro e a época Romana no Alto Tâmega e Cávado* (Phd thesis Universidade de Santiago de Compostela. Unpublished)

Frade, M H S 2002 *Centum Celas – uma Villa Romana na Cova da Beira* (Master Thesis, Universidade de Coimbra. Unpublished)

Giumlia-Mair, A & Schiavo, F lo (eds) 2003 *The problem of early tin. Actes of the XIVth UISPP Congress, University of Liège, Belgium, 2–8 September 2001. Section 11. Bronze Age in Europe and the Mediterranean. Symposium 11.2.*, Oxford: BAR International Series **1199**

Gomes, M E P 1996 *Mineralogia, petrologia e geoquímica das rochas granitóides da área de Rebordelo – Bouça – Torre de D. Chama - Agrochão e as mineralizações associadas*. (Phd thesis. Universidade de Trás-os-Montes e Alto Douro, Vila Real. Unpublished)

Joleaud, M 1929 'L'ancienneté de l'exploitation de l'étain dans le nord-ouest de l'Espagne' *Anthropologie* **39**, 134-6

Kalb, P 1990-92 'As xorcas de ouro do Castro Senhora da Guia, Baiões (concelho de São Pedro do Sul, Portugal)' *O Arqueólogo Português* **8/10**, 259-76

Lackinger, A, Comendador, B, Figueiredo, E, Araújo, M F, Silva, R, Rovira, S 2013 'Copper + Tin + People: Public Co-Smelting Experimentation in Northwestern Iberia' *EXARC Journal* **2013/3**. *Proceedings of the 7th UK Experimental Archaeology Conference Cardiff 2013*. [Internet Source http://journal.exarc.net/issue-2013-3/ea/copper-tin-people-public-co-smelting-experimentation-northwestern-iberia [accessed 27-May-2016]

Lackinger, A, Fernández, C I, Comendador, B, Figueiredo, E, Veiga, J P, Silva, R J C (in press) 'Sacar el estaño de las piedras: Un procedimiento artesanal para la obtención de estaño en la Galicia meridional' *VIII Congreso Internacional sobre Minería y Metalurgia Históricas en el Sudoeste Europeo. Granada, 11-15 de junio de 2014*

Lackinger, A, Herrero, A, Fernández, C 2013 'O Proxecto Urdiñeira: balance de un acercamiento a los campos de la investigación y difusión arqueológicas'. (Sastre, J C, Catalán, R, Fuentes, P coords.) *Arqueología en el valle del Duero: del Neolítico a la Antigüedad Tardía. Nuevas perspectivas*. Madrid: La Ergástula, SL, 323-32

Madroñero de la Cal, A 1994 *Una Posibilidad de rastreo de los orígenes de la metalurgia del estaño en España: interpretación de los petroglifos gallegos desde la explotación y el comercio del estaño antiguo*. Sada: Edicións do Castro

Maia e Costa, H 1966. 'Nota sobre as escórias encontradas no Castro de Carvalhelhos' *Trabalhos de Antropologia e Etnografia* **20**, 173-80

Marina, E F 1987 *The mining industry in Spain*. IGME

Martins, M. 1996 'Povoamento e habitat no Noroeste português durante o 1º milenio a.C.' (Alarcão, J ed.) *De Ulises a Viriato. O Primeiro milenio a.C*. Lisbon, 118-33

Martins, T & Lima, A 2011 'Pegmatites from Barroso-Alvão, Northern Portugal: anatomy, mineralogy and mineral geochemistry' *Cadernos Lab. Xeolóxico de Laxe Coruña*. **36**, 181 - 208

Meijide Pardo, A 1963 'La antigua minería del estaño en el valle de Monterrey' *Cuadernos de estudios gallegos* **18**, 190-234

Merideth, C 1998a *An Archaeometallurgical Survey for Ancient Tin Mines and Smelting Sites in Spain and Portugal. Mid Central Western Iberian Geographical Region*. Oxford: BAR International Series **714**

Merideth, C 1998b 'El factor minero: el caso del estaño y el poblado de Logrosán (Cáceres)' (Rodríguez, A coord.) *Extremadura protohistórica: Paleoambiente, Economía y Poblamiento*. Cáceres, 73-96

Merideth, C 1988c 'La Mina El Cerro de San Cristobal: a Bronze Age tin mine (Extremadura, Spain)' *Papers from the Institute of Archaeology* **9**, 57-69

Meunier, E 2011 *L'exploitation de l'étain dans le Nord-Ouest ibérique entre l'Age du Bronze et la fin de l'Empire romain: bilan et perspectives*. (Master Thesis, University of Toulouse. Unpublished)

Meunier, E 2014 'Thinking NW Iberian tin mining: which basis for which perspectives?' (Fontes, L and Marins, C dir) *Paisagens mineiras antigas na Europa Ocidental: Investigação e valorização cultural: atas do Simpósio Internacional Boticas* (Município de Boticas e Unidade de Arqueologia da Universidade do Minho) 196

Mohen, J P 1992 *Metalurgia Prehistórica. Introducción a la paleometalurgia*. Barcelona: Masson S A

Monteagudo, L 1953 'Localização das Cassitérides e Oestrymnides' *Revista de Guimaraes* **LXVII (3-4)**, 372-416

Monteagudo, L 1954 'Metalurgia Hispana de la Edad del Bronce, con especial estudio de Galicia y norte de Portugal' *Cesaraugusta* **4**, 55-95

Muhly, J D 1973 *Copper and tin: the distribution of mineral resources and the nature of the metal trade in the Bronze Age*. Hamden

O'Brien, W 2015 *Prehistoric copper mining in Europe: 5500-500 BC*. New-York: Oxford University Press

Obermaier, H 1944-45 'Las Kassitérides. El problema de su situación a través de los escritores greco-romanos y de los datos arqueológicos' *Cuadernos de Estudios Gallegos* **I**, 621-32

Penhallurick, R D 1986 *Tin in Antiquity: Its Mining and Trade throughout the Ancient World with Particular Reference to Cornwall*. London: IOM Communications Ltd

Pérez Domingo, A 1831 *Memoria sobre las minas en la Península, sobre la riqueza que han producido, y mejoras de que es suceptible este ramo*. Madrid

Ribeiro, A, Sanderson, D 1996 'SW-IBERIA: Transpressional Orogeny in the Variscides' In David G Gee, H J Zeyen (eds) *EUROPROBE-Lithosphere. Dynamics. Origin and Evolution of Continents*. Europrobe secretariat, Uppsala, 138

Rodríguez Díaz, A, Pavón, I, Merideth, C, Juan, J. 2001 'El Cerro de San Cristobal, Logrosán, Extremadura, Spain. The archaeometallurgical excavation of a Late Bronze Age tin-mining and metalworking site. First excavation season 1998' *BAR. International Series* **922** Oxford

Rodríguez Díaz, A, Pavón, I, Duque, D, Ponce de León, M, Hunt, M, Merideth, C 2013 'La explotación tartésica de la casiterita entre los ríos Tajo y Guadiana: San Cristóbal de Logrosán (Cáceres)' *Trabajos de Prehistoria* **70-1**, 95-113

Rodríguez Díaz, A, Pavón Soldevila, I, Duque Espino, D, Hunt Ortiz, M, Ponce de León, M, Vázquez Paz, J, Márquez Gallardo, J M & Rodríguez Mellado, J, 2014 'La minería protohistórica en Extremadura: el caso del estaño en el Cerro de San Cristóbal de Logrosán (Cáceres)' *Cuadernos de Prehistoria y Arqueología de la Universidad de Granada* **24**, 167-201

Rovira, S 2007 "La producción de bronces en la Prehistoria" (Molera, J, Farjas, J, Roura, P & Pradell, T eds.) *Avances en Arqueometría 2005. Actas del VI Congreso Ibérico de Arqueometría, Universitat de Girona, 16-19 de noviembre de 2005*. Girona: Universitat de Girona, 21-35

Rovira, S, Gómez Ramos, P, Montero Ruiz, I 1996 'Los bronces estañados de la Edad del Hierro: estudio tecnológico' *Boletín del Museo Arqueológico Nacional* **XIV**, 31-7

Ruiz-Gálvez Priego, M 1986 'Navegación y comercio entre el Atlántico y el Mediterráneo a fines de la Edad del Bronce' *Trabajos de Prehistoria* **43**, 9-42

Sà Coixão, A, Silvino, T 2010 'The *Villa* of Vale do Mouro (Coriscada, Portugal)' *Journal of Iberian Archaeol* **13**, 85-95

Sánchez Goñi, M F, Cacho, I, Turon, J L, Guiot, J, Sierro, F J, Peypouquet, J P, Grimalt, J O, Shackleton, N J 2002 'Synchroneity between marine and terrestrial responses to scale climatic variability during the last glacial period in the Mediterranean region' *Climate Dynamics* **19**, 95-105

Santos Júnior, J R dos 1984 '30 anos de escavações no Castro de Carvalhelhos (Boticas – Vila Real)' *Revista de Guimarães* **94**, 411-24

Sarmiento, M 1758-1769 *Onomástico etimológico de la lengua gallega*, published in Tuy 1926, cap. 845 ed. Dr. Lago González, Tuy 1923

Senna-Martínez, J C 2011 'La conexión lusitana: contactos orientalizantes y búsqueda de estaño y oro en el centro-norte portugués' (Domínguez Pérez, J C coord.). *Gadir y el Círculo del Estrecho revisados*. Cádiz: Servicio de Publicaciones Universidad, 271-9

Senna-Martínez, J C 2013 'Un rio na (s) rota (s) do estanho: O Tejo entre a Idade do Bronze e a Idade do Ferro. En, O Tejo Palco de Intereção entre indígenas e fenicios' *Cira Arqueología* **II**, 7-18

Senna-Martínez, J C 2000 'O «Grupo Baiões/Santa Luzia» no Quadro do Bronze Final do Centro de Portugal' (J. C. Senna-Martínez, I. Pedro eds.) *Por Terras de Viriato: Arqueologia da Região de Viseu*. Governo Civil do Distrito de Viseu e Museu Nacional de Arqueologia, 119-31

Senna-Martinez J C, Pedro, I 2000 'Between myth and reality: the foundry area of Senhora da Guia de Baiões and Baiões/Santa Luzia metallurgy' *Trabalhos de Arqueologia da EAM* **6**. Lisboa: Colibri, 61-77

Serpa Pinto, R 1933 'Activité minière et métallurgique pendant l'Âge du Bronze en Portuga' *Anais da Facultade de Ciências do Porto*. **XVIII-2**, 77-85

Silvino, T, Sà Coixão, A 2010 'Le monde agricole romain du nord du Portugal'. *L'Archéologue* **106**, 22-31

Tylecote, R F, Photos, E, Earl, B 1989 'The composition of tin slags from the south-west of England' *World Archaeology* **20**, 434-45

Vera, J A (eds) 2004 *Geología de España*. Sociedad, Geológica de España e Instituto Geológico y Minero de España, Madrid

Veiga Ferreira, O, Castro, L A 1949 'Notícia sobre um pilão de minérios Pré-histórico'. *Estudos, notas e trabalhos do Serviço de Fomento Mineiro* **5**, 44-8

Vilaça, R 2007 'Todos os caminhos vão dar ao ocidente: trocas e contactos no Bronze Final'. *Estudos Arqueológicos de Oeiras* **15**, 135-54

Vilaça, R, Bottaini, C, Sobral de Carvalho, P, Paternoster, G 2014 'O punhal de São Martinho de Orgens (Viseu) no seu contexto local: o ser e o estar' *Revista Portuguesa de Arqueologia* **17**, 127-40

Wachsmann, S, Dunn, RK, Hale, JR, Hohlfelder, RL, Conyers, LB, Ernenwein, EG, Sheets, P, Blot, MLP, Castro, F, Davis, D 2009 'The Paleo-Environmental contexts of three possible Phoenician ancorages in Portugal' *The International Journal of Nautical Archaeology* **38**, 221-53